The Structure of Associations
in Language and Thought

The Structure
of Associations
in Language
and Thought

by James Deese

The Johns Hopkins Press
Baltimore

To Elizabeth and James

✨ *Preface*

By one of those curious tides in scientific and intellectual affairs, the topic of naturally occurring associations is once again interesting to experimental and theoretical psychologists. For many years, the experimental student of verbal behavior largely limited himself to studies of the formation of rote associations in the laboratory. The study of naturally occurring associations—as these are manifest in the language—was left to the clinician, whose primary interest was in dynamic emotional processes. Some twelve or fifteen years ago, however free associations became again a topic of interest to the experimentalists. That interest first centered around the concept of mediation and later around more general notions arising out of the revival of concern among psychologists for linguistics.

It is one of the principal arguments of this book that the interest of psychologists in associations has always been—to a certain extent at least—misguided. Probably, the failure to get to the heart of the matter was not the result of the experimentalists—for once they cannot be blamed for the sterility in some area of study—but the result of the too slavish following of classical philosophic doctrine. If the argument presented here is correct, the heavy hand of stimulus-response analysis rests on the study of association not because of Watson, Thorndike, or Hull but because of Plato, Hume, and James Mill. Nearly the whole of the classic analysis of association centered around the relatively circumscribed and uninteresting problem of what follows what. The central thesis of this book asserts that what is important about associations is not what follows what, but how sets of associations define structured patterns of relations among ideas.

In pursuing this thesis, the book is partly a critique of classical views, partly the presentation of new methods for the analysis of associative structure, partly an attempt to bring together linguistic and psychological analyses of associations in thought, and partly the vehicle for the presentation of some as yet unpublished empirical information. So varied a program cannot fail to slip in some detail, and I hope that some relatively minor failures will not discourage readers from following the major ideas.

The book, I am afraid, falls into what is rapidly developing as a no man's land between empirical experimental psychology (primarily in the analysis of association) and formal linguistic theory. It is far too much to hope that this book may mend that conflict but it is possible that we may be able to define some new areas of investigation that will relieve the pressure at the points of dispute. Some of the classical psychological analysis of thought is sterile. It misses the richness of natural language, even as that richness is evident in raw associations. (Are there any more fascinating data in psychology than tables of association?) On the other hand linguistic analysis, particularly formal linguistic analysis, misses the point for many psychological problems in the analyis of thought. Certain linguist to the contrary not all verbal activity occurs in sentences. Vagrant thoughts and verbal streams in consciousness do provide psychological data, and these are much more important than many investigators—including some formal linguists— are willing to grant. They are even linguistically important, and perhaps they even have something to do with the grammar of well-formed sentences.

This book, then, is primarily about associations. The theory of associations it presents, however is related to problems in linguistics on the one hand and studies of concept formation on the other. The title is not empty; it is indeed an attempt to study associations both in language and in thought.

The final portion of the book is given over to a brief version of a kind of cognitive dictionary. It is meant to be illustrative and the main object in presenting it here is to see how generally useful such a dictionary can be. I suspect that there are uses. There is no one way to make a dictionary—there is room for both Dr. Johnson and Dr. Roget. If the theory sketched here and the sample dictionary are of general enough interest, it may be worth the effort to write a larger dictionary of the language and perhaps of other languages as well. In any event, dictionaries built on psychological principles are long overdue. In very different ways, psychological analysis entered into Roget's thesaurus and into the Thorndike and Barnhart dictionaries. These and other efforts, however, have been designed primarily to show how we can present aspects of the language organized in some way like human thinking. The present dictionary tries to show how we can present human thought as it is organized in the language. It is an associative dictionary, which we may regard at least as a special case of a cognitive dictionary.

So much of any scholarly or technical book depends upon the stimulation provided by colleagues and students. This book is no exception. The author is particularly grateful to W. R. Garner. E. S. Howe has both been a contributor to and critic of the author's views. Though W. S. Torgerson is too new a colleague to be quite so influential, he will perhaps be surprised to find some evidence of his stimulation here. Dr. Iris Rotberg and Dr. Doris Entwisle have both provided data and interest. Dr. Edward N. Lee of the Department of Philosophy at Johns Hopkins read and provided a valuable critique for a large portion of the manuscript. Indispensable have been both the hard work and stimulation provided by students at Johns Hopkins. I am particularly grateful to Gerald R. Miller, Herbert A. Weingartner, Paul E. Johnson, Roy E. Feldman, Herbert H. Clark, and Michael G. Johnson. The preparation of the MS was the responsibility of Mrs. Leonora C. Hunner, who has been patient and helpful in innumerable ways. The whole project, particularly the gathering of original data, has been made possible by a series of NIMH grants. It is with a genuine sense of gratitude that I report the work presented here to have been supported by Public Health Service research grants MH-06550-01, MH-06550-02, and MH-06550-03 from the National Institute of Mental Health.

JAMES DEESE

Baltimore, Maryland
June 1965

Acknowledgments

The author acknowledges with thanks permission granted from the following individuals and publishers for reproduction of certain material: The Academic Press, Inc.; American Psychological Association; Appleton-Century-Crofts; C. N. Cofer; Columbia University Press; Holt, Rinehart and Winston, Inc.; J. Laffal; McGraw-Hill Book Company, Inc.; H. Weingartner.

❧ Contents

List of Tables

List of Figures

The Structure of Associations in Language and Thought

1 *The Idea of Association*

A book on the structure of associations written in the second half of the twentieth century demands a word of explanation that both places it within the main stream of writing on association and provides enough freedom from that tradition to justify its existence. The point of view of this book is that the most important property of associations is their structure—their patterns of intercorrelations. However, nearly all theoretical writing on associations has fixed on another property, that of temporal order. This first chapter is intended to show how attention to this property of temporal order has led to the neglect of structure. The second chapter shows that, while much empirical work on associations has entailed the study of associative structure, it has, at the same time, avoided an explicit statement of the nature of associative structure. The remaining chapters are given over to a theory of associative structure and an attempt to relate that theory both to experimental studies of verbal behavior and to some general properties of language.

The idea of association is almost as old as speculation about mentality itself. This long history is a testimony to the fact that the empirical facts of association are based upon a fundamental aspect of human experience, its temporal order. Almost all the basic propositions of current association theory derive from the sequential nature of events in human experience. Both philosophers and psychologists, old and new, who have written on the topic of association have supposed that the order of events evident in the flow of thought, language, or in the arrangement of tasks in the psychological laboratory is the result of the order of events in the causes of thought, language, and behavior. This time-ordered character of thought and the successive events of language or stimulus-response tasks is so obvious that it is only infrequently commented upon as the origin of the chief associative law, that of contiguity, and that single principle has obscured another basic property of association, that of structure.

1

The view of temporal order, variously stated depending upon the linguistic preferences of the writer, is that one thought leads to another or that stimulus leads to response. The elements of thought or stimulus-response sequences are seldom, if ever, described as occurring save in immediate sequence. One thought leads to another because it causes another; most current psychological theory states this relation in the principle that stimulus leads to or causes response.

It is this succession of one thing after another in the flow of psychological process that gives rise to the classical proposition of association theory, the law of contiguity. The remaining propositions of association theory are, almost without exception, secondary to or dependent upon this primary law. The single important exception is the law of similarity, which occupies a most ambivalent status. It is significant that a great deal of theory is devoted simply to deriving the principle of similarity from contiguity. The fact is, however, that the law of contiguity, in whatever form it is stated or for whatever purpose, is little more than a principle of temporal succession or order. Such a view may not immediately seem to be correct because, I think, we are too sophisticated about association theory, particularly association theory since the time of Locke.

Locke and some of his successors wrote not only psychological theories of association, they wrote associationism into their epistemologies and metaphysics. Much of what has been said about association, particularly when philosophical issues are the matters at hand, goes beyond the property of temporal succession in human experience. Locke is largely responsible for such discussions, and he altered association theory in a fundamental way—a way that has prevented a clear apprehension of the issues at stake in a psychological discussion of association.

Warren[1] begins his sketch of a history of associationism by a famous quotation from Plato, and since this quotation sets forth the basic proposition of much subsequent theory, we shall do well to follow his example. Plato describes the act of recollection in this way:

> What is the feeling of lovers when they recognize a lyre or a garment or anything else which the beloved has been in the habit of using? Do not they from knowing the lyre form in the mind's eye an image of the youth to whom the lyre belongs? And this is recollection: And in the

---

[1] H. C. Warren has left, in various places, materials for a history of associationism. The reference here is to H. C. Warren. Mental association from Plato to Hume. *Psychol. Rev.*, 1916, **23**, 208–230. The quotation from Plato is from *Phaedo* in the Jowett translation.

same way anyone who sees Simmias may remember Cebes. . . . And from the picture of Simmias you may be led to remember Cebes . . ., or you may be led to the recollection of Simmias himself. . . . And in all these cases, the recollection may be derived from things either like or unlike. . . . When we perceive something either by the help of sight or hearing or some other sense, there is no difficulty in receiving from this a conception of some other thing, like or unlike, which has been forgotten and which was associated with this.

Plato is saying that one idea leads to another; sometimes the ideas are alike, sometimes they are unlike; sometimes they are of things that belong together regularly and sometimes about things that only occasionally go together. In so saying, Plato, despite the peculiar theory of recollection that occasions his statement, asserts what nearly every commentator upon associations has said since then.

A better and equally famous quotation is from Hobbes. In *Human Nature*[2] he says:

The *cause* of the *coherence* or consequence of one conception to another is their first *coherence* or consequence at that *time* when they are produced by sense: as for example, from St. Andrew the mind runneth to St. Peter, because their names are read together; from St. Peter to a *stone*, for the same cause; from *stone* to *foundation*, because we see them together; and for the same cause, from foundation to *church*, and from church to *people*, and from people to *tumult*; and according to this example, the mind may run almost from anything to anything.

Hobbes's quotation is better because he states his rule whereby experience produces associations at the outset. The rule is that of temporal contiguity. Furthermore, the examples of associations Hobbes gives are very nearly modern. Save for the improbability of St. Andrew's name occurring to anyone today (except, perhaps, as the name of a golf course) and the rarity of *tumult* as a word, such a sequence might well be that of an educated modern person. It rings true. The important point, however, is that Hobbes says one conception leads to another in thought because that sequence had occurred in sense experience.

The process of association is immediately recognizable, stated either by Plato or by Hobbes. The schemes of one's own thoughts can readily be described in the same way, and it is this fact that is probably responsible for the extraordinary viability of association theory.

[2] T. Hobbes. *Human nature.* London: John Bohn, 1839, p. 15.

The passage from Hobbes describes, more obviously, the flow of language than does the passage from Plato, who casts his associative sequence partly in the form of images. The connections between language, thought, and images provide a complicated and subtle topic, one which has never received a satisfactory treatment at the hands of a contemporary psychological theorist. The modern experimental psychologist works almost exclusively with linguistic associations for the good reason that these provide controllable material for his laboratory studies; he ignores the extra existence of perceptual imagery. Language is the mediator of thought in human beings, and it is that aspect of thought which most distinguishes man from the brutes, so a theory of association cast exclusively in the form of language is not seriously deficient. Such a proposition, or something like it, is frequently encountered in current psychological work in language and thought. We study associations in order to make inferences about the nature of human thought, and these associations are cast in the language which embodies the thought. Without necessarily denying either their reality or their importance, the contemporary psychologist finds images difficult to manage in empirical study. Partly for this reason and partly for others, association theory in modern psychology has become a theory of the succession of elements in verbal behavior. To the extent that verbal behavior is the mediator of thought, modern association theory is a theory of thought. The whole of the current concern with associative mediators, as a matter of fact, is an effort to use the associative properties of *explicit* verbal behavior as a model for the implicit verbal processes of thought.

Hobbes is, then, for the modern reader, a reasonably clear expositor of the simple fact of associations being sequences in language. After Hobbes the topic of association becomes in large measure ancillary to epistemological argument. Such is certainly the case with Locke, who, more than merely giving us the phrase, *association of ideas,* makes the whole analysis of association part of the foundation of his philosophy.

Locke's famous proposition, of course, is that all knowledge is acquired through the senses. This view has had an important and controversial history in psychology, and in no small measure it has been responsible for the central place the doctrine of association has occupied in psychological theory. Locke accepts the basic principle of association as the determiner of the structure of thought and the relation between perception and thought. The ordinal property of thought, as in Hobbes, is reflected in the law of contiguity.

More than Hobbes, Locke is compelled to comment upon the correspondence between the order among percepts and the order among thoughts. This is in part a matter of his concern with epistemology and in part an effort to present a more systematic psychology. In a most general way, Locke simply asserts that the relationship among thoughts is a simple transformation of the relationship among percepts; the correspondence is a direct one. Since Locke rejects any notion of innate ideas, he finds no place for the possibility that the relations between thoughts and percepts are determined by the structure of the mind itself. The *tabula rasa* has no form; it only receives. This Lockean view is implicit in a great deal of the empirical investigation of the higher mental processes that has come out of experimental psychology in the past three-quarters of a century.

In arriving at a correspondence between the relations among percepts and thought, Locke finds it necessary to complicate the law of contiguity. Some associations are temporally ordered—one leads to another—but others occur simultaneously. Thus, the various sensory attributes inherent in an object are perceived together and therefore are associated simultaneously. Ideas, for Locke, are *analytic* elements, and these elements may enter both into successive and simultaneous combinations. They are not necessarily the successive instances in the flow of thought; they are, to use a metaphor common in later writing, the molecules of experience. For our purposes, then, Locke causes confusion in the doctrine of association as a theory of thought. After Locke, association means both the temporal succession between instances in thought (or perception and thought) and the way in which elements or attributes are simultaneously combined in experience.

The broadening of the theory of association introduces one of Locke's most celebrated ideas, the distinction between simple and complex ideas. Complex ideas, as Locke describes them, are analyzable into their coexisting components; these components are always simple ideas. Simple ideas, in turn, may exist in isolation or in simultaneous combination in complex ideas. Here then, complete, is another century's mental chemistry. Complex ideas are the compounds of experience, and simple ideas are the molecules (or atoms).

All of this makes the problem of describing the data of associations more difficult, for Locke does not always clearly distinguish between the associations that are successive and those that are simultaneous. He loses interest in the description of the *process* of thought. (Nothing like the quotation from Plato or from Hobbes occurs in Locke.) He is more concerned with the analysis of the problem of knowing. Therefore, while a major tradition in the study of perception (for example,

Harvey Carr's book on space perception) derives from Locke, much of the modern empirical work on associations, determined as it is by the idea of temporal succession, owes little to Locke.

So it is with much of the rest of the apparatus of Locke's associationism. The distinction between primary and secondary qualities is important in epistemology (and, later, in the study of perception and in metatheories of psychology), but it contributes little or nothing to the psychological study of associations in thought. Therefore, while Locke is one of the central figures in the history of associationism, his influence has been less important in associationistic studies of the nature of thought than it has been elsewhere.

The confusion between epistemology and psychology deepens with Hume, a fact that is altogether important for the history of psychology generally. Hume restates some of the original conceptions of association. In addition to the idea of contiguity, Hume reintroduces association by resemblance and adds, of course, association by cause and effect. Resemblance proves to be a particularly important idea for the psychology of thought and perception, and it provides one of the central ideas in some current views of the structural relations among associations. Hume, unlike Locke, makes a clear psychological distinction between impressions and ideas; ideas for Hume are elements of thought that can be distinguished, on psychological grounds it is to be noted, from the elements of perception.

Hume eventually disposes of the notion of cause and effect by assimilating it to contiguity. In so doing, he implies what is to become empirically the most important of the secondary laws of association—frequency. He does so by declaring causal relations to be very frequent or highly probable temporal successions. Whatever the fate of the principle of frequency as a foundation for inductive inference, it has become the cornerstone of much of the work done by experimental psychologists on association. The cause of the *strength* of associations, by this principle, is the frequency of occurrence of successive ideas or impressions and ideas in perception and thought. Frequency is clearly a secondary principle, for its definition assumes the existence of temporal contiguity. However, in importance it stands at the center of experimental studies of association. Some later associationists will say that isolated contiguities in experience may not be sufficient to produce an overt association between elements, but, if the contiguous occurrences are sufficiently numerous, an association will be formed and strengthened. Thus, the contiguities that are revealed in the successive instances of thought are those that have occurred frequently enough in the past to have acquired some associative strength.

Hereafter, it is possible to draw a clear distinction between the primary laws of association and the secondary laws. The primary laws describe the conditions that are necessary for the formation of associations, and the secondary laws describe the conditions that modify the strength of the resulting associations. The most important of the primary laws, as we have already implied, is contiguity; indeed, the others, if others are stated, are often reduced to or derived from the principle of contiguity. Hume, himself, is responsible for a tradition which reduces the concept of resemblance or similarity to contiguity by mediation (see Chapter II). The secondary laws vary from writer to writer in extent and character, but their fundamental purpose remains the same. They are meant to provide a purely mechanical description of the thought processes, a description that is so mechanical as to make it unnecessary to appeal to obscure powers of the mind in order to describe the great variety of sequences of mental events that may occur in individual human minds.

For a historical exposition of the primary and secondary laws, we might well turn to Thomas Brown,[3] for he states them in close to their modern form. It will be more instructive, however, to examine a more nearly contemporary writer, E. S. Robinson. Robinson, in his book, *Association theory today*, wrote what must surely be the last book on association theory that is almost entirely nonexperimental in nature. (The book was published in 1932.) Robinson is counted as an experimental psychologist, but his book contains no data, experimental or otherwise.

Robinson states two primary laws, contiguity and assimilation. His most general statement of the law of contiguity is as follows:[4] "The fact that two psychological processes occur together in time or in immediate succession increases the probability that an associative connection between them will develop—that one process will become the associative instigator of the other."

The law of assimilation is embodied in two principles. One is stated as follows:[5] "Whenever an associative connection is so established that an activity, A, becomes capable of instigating an activity, B, activities other than A also undergo an increase or decrease in their capacity to instigate B." The other principle is stated by Robinson in this way:[6] "Whenever an associative connection is so established that

[3] T. Brown. *Lectures on the philosophy of the human mind.* Hallowell, Me.: Masters Smith, 1854, p. 373.

[4] E. S. Robinson. *Association theory today: an essay in systematic psychology.* New York: Century, 1932, p. 72.

[5] *Ibid.,* p. 86.

[6] *Ibid.,* p. 92.

an activity, A, becomes capable of instigating an activity, B, that same A will vary in its capacity for instigating certain activities other than B."

Robinson finds it necessary to state two principles of assimilation rather than one because he is influenced by stimulus-response psychology. Robinson's first principle is a statement of assimilation to stimuli (stimulus generalization), and his second principle is a statement of the assimilation of responses (frequently called response generalization). The separation is important, for it represents a new aspect of association theory—the attempt to deal with the two sides of the associative relation separately. It is, in fact, a logical outcome of the directionality implied by the succession of ideas. It occurs at this stage, however, less as the result of a logical development of association theory than as a result of the strong influence stimulus-response analysis has upon contemporary association theory.

The idea of stimulus-response segments as the fundamental unit of psychological analysis comes from reflex physiology and especially from the importance behavioristic psychology attached to reflex physiology. In any event, associations after Robinson are clearly unidirectional. The first element, whether it is conceived of as a percept or a centrally occurring idea, has the property of a stimulus, and the second element has the property of a response. Since stimulus implies an external energy and response implies a movement, a great deal of what has come to be called peripheralism is introduced into association theory after Robinson. The efforts of the peripheralists were directed towards finding sensory properties for the first term in association and reaction properties for the second. Such peripheralism, however, has not been important to laboratory studies of verbal learning and thinking, with a few minor exceptions. The directionality implied by stimulus and response has been important, however, and one of the first places where we find its consequences spelled out is in the dual principle of assimilation stated by Robinson.

Robinson's dual principle of assimilation states that some alteration in the first term in an associative contingency may still allow the succession of the second term by contiguity, and it also states that a given first term may be succeeded not by the usual second term but by a related one. In more recent stimulus-response theory, discussion of stimulus generalization and response generalization is more complicated than the above statement, because such discussion usually deals, in a quantitative way, with particular hypotheses about the dimensions of stimulus and response variation.

Robinson introduces the secondary laws of association in a very general way. He says:[7] "The strength of any associative connection is a function of the conditions of [closeness of] contiguity, frequency, vividness and so on obtaining at the time the connection was formed." Taken together with his two primary laws, such a statement leads to a theory of thought, memory, and other cognitive functions. It also serves as a theory of behavior, if the secondary laws are stated in forms which allow for independent variation in the experimental laboratory. In order to have made an explicit theory of behavior, Robinson would only have had to make some statements about the relations between the constructs (ideas), independent variables (stimuli and conditions), and dependent variables (measures of responding). From McGeoch[8] on, these relations are usually stated explicitly, so the associationistic theory of mind becomes, in contemporary psychology, a theory of behavior, in particular a theory of verbal behavior, of at least a certain kind of language.

For the time being we shall ignore the experimental implications of modern associationism in order to see what kind of a mind it constructs. On the belief that the theory of association is intended to describe the minds of real people it is necessary to suppose that many implicit assumptions are introduced into the theory. Some of these are trivial, but others are quite important.

If we take the dominant trend in association theory seriously and take it literally, which is, I think, the only way to take a theory of mind, we find a theory which describes almost no orderly arrangement among successive mental events. Almost the only principles of order built into the organism, so to speak, are those of stimulus and response generalization. Otherwise, associations are at the mercy of the accidental contingencies of external nature as these are imposed upon the perceptual mechanism. To be sure, Locke and others after him have recognized the apparent orderliness of intellectual processes by appeal to vague *ad hoc* powers, but such notions are outside the scope of association theory, and almost no contemporary theorists make such appeals, even at the expense of drastic reduction in the scope allowed theories. Association theory itself, from Hobbes and Locke on, allows no structure to be determined by internal properties of the mind itself. What the mind does is determined by, or as Robinson and his functional heirs would have it, is a function of, events which happen external to the mind.

[7] *Ibid.*, p. 66.
[8] The reference here is to John A. McGeoch (1898–1941), the most diligent and influential experimental student of associations in the 1930's.

It is this characteristic of association theory which has led to its success as a vehicle for experimental programs in the study of learning, memory, and thinking. The emphasis upon external control of mental events has provided the rationale for experimental programs, programs in which the major information comes from examination of the influence of external agents upon verbal behavior. Association theory does not lead to the kind of study which deposes special and controlled stimulation in favor of the study of correlations between different elements of behavior, as would a psychological theory which stems from, say, faculty psychology. Association theory specifies external control, and this aspect of the theory appeals to the experimentalist.

In association theory, then, almost all of the organization or structure of mental events is determined by the organization of input conditions. The major organization so imposed is the result of frequency of various contingencies in perception. Variation in the frequency of input contingencies leads to variations in the frequencies of associative contingencies, or, more generally, variation in the strength of associations. Theorists specify the relation between frequency of input and strength of associations in different ways, though most contemporay theorists agree that there is some nonlinear relationship between the frequency with which particular associations are made and their resulting strength. The most general assumption, perhaps, has taken the form of a logarithmic law. Such an assumption has led contemporary investigators to look for relations, for example, between the logarithm of frequency of occurrence of words in the language and, say, perceptual thresholds for these words.

Frequency provides the fundamental variable determining organization. Certain other variables, such as duration, have had less important roles in the experimental programs that stem from association theory, although recently several theorists have considered the logical problem of frequency as an integration of durations. Some variables provide difficulty because they cannot be so easily specified physically. How does one, for example, specify the vividness (or intensity, as Robinson insisted) of a word, much less of a thought?

Almost all of the older theorists ignored an extremely important aspect of associative contingencies, namely, their multiplicity. A given element C is not only contingent upon A but also upon B. There is little attention in older work to the concept of *distributions* of contingencies among a relatively small number of basic elements. All authors agree, simply because it is a raw fact of association, that A may come to call up B, but that, on occasion, A sometimes calls up C or D. There is a distribution of contingent probabilities between A, B, and so on. However, until quite recently, many possible implications of the fact that the number of possible associative contingencies is far larger than the number of individual elements have not been systematically explored. Does, for example, the strength of an A-B connection depend upon not only the number of times A and B have been associated but upon the number of different things to which A leads? Modern workers in the interference theory of forgetting have made much of the possible contingencies as the cause of forgetting, but even these investigators have paid little attention to the possibilities of organization within the matrix of possible connections.

Despite the lack of a systematic study of the possible interrelations between members of a finite population of ideas or elements, almost all writers on association have seen the probabilistic conception as enabling us to recover some of the variability that characterizes the flow of thought in people. Such a conception lends itself to a portrayal by association theory of the flow of thought (or speech) as a kind of approximation by Markov process. Each element selects the next by some stochastic rule, and that one, in turn, selects the next. While the deficiencies of such a statistical approach to the flow of speech have received much recent attention,[9] it has not been often noted that such a statistical approach to thought or speech represents a considerable accomplishment. Association theory *does* lead to an approximation to thought, a condition which must surely have attracted the early associationists to the doctrine. That such an approximation falls short of the goal is surely a fatal defect. Even more fatal is the argument put forward by Chomsky[10] and others that such a portrayal must inevitably fail, at least as a means for generating sequences of words as they occur in language.

The deficiencies of association theory are many, and there have been attempts to remedy them, both in earlier writers and in the work of the modern experimental psychologists. Thus, for example, modern theorists, as well as Hobbes and Locke, found it necessary to introduce hedonistic concepts into associationism. A more essential matter for the present problem, however, is the notion of similarity or assimilation, which is introduced usually as an auxiliary primary

[9] See the discussion in G. A. Miller, E. Galanter, and K. H. Pribram. *Plans and the structure of behavior.* New York: Holt, Rinehart and Winston, 1960, pp. 144–148. These authors draw very heavily upon the work of N. Chomsky in the theory of grammar.

[10] N. Chomsky. *Syntactic structures.* The Hague: Mouton, 1957. See also, Miller, Galanter, and Pribram for further references.

law of association. If the present interpretation of the history of association theory is correct, the principle of similarity or assimilation is essentially an alien doctrine. One of the obvious functions of the principle of similarity is to correct shortcomings that result from basing the associative process on a single primary law, that of contiguity. The most commonplace objection that can be raised to the notion of association by contiguity is that sometimes a particular thought leads to the thought of something else which is similar but never, in experience, contiguous. Thus, the thought of a sword easily leads to the thought of a letter opener, though neither the perception of the objects nor the words which represent them are likely to be contiguous in experience. They are, of course, perceptually similar. Nor is it without importance in the history of associationism that their perceptual similarity is accompanied by their common relation to other associations and particular qualities—namely, sharp, pointed, and the like.

The notion of similarity is, at the bottom, structural, and it is a property of the perceiver. Similarity is not a concept in physical analysis. Objects can only be similar or dissimilar to one another in perception (and thought). As it has been used in most associationistic theory, the notion of similarity is tautological. Something is similar when it is similar. Certain of the behavioral theorists have tried to rescue the notion of similarity from such tautology by assuming particular relations between sensory dimensions and response systems. Empirical workers in association have found that, when similarity is defined by one set of operations (say, rating scales), it is usually correlated with the results of some other operation (rote learning of rated material, for example).

The notion of similarity has been extremely useful in perceptual analysis, but it has never been quite satisfactory in the study of language. Part of the trouble is that we are never really clear whether it is the perceptions, the verbal ideas associated with those perceptions, or both which are similar. The principal virtue of the concept of similarity is that it takes the edge from some of the rigid mechanics of association theory; it allows association theory the luxury of variation to suit the occasion of some particular outcome. The result is that it is not really possible to quarrel with the empirical validity of the concept of similarity as one can quarrel with the empirical validity of, say, the principle of frequency. Things are similar which appear to be similar.

Early in modern association theory, Hume invoked both similarity and opposition. He thought that the data of human experience demanded both. Experimental psychologists have, by and large, given up the idea of opposition,[11] and they have tended to identify similarity with generalization in particular dimensions, identical elements, or some other, more or less specialized idea which removes some of the circularity from the unadorned concept of similarity. Sometimes, theorists have tried to derive the notion of similarity from contiguity by way of mediation-produced stimulus equivalence (see Chapter II).

The concept of similarity makes the picture of the mind projected by association theory fuzzier and more rounded in the contours. Furthermore, as we have already hinted, similarity runs the danger of contradicting a basic Lockean principle. It introduces some structure into the mind itself, a structure which is not the result of external nature impressing itself upon the mind but is the result of some conditions intrinsic to the mind. Stimulus generalization is a property of the organism, not of the external world.

Associationism is viable today because it has been overwhelmingly successful in generating experiments for the laboratory student of verbal behavior and thinking. It is flexible enough, via similarity and mediationally produced equivalences, to "explain" a great deal of human thought. Pointing to the importance of associationism here, however, can be a double-edged argument, for it can be said with equal force that associationism has restricted the work of the laboratory student of verbal processes to the variables determined by the preoccupations of association theory.

The fact is that, from Ebbinghaus to the present, the independent variables chosen for investigation in the laboratory have largely been determined by the assumptions of classical association theory. The importance of the unit of repetition, the trial, as a controlling variable is one testimony to associationism. Repeated presentation is seldom regarded by the contemporary investigator merely as a convenient device for allowing a number of processes to go on successively; it is regarded as a carefully controlled device for permitting a fixed number of contiguities or contingencies to take place.

Therefore, much of the outcome of laboratory work, work which is often used to justify the heuristic value of associationism, is directly determined by the assumptions of association theory. Since, as we have seen, these assumptions stem out of the obvious properties of

[11] An exception occurs in Osgood's transfer surface. See C. E. Osgood. The similarity paradox in human learning: A resolution. *Psychol. Rev.*, 1949, **56**, 132–143.

thought available in the casual observation of one's own thoughts, the independent variables of the laboratory have really been determined by armchair observation. At the bottom, such a result embodies the implicit assumption that the *outcome must represent some simple transformation of experience.*

That point is most easily explained by reference to the law of frequency. The relative frequency with which things occur, at any level of analysis, provides some basic data. The student of language, for example, may simply count the relative frequency with which some words occur in some extended sample of a language. Such frequency counts are useful. Some elements occur very much more frequently than others; in the absence of anything better, the best prediction about what particular element is going to occur in a flow of verbal behavior is simply that element which occurs, in the general case, most frequently. The prediction can be markedly improved, in most cases, by making the prediction a contingent one (hence the importance of Markov process).

That some words are more likely to occur than others in contingent relations is a fact so obvious that Hobbes, by examining his own sequence of thoughts, can give us a sequence that makes us say, "Yes, that is reasonable; I might have thought of that myself." We do not need to go to association norms to know that ice is cold, blue makes us think of sky, and the thought of butterflies is more likely to lead to that of moths than to stomach, but more likely to lead to either than to airplanes.

Therefore, one of the observations that comes out of the study of association is that frequent ideas more readily come to mind than infrequent ideas. That, of course, is a tautology. In defense of the associationists, it need be said that there is more to it than that. Marbe's law[12] tells that words which are likely to occur as associations are also likely to occur more rapidly. Such a statement is more than a tautology, and this particular relation is the cornerstone of the modern notion of associative *strength.*

The point is, however, that there *is* a distribution of different frequencies for the occurrence of verbal elements and that such a distribution is immediately obvious, both in absolute and in contingent relations. Hence the importance of the law of frequency in association theory. The simplest way to account for a frequency distribution of the elements in language and thought is to suppose that there is some

---

[12] Marbe's law is generally understood to assert that the reaction time of an association is inversely proportional to the logarithm of its normative frequency.

simple—most certainly monotonic—transformation of the frequency
of input. Hence, the outcome, in terms of the sequences of one's
own thoughts, is determined by the input in the form of a frequency
distribution of relative occurrences.

Such an argument has rarely, if ever, been made explicit by association theorists. It is, however, basic to the importance of the law
of frequency in association theory. In fact, association theorists have
asserted that some ideas occur more frequently than others and that
such is the case because these ideas have occurred more often before.

To be sure, in explication of the law of frequency, classical association theorists sometimes implied that the principle came to them
from observation of the events controlling thoughts. In introducing
the principle of frequency, Thomas Brown reminds us that, as one
repeats something (to be interpreted as presenting an environmental
event repeatedly to one's self), one apparently is more likely to
remember it.[13] However, such a statement is really to be interpreted
as simply one of the alleged facts for which association theory
"accounts."

The law of frequency has become one of the most common—if not
the most important—conditions investigated in laboratory studies of
verbal learning. Frequency is controlled through discrete presentation,
by trials, of the elements of a verbal task. The prevailing modern
assumption is that each successive presentation of an element adds
a decreasing amount to the strength of the resulting association, and
it is commonly agreed that the rate of growth of associative strength
can be modified by such conditions as rate of presentation, and so on.
Until quite recently, however, the possibility that each successive
presentation may invoke a different process within an individual
being tested has been largely ignored. Common sense asserts that a
correct response during learning has a different consequence than
mere presentation or an erroneous response, and this proposition is
reflected in the application of the concept of reinforcement to verbal
learning.[14] The all-or-none issue in associative learning has raised
further questions about the nature of processes correlated with frequency. In any event, the central place given the law of frequency has
played a role in determining the importance of trials as an independent
variable in psychological studies of learning and memory. One could

---

[13] Brown, Philosophy of the human mind, p. 373.
[14] Underwood's concept of reinforcement, not Estes's, is intended here. See
the discussion in W. K. Estes. Learning theory and the new "mental chemistry."
Psychol. Rev., 1960, 67, 207–223.

imagine that, given a different history, the fundamental variable in the verbal learning laboratory might well be something else.

So it is, I think, with nearly all the relations between the primary and secondary laws of association and the independent variables of the laboratory. The variables are the result of the translation of what is evident in experience into controlling events. As is illustrated by the law of frequency, such translation antedates the experimental laboratory. Almost the entirety of classical association theory consists of commonplace observations about how thinking and memory occur, translated into environmental causes by the simple rule that events in the mind must reflect a simple one-to-one correspondence to events that happen in external nature. The experimentalists have transformed these laws, more or less successfully, into the conditions of the laboratory. The laboratory can do little else than "confirm" the classical laws, since these laws derive from the obvious properties of experience, and laboratory studies have seldom ventured far enough away to discover anything else.

There has always been a minority tradition in experimental psychology which has insisted upon the limitations of the classical laws of association. In the main, however, the views of the objectors have made few inroads into the doctrines of association theory. That is so partly because the objections to associationism have not been very strong and partly because, when they have been strong, they have been misplaced. The best that can be said for many of the objections to associationism is that they show a recognition that thought and associations in thought are more highly organized than classical theory seems to allow. Many associationists have agreed that this may be so, but these theorists have restricted themselves to conditions to which only the classical laws apply. In fact, the whole history of technique in the verbal learning laboratory can be reduced, for the most part, to a search for conditions which permit only the operation of the classical laws (hence the domination of the paired-associate technique in the laboratory).

It was the failure of the classical associationists to deal with some of the apparent organization among associations that gave rise to the work of Külpe and the Würzburg school, or at least so Koffka and others have argued.[15] How does association theory account for the

[15] For a discussion of the matter, see K. Koffka. *Principles of Gestalt psychology*. New York: Harcourt, Brace & World, 1935, p. 559.

fact that, when we ask someone to give the opposite to *good*, we get *bad* and not some other high-frequency association, such as *boy*? The answer from a classical associationist might have been that the question is irrelevant. And it is simply not a question to which a modern experimental associationist would address himself.

The Würzburgers, however, did try to answer questions such as this one, and they came up with the notion of "determining tendency" as an added principle of association. The Würzburgers were concerned to show that thought is not the higgledy-piggledy set of sequences that classical associationism seems to portray. In their work, however, they did little more than shore up the classical laws with new, *ad hoc* principles, of which "determining tendency" is an example. It is very difficult to see what the Würzburgers accomplished other than to say, at great length, that thoughts are generally more orderly than association theory supposes.[16]

The early twentieth century saw many such efforts to reinforce association theory with *ad hoc* principles. Müller and Pilzecker,[17] for example, introduced the idea of "initial reproductive tendency." That term refers to the tendency to remember in appropriate order a sequence of words. Such an idea may be thought of as a kind of groping after the modern concept of encoding, and, like the concept of encoding, it is designed to describe some of the orderliness of ordinary thought and speech. Such principles as these, however, provide little more than footnotes for the main current of associationism.

Within experimental psychology there has existed a theoretical tradition that has generally been considered to be opposed to associationism. That tradition, now exemplified in Gestalt psychology, has emphasized the a priori character of the mind. In contrast to Lockean empiricism, that tradition supposes the structure of the mind to alter and transform the information it receives.

In the description of perception and, to a considerably lesser extent, in the description of thinking, Gestalt psychology makes an important contrast with associationism by its stress on structure rather than contiguity. Nevertheless, Gestalt psychology, in its treatment of thinking, has been curiously lacking in the kind of generality characteristic of associationism. The familiar Gestalt laws are, in their

---

[16] Such a statement ignores, of course, the imageless thought controversy and its consequences.

[17] G. E. Müller and A. Pilzecker. Experimentelle Beiträge zur Lehre vom Gedächtnis. *Zeit. Psychol.*, 1900, Ergbd. I.

original statement, laws of form perception. Some of them have been generalized to other aspects of perception and, largely by metaphorical extension, to some aspects of thinking and problem-solving.

Various Gestalt theorists and experimentalists have given attention to the classical phenomena of associations as they are studied in the laboratory, but the major principles of Gestalt psychology have been applied to these phenomena only indifferently. Koffka discusses structure in associations, but the structures to which he refers are largely those of perception, and they are secondary to a general principle of contiguity. Contiguity, in a word, is modified by the laws of perception. Such a general view leads Koffka to treat at length so disappointing an issue as the role of rhythm (indeed the impossibility of avoiding rhythm) in the rote memorization of nonsense syllables. The von Restroff phenomenon and other effects[18] like it imply that not every association can be made contiguous with every other association to quite the same degree, but various secondary laws of classical associationism imply the same thing. Gestalt psychology has very little to say on the topic of the organization of associations or why associations occur in the patterns they do.

Very recently Asch and Ebenholtz[19] have argued against the directionality of associations and presented experiments designed to show that associations do not necessarily have a forward or stimulus-response direction. This argument makes a clean break with the history of associationism, which, as we have seen, derives its basic principle of contiguity from the time-ordered property of thought. Furthermore, asserting that there is no directionality in associations implies a very different kind of organization than that implied by the classical theory. It is beside the point to assert that modern experimental associationists recognize "forward" and "backward" associations. It is clear that, except for theorists like Asch and Ebenholtz, "backward" associations are regarded as little more than unfortunate artifacts of methods of presentation and practice.

There remains to be discussed the concept of *Aufgabe*. The work of the Würzburg school, as we have already said, did not really depart from the main tradition of association theory. The Würzburg investigators, in fact, were more concerned with associations as data than were the major Gestaltists. Associations provided data for the Würzburg laboratory, although these associations seem to be regarded as

[18] These effects refer to an enhancement of learning or recall which results from some unique characteristic of a verbal item.

[19] See, for example, S. E. Asch and S. M. Ebenholtz. The principle of associative symmetry. *Proc. Amer. Phil. Soc.*, 1962, 106, 135–163.

secondary to introspective data. Introspection gave rise to the notion of imageless thought, and it was the inability of the introspection technique to decide the issue which eventually led to its disfavor in the psychological laboratory.

The Würzburgers also used the association technique, however, and they assumed the laws of association. Associations were modified by the *Aufgabe*. The *Aufgabe* provided an organizing principle that gave direction to associations. The Würzburgers tried to show that the *Aufgabe* was under some kind of experimental control, but it was control of the weakest variety—that produced by instructions. It led to little more than confirmation of traditional classifications of associations, and it directed attention away from the central issue, namely, the internal organization among associations.

If this brief dismissal of dissenting traditions in the treatment of organization among associations is substantially correct, we are left with the dismal conclusion that no major point of view in psychological theory has attempted to provide a description of the structures apparent in the sequences of associations. The principles of organization that come from association theory itself imply almost complete anarchy. The classical laws say, in effect, that anything can be associated with anything else with about equal ease, providing the conditions of original presentation are right. Therefore, what organization exists in manifest associations is the result of the accidental contingencies of events in nature as these impress themselves upon the perceiving mind. They have nothing to do with the grammars of human languages or any other highly organized system in thought. To this picture, the Gestalt psychologists do little more than add the possibility of certain natural groupings in association based upon the Gestalt laws of perception. The accidental contingencies are altered by the laws of perception, but that is about the end of the matter. Koffka writes about some "intrinsic relations," but beyond pointing to some examples in perception, these intrinsic relations go unspecified. Such principles as the law of fittingness[20] are not principles at all, but circular reifications of examples culled from the experimental literature and from casual observation. Finally, Gestalt psychology has never implied that contiguous presentation is not the cornerstone of association. The Würzburgers add only *ad hoc* notions that return some of the properties of association, rather mysteriously, to volition. To the Gestaltists and Würzburgers alike, associations are reflections of past experience.

[20] Koffka, Principles of Gestalt psychology, p. 427.

The theorist who comes closest to describing the organization of relations among associations is Bartlett,[21] although he almost never mentions the term "association" and deals not at all with any of the traditional problems of associationism. Bartlett's problem is the description of memory as a process of reconstruction. He says, at great length, that new structures or schemata develop as the result of recall; therefore, each recall has the potential to alter what is remembered. There is, then, in Bartlett the implication that reconstruction in memory comes from simplified structures which have the power to organize any particular bit of past experience and place it in relation with some other bit of past experience. It is but a short step to propose that the sequences of thought evident in associations are also constructed from structural relations. Therefore, the sequences in manifest association do not necessarily reflect contiguous relations in original presentation or learning.

Bartlett gives us almost the first suggestion that associations are not simple, direct echoes of previous experience. Particular sequences may be created by structures in much the same way that the transitional sequences in a language are, or can be, created by grammatical relations. We should, then, regard Bartlett as one theorist who offers a unique alternative to the theory of association—one that, by its emphasis on construction or generation, provides an alternative to the classical theories of the associative process that is surprisingly analogous to the alternative that transformational theory offers in the study of grammar.

If we are to free ourselves from complete devotion to the principle of contiguity, we must, as Bartlett did, be willing to consider that our memories are not simply reflections of the contiguities in previous experience. If that is so, we should be willing to admit the possibility that obtained associations may never have occurred together in the experience of the person who yields them; they may, instead, be the result of schemata which serve the function of bringing together structurally related elements from diverse experiences. One way of considering such a possibility is to examine, with an eye unprejudiced by the doctrine of contiguity, the patterns that exist among associations between words as these are given by people. That is the task of the next few chapters.

[21] Principally in F. C. Bartlett. *Remembering: A study in experimental and social psychology*. New York: Cambridge, 1932.

2   *The Empirical Study of*
Associative Organization

The beginnings of empirical study of associations are easily dated by the work of Galton (1880), Wundt (1883), and Ebbinghaus (1886). Galton and Ebbinghaus, between them, nicely exemplify the two major traditions in the study of associations. Galton invented something like the modern free-association test, and Ebbinghaus invented the nonsense syllable which he used in the experimental study of the formation of new associations.

Both men were squarely in the main tradition of associationism, but Ebbinghaus's commitment to an experimental program rather than to simple observation more thoroughly identified his work with the ideas of classical associationism. Galton's technique and its various modifications yield endless examples of associations like those used by earlier writers to illustrate the classical laws, but his technique was not limited by the classical laws to the extent that Ebbinghaus's was. The history of the experimental study of associations from Ebbinghaus on has illustrated the almost complete dependence upon the principle of contiguity for defining experimental arrangements. The serial-anticipation technique and the paired-associate technique are the best-known testimonies to the classical laws. It is only the exceptional technique, such as Bousfield's clustering analysis, that escapes the influence of the principle of contiguity in presentation of the material to be learned. Therefore, in order to examine the organization among associations without commitment to the classical laws, we must turn to the tradition that stems from Galton and the study of naturally occurring associations.

In much of the empirical work on naturally occurring associations we find little or no theoretical argument, in the sense that theory has been understood in the experimental tradition. We do find attempts to classify associations, and these classifications, in their underlying schemes, provide a kind of theory. The classifications are not always related to psychological processes, however, so sometimes the theory is latent rather than manifest. Furthermore, these classifications owe little or nothing to any of the classical laws save that of similarity.

The classification schemes are partly psychological, partly logical, partly linguistic, and partly philosophic (epistemological). These classifications are more often than not rooted outside the association process itself and applied to that process by brute force. They attempt to impose upon associations the relations found in grammars, dictionaries of various sorts, and psychodynamic theories, as well as views about the organization of the physical world.

Galton[1] classified his own associations, quite characteristically for Galton, in a psychological but not very systematic way. He grouped associations into those dependent upon images, those which were "histrionic representations" of attitudes and the like, and those which were "purely verbal." Wundt,[2] also quite characteristically, makes his fundamental devision out of his theory of introspection. The first division made by Wundt is into internal and external associations. External associations reflect previous perceptions of relations in the world—for example, *nose-face*. Internal associations depend upon thought processes of the individual, as in the example, *charity-kindness*. This distinction runs through the work of Wundt's successors (Kraeplin and Aschaffenburg, for example). It is related to Ziehen's[3] classification into those associations that are made without judgment (*rose* makes one think of *red*) and those by judgment (a *rose* is *red*).

Among the earliest and most familiar of the classifications based upon a logical structure of relations is that which divides associations into those that are supraordinate (*dog-animal*), those that are subordinate (*animal-dog*), and those that are co-ordinate (*cat-dog*). Such a classification organizes associations into a branching tree in which sequences are possible (in both directions) along the branches between adjacent nodes and transversely at any given level. Such a scheme, however, inevitably leaves a wastebasket class which includes all of the associations that cannot be fitted into the scheme. Sometimes the scheme is incorporated into a larger one. Wundt, for example, places the subordinate and supraordinate relations into a single class, the co-ordinate into another, and makes a third class of dependent relations (causality and purpose). Of course, a wastebasket class still remains even with the addition of the third kind of relation. There

[1] F. Galton. Psychometric experiments. *Brain,* 1880, 2, 149–162.
[2] W. Wundt. Über Psychologische Methoden. *Philos. Stud.,* 1883, 1, 1–38.
[3] T. Ziehen, *Die Ideenassoziation des Kindes.* Berlin, 1898.

is something fundamental about subordinating and supraordinating associations, however; nearly every scheme finds a large place for these relations.

The investigators of the Würzburg school introduced the concept of imageless thought, and such a notion leads to the classification of associations into those with and without images (Mayer and Orth).[4] The imageless thought question was a major issue for the introspective experimentalists, but, despite its importance to these people, I do not think that it has ever had much implication for the study of the organization among associations.

Among the earliest techniques used in psychoanalysis for the tapping of the unconscious was free association. The psychoanalytic use of free association opened a whole new area in which the study of associations was important. A great deal of the psychoanalytic use is evaluative and rather specific to the dynamics of psychoanalytic theory, but some of the psychoanalysts have also classified associations. A representative psychodynamic classification is that by Jung and Rilkin.[5]

From the vantage point afforded by more than forty years, the classification by Jung and Rilkin is curiously naïve. It depends much more heavily than one might have otherwise supposed upon the system devised by Wundt. There is the familiar division into inner and outer associations, and there is a residual group, one that seems to include most of the psychodynamically interesting associations. These include egocentric reactions, verbal linking, repetition, perseveration, and "meaningless" (that from psychoanalytic writers!) reactions. There is, of course, also the clang association.

The statistical analysis that Jung and Rilkin present is dull and uninformative. Despite the promising and important position occupied by the free-association technique in psychoanalytic work, the formal attempts to present organized normative information about association proved to be disappointing.

Wells,[6] in his clinical manual, adopts a rather simplified version of the system favored by Jung. He arrives at the following classes:

1. Egocentric or subjective

[4] A. Mayer and J. Orth. Zur Qualitativen Untersuchung des Assoziation. *Zeit. Psychol.*, 1901, 26, 1–13.

[5] C. G. Jung and F. Rilkin. The associations of normal subjects. In C. G. Jung. *Studies in word-association.* Trans. M. D. Eder. New York: Moffat, Yard, 1919.

[6] F. L. Wells, *Mental tests in clinical practice.* Yonkers-on-Hudson, N.Y.: World, 1927.

2. Supraordinate
3. Contrast
4. Miscellaneous
5. Speech habit

Wells classifies in order to make inferences for diagnostic purposes. These inferences are based upon the relative frequency of occurrence of different classes of association in criterial groups of subjects. Like that of Jung and Rilkin, Wells's approach is largely psychometric; he shows little or no interest in the content of the associations themselves.

Rapaport[7] serves as an example of a clinically oriented investigator who makes full use of associative data. He describes two ways in which associations can be used in clinical diagnosis, and both of these force him to consider the problem of classification. One use of associations brings Rapaport to a consideration of the meaning or content of associations. Here, he falls back upon some notions about the origin and meaning of associations which stem from psychoanalytic theory.

In order to classify an association, Rapaport must make some interpretation of the meaning of the association. An association to a particular stimulus yields a clue to the generalized dynamic or emotional response system aroused by that stimulus. Thus, says Rapaport, the response *tyrant* to *father* allows us to make some inference about the meaning of *father* for that individual. Therefore, Rapaport implies that responses in free association yield information about the meaning of the stimulus, and he implies that associations should be classed and sorted on the basis of their meanings. This view is very different from that implied by classical association theory, which would have the response determined by contiguous relations to the stimulus. The difficulty with Rapaport's notion is that the meaning and dynamic interpretation of any given association must be arrived at by intuitive judgment. Furthermore, most associations are considerably less obvious than the above example.

Rapaport's second use of associations is generally psychometric. In psychometric use the specific content of free associations is unimportant. What is important are the other characteristics of associations, their latencies and relative frequencies of occurrence. Any classification based upon these characteristics necessarily evokes a system based upon events outside the association process. Such would be the case, for example, if we classified associations on the basis of the relative

[7] D. Rapaport. *Diagnostic psychological testing; the theory, statistical evaluation and diagnostic application of a battery of tests.* Chicago: Yearbook Publishers, 1950, Vol. I.

frequencies of responses given by schizophrenics and normal individuals, or if we classified associations into slow and fast ones.

Rapaport's awareness of the normative, psychometric use of free associations leads him to certain views about affective processes in association. For example, he asserts that lack of ego strength makes it easier for affective influences to disrupt the ordinary attitude of conforming to the instructions of the association test. The result may be the production of a deviant response—one not ordinarily given by normal individuals. Important, in this context, is the view stated by Rapaport that high ego strength prevents the content of the reaction from revealing sources of affective difficulty. One cannot detect the affective meaning of a stimulus from the typical response given by the ordinary individual. Such a point of view leads most dynamic theorists to reject statistically common associations as uninteresting. One must, as it were, pick and choose among associations to find the interesting and meaningful (that is, pathological) ones.

The notion that something like ego strength filters association, however, need not lead to the dismissal of associative data in the study of meaning generally. Words filtered through ego-protective devices have meanings too, though these meanings must always be regarded as altered by the presumed protective processes. If the initial or strongest response has been displaced by one more acceptable to the ego, the displacing response is not picked simply at random. Needless to say, there is no firm and incontrovertible evidence for such a process of selection at work, much less any generally agreed upon method for distinguishing between associations filtered by ego processes and those not so filtered. The fact remains, however, that in an ordinary testing situation we may not have all or even the psychologically most important meanings revealed.

In any event, Rapaport's assumption that common responses are uninteresting is a fairly general one among those who make clinical interpretations of free associations. Such a view leads to the neglect of some potentially interesting (perhaps even dynamically interesting) properties of the ordinary, popular, or normative response.

Implicit in Rapaport's analysis of associations is the psychoanalytic view of the nature of intellectual processes. In a more general way than we have already implied, psychoanalytic theory provides a point of view about intellectual processes, one that could lead to a particular view about the structure or organization of associations if it were to be stated in explicit and particular detail. Furthermore, as we shall see, empirical techniques for the analysis of organization in manifest free associations may have implications for psychoanalytic theory, particularly if we rid ourselves of the assumption that popular or frequently occurring associations have no dynamic implications.

There are some other important general respects in which psychoanalytic and other dynamic theorists have differed from other psychologists who have studied associations. The most important of these is the emphasis in dynamic theories upon the part played by intraindividual conditions as determinants of the course of manifest associations. I do not mean to imply that association theorists of the traditional variety have totally neglected factors arising from within the individual, but, in their work, they minimize the importance of these. In part, such a result reflects the experimentally oriented preoccupations of many of those who have studied associations. Psychoanalytic and other dynamic theorists have, to the extent that their own preoccupations have allowed, accepted the laws of association, but these theorists regard the laws of association as of little importance in determining the significance of individual associations. They have been less concerned with external conditions than internal conditions as determiners of behavior.

The problems which interest dynamic theorists are not, in general, those that are ordinarily considered to be important in the study of learning, except possibly as learning is influenced by such presumed effects as perceptual defense. Dynamic factors, however, are more clearly at work in forgetting and parapraxis (minor errors of speech), according to the assertions made by various dynamic theorists.

Contemporary association theorists in the experimental tradition would probably describe both forgetting and parapraxis, if pushed to do so, as the result of interference between associative contingencies. In psychoanalytic theory, on the contrary, such things as forgetting and slips of the tongue are presumed to be determined by stable characteristics of the personality. Here, then, is a fundamental dichotomy. The experimental associationists invoke the classical laws of association as these are exemplified in the laboratory. The dynamic theorists tell us that these phenomena are determined by wishes, conscious and unconscious, affective value, and other, similar effects. The evidence, of course, is on the side of the experimentalists, but they are very cautious about generalizing their results to the ordinary conditions of thought and language.

Whatever appeal there is to the views of the dynamic theorists about associative processes, these views do not have the empirical power that comes from the active experimental program of the modern associationists. In fact, modern associationists have demonstrated considerable laboratory control over the conditions responsible for many verbal processes. Dynamic theorists, on the other hand, give us a rich (but not always completely convincing) range of examples from the clinical literature. They provide almost nothing in the way of evidence capable of withstanding hard, critical scrutiny.

In brief, dynamic theorists are apt to see a common thread running through many associations given by a particular individual, and they see the relatedness of associations as a problem for personality theory and, only in a trivial way, a result of the laws of association. In such a view, these theorists come close to the idea of structure as a fundamental determinant of association, but they are never able to marshal evidence or a method for presenting a strong empirical case for their views.

To be sure, the dynamic theorists have only indifferently applied themselves to the description of intellectual structure. Armed with a number of ideas about the dynamic interpretation of dreams, associations, and the like, they have constructed pictures of personalities and histories of personalities by linking together the bits and pieces they find in free, expressive behavior. Free associations have been a favorite source of data because of the assumption that they, more nearly than any other intellectual product, escape the censoring of the ego. To the extent that dynamic theorists have been interested in intellectual content, they have concentrated on the deviant and unusual and, in some instances, the symbolically interesting aspects of free association. Few dynamic theorists and almost no psychoanalytic theorists wish to make anything of the free associations of high frequency of occurrence. It is of little concern (save for such value as is in normative information) that the most common response to *man* is *woman* or that the most common response to *woman* is *man*. These are obvious; they are given by nearly everyone. Therefore, they have not been regarded as providing much information about underlying dynamics.

So, in general, dynamic theorists have ignored the statistically common free associations. I am inclined to think that the clinical preoccupations of these theorists—the concern with the description of a single case—have led them to regard any statistically general phenomenon as uninteresting. In taking such a position, however, they have neglected an opportunity to describe the organization of associations, an organization which could lead to a new interpretation of deviant and unusual responses. Yet, despite the lack of explicit interest in organization among associations, some dynamic theorists have dealt with problems in which the organization among associations is a fundamental question. An example comes from the father of modern theory about schizophrenia, E. Bleuler.[8]

Bleuler is concerned with thought processes in schizophrenia, and he says that the basic intellectual symptom of schizophrenia is that associations become disrupted. The schizophrenic has unusual and "unlogical" associations, remote associations, and clang associations. Bleuler reproduces several schizophrenic linguistic productions, and these are meant to illustrate the role of deviant associations in schizophrenic verbal processes. About one of these productions, Bleuler comments that it seems to be dominated by a single supraordinate concept, that of things *Oriental*. The actual sequence of words in the production, Bleuler suggests, appears to be an almost random drawing from a collection of words which are associations to that particular supraordinate concept.

Bleuler gives an impressionistic account of what has happened to the chain of associations in the records he presents. Clearly, it is his impression that the associations are organized. Under normal conditions they are organized in one way; in pathological conditions they are organized in another way. There is, of course, no explicit description of the structuring he implies. Bleuler's skeptical reader is left with the impression that, for every conclusion Bleuler draws, just exactly the opposite conclusion could have been drawn with equal force.

In summary, Bleuler says:[9]

> The innumerable actual and latent ideas which determine associations in normal trains of ideas may be rendered, singly or in any combination, ineffective in schizophrenia. In turn, ideas may come into play that have little or no connection to the main ideas, and should have been excluded from the train of thought. Thereby thinking is rendered incoherent, bizarre, incorrect and abrupt. At times all threads fail, and the train of thought is arrested; after such blocking, ideas lacking any recognizable connection to previous ones may emerge.

Certainly, the intellectual and verbal processes of the schizophrenic mind suggest chaos. But, one may ask, is schizophrenic speech incoherent because it is intrinsically disorganized, or is its individual organization simply different from that of the normal mind? Indeed, is it possible that the associations (and the accompanying patterns of

---

[8] E. Bleuler in D. Rapaport. *Organization and pathology of thought.* New York: Columbia Univ. Press, 1951.

[9] *Ibid.*, pp. 596–597.

speech) of schizophrenics are more highly organized than those of the normal individual but merely lacking in conformity to the ordinary modes of thought? These are questions that cannot be answered without explicit methods for determining the nature and extent of associative structure.

These few remarks about psychodynamic views of association serve to remind the reader that the problem of associative structure has been a persisting and important one in the study of personality and personality deviation. For the most part, attempts to discover underlying structures among associations have been limited to and determined by the well-known classifications of association, classifications that are usually based on logical and linguistic relations as well as associative ones. The remarkable feature of this work is the fact that it has been so concerned with associative structure without an explicit technique to investigate that structure.

Let us now turn to the experimental tradition and its contributions to the study of organization among associations.

We have already seen that the experimental tradition is dominated by the classical laws of association and that these laws, in their simplest application, provide for a rather erratic and haphazard organization in associative processes. For, at the bottom, associations are determined by the accidental contingencies of experience.

The law of contiguity is responsible for the experimental arrangements by which material is presented to subjects in studies of verbal learning. The methods of paired associates and serial arrangement, as well as their various modifications, rely upon the repeated presentations of contiguous verbal elements. Interestingly enough, from the very beginning—Ebbinghaus's work on remote associations—the simplest meaning of contiguity, that of adjacent order of presentation, turns out to be inadequate. Remote associations are possible, and there is a kind of order of remoteness which determines the rapidity with which associations are formed.

Until Bousfield's recent work with the method of clustering, however, almost all of the experimental study of association was based upon contiguity in presentation and stimulus-response relations in analysis. The scattered studies, largely from the laboratories of the Gestalt psychologists, which dealt with some particular application of perceptual organization to rote learning of lists of words or nonsense syllables are few and unimpressive in content, and these, almost without exception, rely upon contiguous presentation to define the basic structure.

There is one principle of organization, derived from contiguity, that has become increasingly important in recent years. That is the principle of mediation. Mediation can be employed both to dispense with a special concept of similarity or generalization and to provide a description and reconstruction of naturally occurring associative structures.

The idea that two verbal elements can be associated by the mediation of a third, contiguous to both, is very old in association theory; it is explicitly mentioned by Hume, who uses it in order to derive the principle of resemblance from the law of contiguity.[10] The principle has been important from the beginning of experimental work on associations, and it has become of primary theoretical interest in recent years.

Ideas about mediation are an essential ingredient of stimulus-response behaviorism, and the sheer numbers of versions of the concept have become bewildering in recent years.[11] Our purpose here is not to explore this variety but to illustrate the use of the concept to describe associative structures. There is, therefore, no better place to begin than with Cofer's and Foley's[12] attempt to give an account of the complexities of relations in ordinary language by a strictly behavioristic version of the notion of mediation. Their paper provides a convenient point of departure for a systematic discussion of the relations between mediation and associative organization.

Cofer and Foley start with the Pavlovian conditioned response. They aim to derive what they term "mediated generalization," something which they see as parallel to primary stimulus generalization. Primary stimulus generalization implies some psychological or topographic organization among stimuli such that one stimulus "resembles" another in its effect upon the organism. Primary stimulus generalization itself is unlearned, but, when an organism learns to respond to one stimulus, it also learns to respond, by generalization, to stimuli to which it is not specifically trained. Cofer and Foley wish to show that

---

[10] For a discussion of the history of mediation, see A. E. Goss. Early behaviorism and verbal mediating responses. *Amer. Psychologist,* 1961, 16, 285–298.

[11] Goss's history, cited above, is just about exhaustive, but Gough more thoroughly sees the generality of the idea. See P. Gough. The mediation phenomenon. Studies in verbal behavior, Report No. 6. Minneapolis: Univ. of Minnesota, 1961.

[12] C. N. Cofer and J. P. Foley, Jr. Mediated generalization and the interpretation of verbal behavior. I. Prolegomena. *Psychol. Rev.,* 1942, 49, 513–540.

some instances of generalization are not primary but can arise through learning. They do not imply that all generalization is learned; in theory, however, their analysis would make it possible to abandon primary stimulus generalization and describe all associative organization by the principle of mediated contiguity.

The arguments made by Cofer and Foley are briefly summarized as follows. A stimulus, CS_1, is conditioned to elicit a response, R_x; the conditioning, of course, is by the principle of contiguity. Also conditioned to R_x are stimuli CS_2, CS_3, . . . CS_n. Then CS_1 is conditioned to R_y, but, while being so conditioned, CS_1 also elicits R_x implicitly. The response, R_x, has stimulus properties. Therefore, R_y is not only conditioned to CS_1, it is also conditioned to the stimulus aftereffects of R_x (s_x). Such conditioning is also by the principle of contiguity.

The result is that any stimulus, CS_n, previously conditioned to R_x, comes to elicit R_y through the mediation of R_x (s_x) without direct conditioning. Here then is a principle of organization built upon a chain of stimulus-response connections. It is, in its essentials, the stimulus-equivalence paradigm of mediation, but it is clearly explicated as a stimulus-response chain. The hypothetical intervening links have the properties of overt stimulus-response sequences. The derivation allows Cofer and Foley an extraordinary freedom in describing existing verbal organization.

Once the naturally occurring relations among words (as they exist in the free-association test, for example) have been recovered, it is possible to make inferences about what combinations of words, serving as CS's, originally elicited certain other words, R_x's. Synonyms provide an easy case, on the assumption that they serve as equivalent CS's in eliciting common R_x's. That is simply to say that words which are synonyms elicit certain learned responses in common. The same might be said of homophones, except that these can also be treated effectively by the primary stimulus-generalization principle.

By the use of synonymic and homophonic examples, Cofer and Foley are able to generate a structure like that shown in Figure 1. Notice that the R_x's are left out of the diagram. By including these R_x's, the diagram would have been more complicated, but it would have served as a more adequate explanation by the principles elected by Cofer and Foley.

The Cofer and Foley analyses, as well as some other early experimental analyses of mediation, are important to our present purposes because they are essentially stimulus-equivalence cases of mediation. Recently, a considerable number of experimental psychologists have

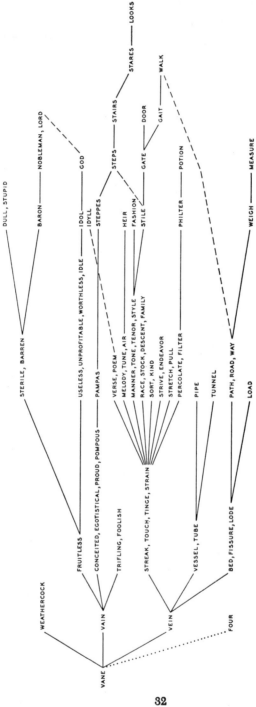

FIGURE 1: Formal representation of certain possible phonetic and semantic (mediated) generalization gradients. (Reproduced from C. N. Cofer and J. P. Foley, Jr. Mediated generalization and the interpretation of verbal behavior. I. Prolegomena. *Psychol. Rev.*, 1942, 49, 528.)

turned their attention to the study of the complete variety of possible mediational relations between three or more terms. More exhaustive than any other in this effort is the work of J. J. Jenkins and his associates.[13] In Jenkins's work the cumbersome notation, as well as the derivation, from classical conditioning is dropped and replaced by simple diagrams in which stimulus terms appear on the left and response terms on the right. Three examples of Jenkins's mediation paradigms appear in Table 1.

TABLE 1: The Three Principal Types of Mediation Paradigms

Stage	Chaining	Stimulus equivalence	Response equivalence
Learn:	A..........B	A..........B	B..........A
Then learn:	B..........C	C..........B	B..........C
Test for:	A..........C	A..........C	A..........C

Mediation among associations implies at least three terms: an original instigator of the associative process, the mediator, and the final response. Logically, therefore, all cases of mediation between three terms can be generated by taking three elements two at a time. When that is done, as Jenkins shows us, eight mediation paradigms result. These, however, reduce in type to three, a chaining paradigm, a stimulus-equivalence paradigm, and a response-equivalence paradigm. Examples of each of these three types are illustrated in Table 1. The Cofer and Foley example is, in principle, like the stimulus-equivalence case.

The curious feature about these three types of mediation is that only one clearly and simply conforms to the major canons of association theory, as we outlined them in the last chapter. That type is the chaining paradigm. Hence the elaborate arguments needed by Cofer and Foley to reduce stimulus equivalence to stimulus-response chaining. In the direct-chaining paradigm there is both contiguity between terms and direction. The stimulus leads to response, and it is clear that the response is mediated through an intervening term that is both a response to the original stimulus and a stimulus for the final response.

Even more curious is the fact, as Jenkins tells us, that the other mediation paradigms "work" and do so about as well as the chaining paradigm. That is to say, they produce transfer in paired-associate tasks, and such transfer is about equal for all cases (except "reverse

[13] See J. J. Jenkins. Mediated associations: Paradigms and situations. In C. N. Cofer and B. S. Musgrave. *Verbal behavior and learning.* New York: McGraw-Hill, 1963.

chaining"). There are many reasons why this could be so, including some that are artificial in the testing situation.[14] For our purposes, however, it is sufficient to notice that the chaining paradigm is clearly not the only one that works.

It is convenient to collapse Jenkins's types still further and distinguish only between chaining paradigms and equivalence paradigms. A clear operational distinction between stimulus equivalence and response equivalence is difficult to make when one deals entirely with verbal materials, simply because it is difficult to maintain a distinction between verbal elements as stimuli and verbal elements as responses. The morphological features of language are reflected in both perceptual and behavioral aspects. In the classical paired-associate experiment the first term is called "stimulus" and the second term "response," but it is fair to say that no one is fooled by these names. Everyone knows that subjects must read (perceive) both terms and that most subjects probably implicitly say to themselves the stimulus term during the experiment. The designations, stimulus and response, only describe what happens to a fair degree during the anticipation phase, when the subject must produce the "response" when he sees the stimulus. A number of recent papers demonstrate the obvious point that subjects also learn, to a degree, to give the stimulus when presented with the response.[15]

The problem of disentangling the stimulus and response aspects of the elements in paired-associate learning has led to a very esoteric literature, germane to certain problems but not those before us now. Since we are not concerned with these problems, we may accept mediation as of two basic types, chaining and equivalence, whether stimulus or response. Chaining is the obvious associative case, but equivalence is the more generally interesting one. For one thing, it immediately suggests a grammar of verbal behavior (and ideas), for the essential feature of learning the morphology of our native tongue is learning that certain words (or morphemes) belong in certain contexts and not others. Thus, the word *friendly* belongs in an adjectival position and the word *friend* in a nominal one. Much of the work on structural grammar assumes that people learn linguistic form classes by a kind of equivalence relation, a situation that we shall more completely explore in later chapters.

---

[14] See the general discussion following Jenkins's chapter in Cofer and Musgrave, *Verbal behavior and learning.*

[15] See, for example, B. J. Underwood and G. Keppel. Bidirectional paired-associate learning. *Amer. J. Psychol.*, 1963, **26**, 470–474.

The chaining paradigm has been the preferred one for modern psychological theory, not only because of its connection to the classical laws of association but because of the role peripheralism has played in modern theory. The significance of the chaining paradigm is that it presumes an implicit process which possesses some, if not all, of the properties of overt response. It occurs to the exclusion of other elements (two antagonistic and simultaneous responses being impossible), and it has the stimulus properties assigned to overt responses of the same character.

Therefore, many modern students of verbal behavior have tried to reduce the equivalence paradigms to some form of chaining. That is essentially what Cofer and Foley accomplish when they cast their argument in the form of classical conditioning. If, however, we maintain a distinction between chaining and equivalence paradigms, we have some basis for the classification of associations. Associations, by such a system, would be either direct, chain mediated, or mediated by equivalence. The chained associations have nearly all the aspects of direct associations, since they are simply direct associations in which the middle terms are latent rather than manifest. Equivalence, however, leads to a kind of classification, as is implied by the above comment about grammar. The verbal elements in a language become grouped as the result of their connection to common elements; they do not necessarily ever have to be contiguous to one another directly. A and C are associately related because they both lead to B; in a structural grammar, *friendly* and *good* are grammatically equivalent because (to oversimplify) they can both occur in the frame, "he is a ——— man."

It is always possible, of course, to argue that the apparently noncontiguous relations between equivalences arise out of some latent stimulus-response chains. Whether or not the argument is useful is not central to the issue of structural analysis of associations. What is important is that the equivalence paradigm frees associative classification from the *necessity* of looking for temporally contiguous relations between terms that are associated. Whether or not one actually looks for such contiguities depends upon whether or not one is a stimulus-response theorist, not upon the nature of the relations themselves. Therefore, there is at least the possibility, in the equivalence paradigms, of the description of associative structure without direct contiguities between the terms in manifest, overt associations. It is interesting to note, in this connection, that much of the use of associations by dynamic theorists seems to imply equivalence rather than chaining. A symbol comes to stand for something not because of contiguity but because the symbol is in part equivalent to something else.

Finally, we obtain a somewhat different picture of the origin of equivalence relationships by examining the original set of ideas W. A. Bousfield developed in connection with his studies of category clustering.[16] It is worth discussing in this context in order to illustrate that equivalence relations need not arise from directional chains. Bousfield's experimental situation is quite simple. A subject is presented with a list of words. These words belong to several different classes, and these classes are semantically defined. The words are presented in random order with respect to class membership. After presentation, the subject recalls the words in any order that suits him. The results show that people tend to reorganize the presented list so as to emit, in recall, words of the same class in contiguous position. The contiguity of position in recall may be said to be evidence for association between these words, association which arises out of previous experience. Furthermore, the clustering effect itself shows the psychological reality of the original classes, and the extent of clustering may be used as an index of the degree of organization within the classes.

Bousfield's work is particularly important in the present context because he took the view that these associations do not arise from the classical laws. Bousfield assumes a principle of mediation, but the mediation is not by associative contiguity. The clustering occurs, Bousfield argued, because there was mediation by a category or concept name or some nonverbal equivalent of a category. In the recall process, the occurrence of two or more co-ordinate items activates a supraordinate structure. Such an activation provides a "relatedness increment" to the remaining individual items, and it increases their probability of being recalled together.

Bousfield indicates his debt to Hebb,[17] and, indeed, Bousfield's account of the development of supraordinate associative categories is modeled after Hebb's account of the development of form perception. Bousfield's notions, however, owe little to Hebb's vocabulary, a vocabulary which is determined by Hebb's neurophysiological interests. Nevertheless, the source of the ideas employed by Bousfield in explanation of clustering arise outside the main stream of associationism.

---

[16] Bousfield's earlier theoretical views, summarized here, may be found in W. A. Bousfield. The occurrence of clustering in the recall of randomly arranged associates. *J. gen. Psychol.*, 1953, 49, 229–240.

[17] D. O. Hebb. *The organization of behavior.* New York: Wiley, 1949.

Bousfield assumes that his subjects have had some experience at making discrete combinations of words, A with B, C with D, and A with D, and so on. He does not say so, but it is at least possible that these could arise independently of contiguous presentations in experience (and hence fail to conform to the law of contiguity). Borrowing from Hebb, Bousfield asserts that these relations of parts to one another grow into a structure, such that presentation of any one of the parts, D, for example, will raise in strength all the other parts (that is, make them more likely to occur). The network of relations between the parts form a supraordinate structure which may or may not have a class or concept name. In recall, the occurrence of one member of such a structure will arouse the concept schema, and that, in turn, is responsible for the occurrence of one or more additional words from the same structure.

Bousfield is not constrained to go further, for he is simply concerned with the description of grouping in recall. He leaves the development of categories in very general terms and then goes on to make some guesses about the effects of number of repetitions, and so on, upon the tendency to activate supraordinate structures. Surprisingly enough, he largely ignores the question of categorically relevant intrusions in recall. If recall is entirely determined by a concept schema, list membership ought to be ignored in favor of the most representative items from the category.

The equivalence relationship, by Bousfield's analysis, can be taken to explain direct overt elicitation of one term by another. The grouping together into concept schemata leads, in behavior, to the sequential emission of verbal items. Therefore, if we were to generalize Bousfield's views beyond the specific problem of category clustering, we should say that the organization apparent in the flow of verbal behavior is the result of sequences of that behavior being under the domination of one or another concept schemata. Such an account is very much like Bleuler's description of the organization of sequences of thought in schizophrenia, to which we referred earlier in this chapter.

One further aspect of Bousfield's notion has implications for the structure of associations. Suppose a new term enters into some kind of relation with an existing term. If, for example, A becomes associated with a new term, E, the new term is then equally associated with all the other members of the category. It would, by virtue of association with A, exist as a co-ordinate member of the system. Such a case, however, should not be interpreted simply as mediation by associative equivalence, for Bousfield does not invoke the directionality that would be implied by a mediational description. E may elicit A, B, C, or D, and A, B, C, or D may elicit E. There is simply a new term in the structure.

Structures grow by a kind of accretion. Though Bousfield does not explicitly deal with the problem, one would suppose that categories themselves, under some circumstances, would become co-ordinate members of supersystems. Therefore, one can imagine Bousfield's scheme of organization to be like a branching, hierarchical classification. In Bousfield's view, one does not go directly from one subsystem (species) to another; it always is necessary to detour via the next higher or supraordinate order, though the supraordinate concept itself may never appear in any behavioral sequence.

Almost the entire purpose of Bousfield's category description of verbal organization is to give a coherent picture of clustering and similar effects. It can, however, be regarded as a more general organizational scheme, one that yields a classification of associations. It does so, however, by restricting associations to a particular case. Hence the category norms[18] Bousfield uses are not quite the same as norms for free associations. Subjects who provide his norms are asked to give examples of categories—of vegetables, chemical elements, or kinds of footgear. This is precisely the weakness of the categorical description of verbal organization; it is by its very nature a special case. If we think of the category organization as representing a scheme of ideas, we must accept the proposition that some ideas do not fit the scheme. The major reason for devoting so much space to Bousfield's system at this point is its explicit freedom from dependence upon the principle of contiguity as explanation. Category clustering can be regarded as a kind of equivalence, but it does not arise out of an explicit consideration of the possibilities of contiguity via mediation, as does the analysis presented by Cofer and Foley.

In summary of these first two chapters, we may say that association theory has its appeal because it seems to describe the haphazard nature of the order of ideas in thought. It is based on the temporal order of succession of elements in language and thought, and it asserts that these elements occur in the order in which they do because that is the order in which they occurred in some previous experience. Yet

---

[18] B. H. Cohen, W. A. Bousfield, and G. A. Whitmarsh. Cultural norms for verbal items in 43 categories. Technical Report No. 22. Storrs, Conn.: Univ. of Connecticut, 1957.

associations are not totally disorderly, for a given thought does not lead to any other thought. Hence, despite the almost complete dependence of association theory upon the principle of contiguity, various investigators and commentators have tried to derive more logical schemes for the classification of associative dependencies in language and thought. No classification scheme has been entirely satisfactory, however, because each is in some way an attempt to impose a non-associative principle of organization upon associations. Thus, logic, grammar, and various semantic schemes have been brought into use in the attempt to describe the structure of associations.

The free-association test itself has survived as a technique of psychological investigation because it is an instrument for detecting the sequences of thought as these seem to exist in their most unconstrained form. The free-association test is, of course, not entirely free. The results of any particular test are determined by a number of things, many of which are trivial and situational but, at the same time, impossible to avoid. Nevertheless, of all of the ordinary psychological techniques that have been used to study the sequence of thought, the free-association test comes closest to being context-free. Therefore, the proper instrument with which to begin the study of verbal organization in thought is the free-association test. However, we should rid ourselves of any preconceptions about how the individual contingencies revealed between individual stimuli and responses in free association arise or how they ought to be organized or classified. These free associations are related to meaning in a very fundamental way, and the nature of that relation is the subject of the next chapter.

3

The Concept of Associative Meaning

In his well-known book, *Language,* Bloomfield defines the meaning of a linguistic form as "the situation in which the speaker utters it and the response which it calls forth in the listener."[1] Such a statement clearly reflects the behavioristic influence upon Bloomfield; it is couched in the language of stimulus-response psychology. The statement is, however, not quite so objective as it first appears, for what Bloomfield means by the "speaker's situation" is something more like what ordinarily would be described as the "speaker's intention" rather than the "stimulus" of classical behaviorism. In fact, in retrospect it is easy to see that Bloomfield could have more perfectly achieved objectivity by ignoring the "speaker's situation" entirely, or, perhaps more accurately, by assuming that meaning for the hearer and the speaker is the same. Such an assumption reduces the definition of meaning to the hearer's *responses* to particular linguistic forms, and it assumes that there are similar potential responses on the part of the speaker, which prompt him to utter the forms in question. However, Bloomfield was under the strong influence of early behaviorism's attempt to reduce the act of communication to stimulus and response.

A useful start to the psycholinguistic analysis of meaning can be made with the definition provided by Bloomfield. He, however, goes on to assert:[2]

> In order to give a scientifically accurate definition of meaning for every form of a language, we should have to have a scientifically accurate knowledge of everything in the speaker's world. The actual extent of human knowledge is small compared to this. We can define the meaning of a speech-form accurately when this meaning has to do with some matter of which we possess scientific knowledge.

[1] L. Bloomfield. *Language.* New York: Holt, 1933. p. 139.
[2] *Ibid.,* p. 139.

Still further, he remarks:[3] "In practice, we define the meaning of a linguistic form, wherever we can, in terms of some other science." What Bloomfield is plainly doing in these statements is ruling meaning out of linguistics or psycholinguistics and into the definitional schemes of the several sciences. He helps to establish the point of view held in structural linguistics and elsewhere which asserts that meaning cannot be studied scientifically.

The result is that a very promising beginning to the psychological study of meaning, one suggested by Bloomfield's initial assertion, is never realized. By picking up at the point before Bloomfield ruled meaning out of linguistics per se we can, I think, come to a conception of meaning that has systematic use in linguistics and psychology. That implies we are to consider meaning as revealed by the responses elicited in human beings to individual linguistic forms, not as revealed by the definitions provided in a scientific study of objects in the world. Furthermore, when we take such a position, we can make the study of associations relevant to the concept of meaning.

One difficulty encountered in defining meaning as the response of a hearer (or speaker) is that any particular linguistic form, at various times, elicits a variety of responses in the same person. Therefore, the meaning of any form is not given by a single response or, indeed, by a collection of responses at some particular time, but by the *potential distribution of responses to that form*. Such a notion provides the general basis for the ideas presented in this chapter.

The idea of meaning as the distribution of potential responses is intuitively appealing, but it runs the danger of being too general a notion to be useful. Obviously, we cannot, in empirical fact, specify the sum total of the responses which can be elicited by any linguistic form from each and every speaker or even from a representative sample of speakers of a given language. Such a distribution is open-ended or potentially infinite. New elements are continuously added. Such a concept of meaning can be made useful in application only by restricting the definition to some particular distribution for which it is possible to obtain empirical approximations.

The most obvious and straightforward case to which the concept of meaning as the distribution of responses can be applied is that of the distribution of free associations. The free-association test yields distributions of responses to particular linguistic forms across a population of speakers of a language, and the entire history of fifty

[3] *Ibid.,* p. 140.

years of psychological investigation of the matter asserts that these
are the most direct and immediate responses elicited by the linguistic
forms which serve as stimuli. The free-association test, as it is ordinarily administered, is not context-free, but it is perhaps as close to
a context-free testing situation as anything that can be devised. The
subject of a free-association experiment is instructed to respond to
the stimulus as a single, independent item. He does not respond to
the stimulus as if it were embedded in a sentence or some discourse.
However, the particular response an individual is likely to give to a
stimulus is in part under the control of earlier responses he may have
given, as well as earlier stimuli he may have responded to. Furthermore, despite explicit instructions to the contrary and willingness to
co-operate, subjects do edit their responses. Furthermore, and most
generally, the nature of the free-association test restricts potential
responses to verbal ones. Therefore, at best, the distribution of
responses obtained from a free-association test is a distribution of
intraverbal meaning. It yields no direct picture of the images and so
on elicited by a particular stimulus.

Despite these limitations, the free-association test provides a useful
approximation to the hypothetical potential distribution that defines
the most general case of meaning. It is the most nearly context-free
of all the techniques of eliciting verbal responses to particular stimuli.
Therefore, it is possible to assert that the distribution of free associations is less restricted than the distribution of utterances to some
linguistic form under any other set of instructions or constraints. Free-
association instructions, for example, clearly provide less restriction
upon distribution of responses to the stimulus, "Tell me what _____
means." Free associations are not limited to particular form classes or
by any prior conception of the "logical" or "hierarchical" structure of
meaning.

These two characteristics, the limitation of the obtained associations
to verbal responses and the minimal influence of context, are the
important features of the distributions of responses to stimuli in free
association. Therefore, these are the two chief characteristics of what
shall hereafter be called *associative meaning*. In using the term
"associative meaning," I do not mean to imply the operation of the
classical laws of association in the production of meaning. The term
is meant simply to describe the major characteristics of the distributions of responses obtained in the free-association test. The term
"meaning" itself we shall use to refer to the hypothetical complete and
unconstrained distribution from which the associative distribution is

drawn. This statement implies that *associative meaning* is a subset of
the set *meaning*. We shall, in the later chapters of this book, present
evidence to show that associative meaning is the largest subset that it
is possible to obtain empirically by any single technique. Obviously,
any other restricted distribution can be described by the appropriate
adjective. Thus, we may characterize Bousfield's norms as yielding
categorical meaning. We may characterize the set of entries (typically
in the form of sentences or phrases) in a dictionary as *dictionary
meaning*. Obviously, we are concerned with the schematic meaning
of lexical forms, not the meaning of particular and individual sentences.

Though we may, under some circumstances, be interested in the
absolute character of some distribution of responses given to a particular word as stimulus, more often we are interested in the relations
between the distribution to that word and the distributions to other
words. Meaning is a relational concept. That is to say, it describes the
nature of some relation between words and natural phenomena or
between words and words. In the analysis of language and thought
we are mainly concerned with the relations between linguistic events.
Therefore, our interest in associative meaning centers on the relations
between distributions to different linguistic forms as stimuli rather
than on the relations of those distributions to natural phenomena
generally.

The distribution of responses evoked by a particular word as
stimulus defines the meaning of that word. The only ways in which
such meaning can be specified are (1) by the nature of the distribution itself and (2) by the relations that distribution has to distributions
of responses to other linguistic forms as stimuli. Therefore, in large
part, our enterprise will consist in the study of the relations between
words in associative meaning and the reduction of the associative
meaning of some linguistic forms to the meaning of others. In later
chapters we shall be concerned with the problem of reducing these
relations to underlying schemata or structures.

Our problem for the present chapter is the comparison of distributions of responses obtained to two or more stimuli in free association.
The comparison of such distributions yields a technique for the classification of associations, and that classification is one rooted in the
associative process itself. It is determined solely by the relations
among the associative distributions, not by any extra-associative
principles of organization.

We might, it should be noted, also study the distributions of stimuli to particular responses. These distributions, however, are less interesting than the distributions of responses to stimuli. They do not specify the meanings of associative concepts; rather they specify the distribution of linguistic forms in a language that have common meanings. They can, in theory at least, tell us how responses are mapped over the stimuli that comprise the perceived world (or, more particularly, the world of verbal stimuli), but, when they are used in this way, they are subject to a serious problem of sampling, a problem to which we shall have occasion to return later. One is fairly certain to observe all the statistically important responses to a given stimulus in even a very modest sample. It is considerably more difficult, however, to specify all the *usual* stimuli for any given response.

We aim, then, to study the intraverbal associative meaning of stimuli by characterizing the relations among the distributions of free associations to stimuli. In order to pursue this problem, however, several practical questions of technique and methods of analysis arise, and these must be settled before we can go on to the general issue.

Any general review of methods for studying associations[4] illustrates the variety of options available for the determination of distributions of free associations. For a point of departure, we shall take as the distribution of responses to any stimulus, the collection of responses to that stimulus, each response elicited from a different subject. We obtain only one response per individual per stimulus because we know that subjects have memories, and consequently a second response to the same stimulus is likely to be influenced by the first. The association is no longer free. Furthermore, the degree or amount of constraint is unknown, so there is no further analysis possible. In an ideal condition we should take only one response from a single individual and present him with only one stimulus. Otherwise, we run the danger of having responses to other stimuli influenced by the responses to the first. Such contextual effects, while undoubtedly present, are of minor influence, and any attempt to eliminate them is, to say the least, impractical.

In fact, the constraint introduced into the second and succeeding responses to the same stimulus does not provide an insurmountably difficult problem in analysis. A technique introduced by Garskof and Houston,[5] about which we shall have more to say later, deals with the

---

[4] For example, Chapter 3 in R. S. Woodworth and H. Schlosberg. *Experimental psychology.* Second ed., New York: Holt, 1954.

[5] B. E. Garskof and J. P. Houston. Measurement of verbal relatedness: An idiographic approach. *Psychol. Rev.,* 1963, **70**, 277–288.

problem of multiple responses to the same stimulus from the same subject. Furthermore, an examination of some data provided by Laffal and Feldman[6] shows that certain characteristics of associative meaning are very resistant to the constraint created by obtaining multiple responses from the same subject. It is, however, best to begin with the situation which introduces the least constraint into the testing situation, and that situation is provided by the most widely used technique of obtaining free associations, which is to obtain only one response at a time from each subject.

The distribution we obtain by the standard free-association technique is one characteristic of a sample of individuals. If the sample is an appropriate one, it will enable us to describe the structure of associative meaning of the words used as stimuli for a population of users of a given language. It is important to note, however, that the structure of associative meaning we obtain by comparing distributions of responses to different stimuli is not the meaning for a single individual but that for a population of individuals. It is, strictly, a kind of socially agreed upon meaning, we may take the structure determined for a population as representative of the major characteristics of the structure for a single individual. In theory, it is analogous to describing the characteristics of a single undergraduate at a given college by the average characteristics of all undergraduates at that college. The analogy cannot be pushed too far, however. If people do not possess meanings in common, they cannot, of course, communicate. We shall argue that common meaning in communication is to a considerable extent determined by the existence of commonality of associative structures in different people. Therefore, the determination of associative meaning by combining responses from different people into a distribution should yield a picture of the linguistic commonality that exists among these people. If there are no meanings shared in common between individuals in a sample, there should be only haphazard and unreliable relations between distributions to different stimuli and no orderly associative structures should emerge. It does not follow so readily that there is a community of personality characteristics in a sample of individuals.

The relationship between any pair of linguistic forms, then, is determined by a comparison of distributions of responses from different individuals. If the associative meaning of any stimulus is given by the distribution of responses to that stimulus, then *two stimuli*

[6] J. Laffal and S. Feldman. The structure of single word and continuous associations. *J. verb. Learn. verb. Behav.*, 1962, 1, 54–61.

may be said to have the same associative meaning when the distribu-
tions are identical, and they may be said to share meaning to the
extent that these distributions agree.

Distributions may be said to agree when they possess examples of
the same linguistic forms. A measure of the relation between two
stimuli in associative meaning, then, depends upon the co-occurrence
of common elements. Such co-occurrences define the intersection of
distributions of associative meaning. In the past few years, a number
of different investigators have developed indices for describing associative measures of relatedness among words. Many of these indices,
summarized in a review by Marshall and Cofer,[7] describe ways of
comparing associative distributions. The measure to be described
below most resembles and depends upon assumptions made by
measures developed by Jenkins and Cofer[8] and by Bousfield.[9] Much
of the argument presented below is an extension of arguments
presented by these investigators.

It is rare that a linguistic form occurs as a response to itself in free
association. Frequently, subjects in a free-association experiment are
instructed in such a way as to discourage the emission of responses
identical in linguistic form to the stimulus. Even when such instructions are not explicitly given, subjects rarely give responses which are
merely echoes of the stimulus. It could be argued that such is the case
because there are social sanctions imposed upon merely echoic verbal
responses. In any event, the almost total absences of echoic responses
raises a problem which is of fundamental importance in the measurement of relatedness in associative meaning through intersecting
distributions of responses. Pairs of words often appear to be associatively related when they yield no *overt* associations in common. These
cases are always words for which the responses to one include many
examples of the word which is the stimulus for the other. An example
in data collected from Johns Hopkins University undergraduates is
the pair, *soft-loud*.[10] These words elicit one another as associates, but

[7] G. R. Marshall and C. N. Cofer. Associative indices as measures of word
relatedness: A summary and comparison of ten methods. *J. verb. Learn. verb.
Behav.*, 1963, 1, 408–421.

[8] P. M. Jenkins and C. N. Cofer. An exploratory study of discrete free associations to compound verbal stimuli. *Psychol. Reports*, 1957, 3, 599–602.

[9] W. A. Bousfield, The problem of meaning in verbal learning. In C. N. Cofer
(ed.). *Verbal learning and verbal behavior*. New York: McGraw-Hill, 1961.

[10] Here and in other places references to associations collected from Johns
Hopkins University undergraduates describe data collected on samples of from
fifty to two hundred students during the period from 1957 to 1964. Portions of
these data have been published elsewhere.

in a sample of fifty responses to each, they possess no other words in common. Even in a larger sample they would show little agreement in associative distributions. These words, then, would have little associative resemblance if one considers only the overt responses in common. Yet intuition leads one to suppose that they are highly related.

This difficulty has been recognized by many investigators. One solution has been to adopt the assumption that a word serving as a stimulus in free association not only yields the overtly given associate *but also yields itself as a response.* Therefore, such an assumption asserts that each example of a free association yields two responses, one the assumed implicit response which is identical to the stimulus and the other the overt response. At any time, N free associations are obtained; therefore, the assumed size of the distribution of associations is $2N$. Half of these associates are, by assumption, the stimulus word itself.

Bousfield, Cohen, and Whitmarsh[11] have called the assumed implicit response the "representational response." The term is meant to describe a response which identifies or represents the symbolic stimulus. Such a view of the implicit response, however, raises a problem not examined by Bousfield and his associates. These investigators make the assumption that the implicit response is always identical in linguistic form to the stimulus—that it is, in fact, the same morpheme or morphemes. For a great many words as stimuli, particularly when the words are read, such an assumption creates no difficulties. It does so in certain other cases, however, and these cases have the interesting consequence of providing some independent support for the assumption of a representational response in a measure of associative relatedness.

Rare or unusual words provide one case. If the word is rare enough not to be recognized as a word by some of the individuals in the sample, or if it is recognized as some other, more common word, there will be variation from subject to subject in the representational response. Such variation can usually be detected, in an intuitive way, by an inspection of the content of the obtained associations. An example, again taken from the Hopkins data, is the word *abbess*. Casual inspection of the distribution of free association to this word strongly suggests that many subjects were reacting to that word in the

[11] W. A. Bousfield, B. H. Cohen, and G. A. Whitmarsh. Verbal generalization: A theoretical rationale and an experimental technique. Technical Report No. 23. Storrs, Conn.: Univ. of Conn., 1958.

same way they would react to *abyss,* while others were reacting in a quite different and more appropriate way. Such confusions among linguistic forms may be responsible for many unusual effects in free association, as well as some of the more interesting forms of word play, puns, and the like.

A closely related problem is that of formal homophony. In a phonemic (in contrast to graphemic) presentation, the words *earn* and *urn* will elicit, from most subjects, free associations appropriate to the word *earn.* In a fair-sized sample, however, responses appropriate to *urn* do occasionally appear. Furthermore, some evidence suggests that the representational response for such homophonic pairs is strongly under the control of context, even when that context would not otherwise exert much influence upon the distribution of obtained associations. Thus, in eliciting a series of free associations from a subject, preceding the phonemic sequence \ərn\ by stimulus words like *wages,* and *salaries* will produce a set of associations totally different from that produced when the identical phonemic sequence is preceded by *funeral* or *vase.*

It is this kind of result which provides some objective argument for the reality of the representational response. For it would not be possible to obtain differences in distributions of free associations to precisely the same phonemic string depending entirely upon context, if the context did not force the occurrence of one representational process to the exclusion of the other. Such homophones, of course, frequently provide distinctly different distributions when they are visually presented. In the Hopkins data, there are no responses in common between the distributions for *earn* and *urn.*

Therefore, it is clear that one cannot assume that the representational responses for all words in the languages will be the same from subject to subject. Nevertheless, the assumption of identity of the representational response is a useful approximation that works for very many, perhaps most, words in the language when a reasonably verbally skilled set of subjects is tested.

The assumption of a representational response identical to the stimulus allows for easy recovery of the frequency of that response. It is possible, however, to estimate the frequency of other forms occurring as representational responses by content-scoring of the obtained associations. The assumption of identity works well with ordinary words—words of high or moderate frequency of usage—and it even works for homophones when one member of the pair is of very low frequency of use in the language at large. In all subsequent

TABLE 2: Frequencies of Associates in Common to Nineteen Words Highly Related in Associative Meaning

Responses	\multicolumn{19}{c}{Stimulus words[a]}																		
	1	2	3	4	5	6	7	8	9	10	11	12	13	14	15	16	17	18	19
1. Moth	50	2	50					1											7
2. Insect	1	50	25						8										6
3. Wings	2		12	4					3										5
4. Bird		9		50	3				2										4
5. Fly	10			15	4			1				9					2		3
6. Yellow					50	50	2	2			1	1		4	10		1		2
7. Flower		24				2	50				1	2		1				2	
8. Bug					4			50				1							
9. Cocoon									5										2
10. Color									50	50									
11. Blue				1	1					8						40			
12. Bees	2	1				5	2	2	1		50								
13. Summer						2	2					50	50	1	1				
14. Sunshine												1	1	50					
15. Garden					1		6							1	50				
16. Sky											6					50			
17. Nature						1											50		
18. Spring	1																		50
19. Butterfly	4								8				3	4				1	
20. Light																			2
21. Pretty							3									1			
22. Ant		3			1			5		1									
23. Bright														4					
24. Airplane			4	3	1														
25. Feather			2	2															
26. Flight			1	2															
27. Tree				2	1												6		
28. Plane			2		5									1					
29. Red						6	1			16	13		1						
30. White						1				5	2						2		
31. Green						5	2				4				3				
32. Sun						2													
33. Beetle								1											
34. Spider								1											
35. Gold						1					1		1						
36. Black						1				8	2								
37. Winter													17	8					
38. Warm										1			3		5			4	
39. Plant							2			1								1	
40. Gray						1					2						1		
41. Brown						1													
42. Vacation													2					1	

SOURCE: J. Deese. On the structure of associative meaning. *Psychol. Rev.*, 1962, **69**, 166.

[a] The numbers of the stimulus words correspond to the first 19 response words.

49

data presented in this book, the assumption is made that the representational response is identical in linguistic form to the presented stimulus.

The most direct way to introduce a formal definition of intersection in associative meaning is to examine a collection of words for which the various relations in associative meaning may be computed. Such a collection is presented in Table 2. The words in this table are of little intrinsic psychological or linguistic interest, but the collection as a whole is useful because the words are all highly related in associative meaning. That the words are so related has been assured in a quite mechanical way. One word in the collection is *butterfly*, and all the other words are commonly occurring associates to *butterfly*. Associations were obtained to each of these words from a sample of fifty Johns Hopkins University undergraduates. The words all appear as stimuli across the top of the table. Any response *in common* between two or more of the stimuli appear in rows. Since each word possessed some free associations not in common with any of the others, the sums of the rows will not be the same.

Since the associations presented in Table 2, under the assumption of the representational response, were obtained from a sample of fifty subjects, the total number of responses possible to each stimulus is one hundred. The individual columns do not total one hundred in Table 2 because only those responses in common between the various stimuli appear. Notice that the frequency for the representational response (50) is entered in the cells locating stimulus-response intersections. Also note that not all possible identical stimulus-response cells need have entries in such a table, for the table only lists responses common to two or more stimuli. If a particular stimulus never appears as a response to another stimulus, it need not be entered as a response to itself in such a table. Such occurrences will be rare, however, in collections of highly related words.

The simplest measure of associative intersection among words may be obtained by introducing the assumption that *there are no within-individual constraints in the distributions of associates*. Such an assumption can be interpreted to mean that each individual contributing an association to a sample is equally likely to give the association contributed by every other contributor. That assumption is, of course, an oversimplification. Individuals do sometimes give unique and idiosyncratic associations. The assumption, however, provides a reasonable approximation to the true state of affairs when subjects are relatively homogeneous. It is analogous to the assumption introduced into the law of comparative judgment by the famous Case II.[12] Like Case II of the law of comparative judgment, it yields a result which is descriptive of any one individual from that sample only in the case that the assumption is correct. In fact, it results in a description of a kind of adjusted average for the entire sample.

The assumption of absence of within-subject constraint makes it a matter of indifference which subject in a sample produces any particular response. Subject A may yield a particular associate to stimulus I, while subject B may yield the same associate to stimulus II. The two stimuli are assumed to yield a response in common on the grounds that the response of either subject is representative of a potential response in the other. Either subject might have given the response to either of the stimuli. To the extent that within-subject constraints do actually exist, however, a response given by one individual is not likely to be given by another. The result is that the obtained values for an index of commonality of associative meaning will be lowered.

We may take the conditional frequency of occurrence between pairs of stimuli as the measure of the commonality in distributions of responses to those stimuli. A response is said to have a conditional frequency of occurrence only if it occurs in both distributions. As a consequence, the joint frequency of occurrence is always the smaller frequency of the pair. The commonality in distribution, then, is the sum of the conditional frequencies of occurrence divided by the geometric mean of the N's of the two distributions. Therefore,

$$\text{I.C.} = \frac{S_A \quad S_B}{\sqrt{N_A \cdot N_B}}$$

$S_A \cap S_B$ is the intersection of the two stimuli, with R_C as the sum of the responses in common and the denominator as the geometric mean of the two distributions. If the two distributions are equal in size (the same number of associations having been obtained to each stimulus), the denominator is simply the N for one distribution, and it is the number of possible conditional occurrences.

Such a measure may be readily derived from the expression of the product-moment correlation in terms of common elements,

$$r_{AB} = \frac{N_C}{\sqrt{N_A + N_C} \ \sqrt{N_B + N_C}}$$

[12] I am indebted to E. S. Howe for pointing out that the analogy is to Case II and not Case V as I have asserted elsewhere.

Here, N_C refers to the elements in common, N_A to the elements in the distribution of elements in A not in B, and N_B the distribution of elements of B not in A.

If it were possible to obtain distributions of associations to repeated presentations of the same stimuli without the artifacts introduced by repeated presentation, these two equations would define the measure of relation for single individuals. Various schemes for estimating distributions from single individuals will be discussed in a later chapter.

The only feasible alternative to the assumption of absence of within-individual constraints on the distributions of associates is the assumption made by taking the obtained associations as a measure of constraints that do exist. Such an assumption is equivalent to saying that, if an individual does not give a particular response to a given stimulus, that response does not occur in his distribution of responses to that stimulus. Such an assumption is clearly inappropriate when but a single response is obtained from each subject, and, if it were used in determining the index of intersection (by counting joint frequencies only when they were given by the same subject), it would result in gross underestimation of the commonality in associative meaning even for particular subjects, much less over a population of individuals at large.

An example of the calculation of the index of commonality may be taken from the first two columns of Table 2. These present the responses to *moth* and *insect* respectively. *Insect* yields *moth* twice, and this is also the common frequency of occurrence (by assumption of the representational response). *Insect* occurs to *moth* once, and *fly* occurs to both with the smaller frequency being nine. Therefore, the sum of the frequencies in common is twelve, which, when divided by the total number of possible occurrences in common, yields an index of 0.12.

The measure of relation in associative meaning between two words may, in theory, vary from 0.00 to 1.00. The latter value, however, will happen only if the responses to both stimuli in a pair consist entirely of instances of the stimulus for the other—that is to say, when responding is completely reciprocal. Such a result is a consequence of the assumption of the representational response. In practice, of course, such a result never occurs. An approximation to it, however, is very common and of considerable importance. Certain adjectives yield other adjectives as associates with very high frequency of occurrence (see Chapter VI). These usually constitute reciprocal pairs in which the relation of associative meaning is almost entirely determined by the frequencies of the reciprocal responses. Such pairs receive almost their entire intraverbal associative meaning from one another, and they are pairs which function in equivalent verbal positions. They are likely, in discourse, to appear in the same sentence, even though they are not synonyms for one another. As a matter of fact, they are usually antonyms. Pairs of adjectival antonyms constitute the most common scheme for the meaning of English adjectives, and as the above discussion would imply, these antonym pairs define orthogonal dimensions.

Such pairs are related, of course, in the traditional associative sense. They elicit each other. Notice, however, that the maximal associative relation, in the present sense, occurs only if the pairs are nearly symmetrical. Occasionally one finds pairs of words in which one member frequently elicits the other, but the second only infrequently, if at all, elicits the first. Such a pair could reach a maximal commonality of associative meaning of only 0.5. These pairs do occur, and they occur under particular circumstances. The most general case (at least for adjectives) for such pairs is that in which one member of the pair is part of a basic adjectival pair-scheme, while the other is a less frequently occurring synonym of one of the members of the schematic pair. For example, *frigid* sometimes elicits *cold* (and, in this sample, most frequently elicits *woman*), but *cold* almost never elicits *frigid* (and most commonly elicits *hot*). In this way, the associative meaning of certain less frequently occurring adjectives tends to collapse on the various pair-schemes.

These patterns within a particular form class or part of speech are more characteristic of the associations of adults than children.[13] Children are more likely than adults to give syntagmatic associates. Thus to *good*, a child is more likely to respond with *boy* than would an adult (who would most probably give *bad*). Ervin[14] and others have argued that the within-form-class or paradigmatic associations of adults arise by mediated equivalence. Thus, the sentence, "He is a _____boy," is liable to give rise to the use of both *good* and *bad* in the missing position. Through occurrence in a number of such sentences, *good* and *bad* come to elicit one another through mediated

[13] See D. R. Entwisle, D. F. Forsythe, and R. Muus. The syntactic-paradigmatic shift in children's word associations. *J. verb. Learn. verb. Behav.*, 1964, 3, 19–29, for an account of the literature on this problem.

[14] S. M. Ervin. Changes with age on the verbal determinants of word association. *Amer. J. Psychol.*, 1961, 74, 361–372.

equivalence. Because the process of development of equivalence is incomplete in children and still growing, children are less likely to produce the mediated equivalences than adults and, instead, produce common sequences in English.

Notice that such a process of development of mediated equivalence does not depend upon directional chained associations, and its description by the chaining process is circumstantial and cumbersome. One might more simply say that individuals tend to make equivalent or partially equivalent (intersecting) linguistic forms which occupy identical positions in ordinary utterances. An associationist might object that such a description fails to make contact with a large body of experiment and theory from the learning laboratory. It might equally well be said, however, that it does make contact with current conceptions of grammatical structure and with both practical and laboratory programs, designed by linguists, for the learning of grammar.[15]

If two stimuli have precisely the same distribution of responses, except that they never elicit each other, the maximum value the index of commonality can take is 0.5. In a word, the potential associative intersection is lower than if the words elicit each other. Pairs of words which have intersecting distributions of responses except for themselves are not uncommon. An example from the Hopkins data is the pair, *piano* and *symphony*. These both elicit *note, song, sound, noise, music,* and *orchestra* in varying frequencies, but they do not elicit each other. Intuitively at least, it would seem that such pairs would much less frequently occupy positions in identical sentences than would, say, *good* and *bad*. We shall examine this supposition at greater length later; suffice it to say here that such pairs characteristically occur in certain groups of nouns in English.

Some kinds of such pairs—pairs which do not include one another in their distributions—are also found among words which possess common morphological features which serve to mark their form class. The several classes of morphologically marked adjectives provide examples. Compare *childish* and *freakish* or *fragmentary* and *rudimentary*. In brief, some words may have commonality in associative meaning *only* because of the grammatical position they occupy. Therefore, if our present point of view is useful it further erases the distinction between

---

[15] It is very difficult to provide a single reference for this assertion because the point of view that people learn morphological equivalences by contextual interchangeability is very diffuse in modern linguistics. For an English grammar text which exemplifies the approach, see P. Roberts. *Patterns of English*. New York: Harcourt, Brace & World, 1956.

grammar and meaning. A form class is a large but weak set of equiva-lences. As the equivalences become stronger (that is, as the intersec-tions between distributions become larger), the sets become smaller, and we are more likely to describe the relation between the linguistic forms as one of meaning rather than grammar. The distinction, in the present context, between grammar and meaning is difficult to maintain in view of the great usefulness of regarding both grammatical and meaningful relationships among distributions of associations as arising from equivalences of frames in ordinary discourse.

Finally, one other result stems from the assumption of the repre-sentational response. It is that every word must have at least some associative meaning in common with at least the words it yields as responses. Hence, the obvious result is that we may use the content of free associations to determine some (but not all) of the words related to the stimulus in associative meaning. Inspection of the content of free associations is a rather weak way of discovering the patterns of relations that exist in associative meaning. We may happen upon an occasional *tyrant* to *father* that is of interest, but if we restrict ourselves entirely to the inspection of the responses that occur to *father*, we miss the important fact that the words *powerful, big, old, angry,* and *man* occur both to *tyrant* and *father*. It is this point as much as anything else which describes why dynamic theorists have sometimes over-looked psychologically important relations among words.

Table 3 is a matrix of indices of commonality in associative meaning calculated from the data in Table 2. The assumption that a word always elicits the same associates as itself is responsible for the entries of unity in the main diagonal. The data in Table 2 are typical for any collection of words that are highly related in associative meaning. In-deed, it is just about impossible to obtain any collection of stimuli larger than three, each member of which has some intersection with at least one other member in the set, which does not conform to the general pattern in Table 3.

The skewed distribution of indices of commonality evident in Table 3 (the median index being 0.02) is characteristic of any collection of highly related words. Such a pattern is also evident in Table 4, which is a matrix of intersects for four highly related words, *man, woman, girl,* and *boy.* There are two large values in this table and four small ones. The two large values define fundamental contrasts (*man-woman* and *girl-boy*), while the four smaller indices show how these contrasts are related. It is, perhaps, intuitively satisfying to know that *boy* and *girl* are both more related to *woman* than to *man.*

TABLE 3: Intersection Coefficients for Associations in Common between the Words in Table 2[a]

Stimulus words	Stimulus words																		
	1	2	3	4	5	6	7	8	9	10	11	12	13	14	15	16	17	18	19
1. Moth	100	12	12	12	11	01	00	04	11	00	00	02	02	05	01	01	01	01	15
2. Insect		100	09	09	17	01	01	33	10	01	01	03	00	00	00	00	01	00	12
3. Wing			100	44	19	00	00	03	02	00	00	10	00	00	00	00	03	00	13
4. Bird				100	21	01	00	03	02	01	01	10	00	01	00	01	05	00	12
5. Fly					100	01	01	08	06	01	02	06	00	03	00	02	04	00	11
6. Yellow						100	07	00	00	17	23	02	02	07	05	02	04	03	05
7. Flower							100	02	00	03	07	02	01	06	18	02	06	02	06
8. Bug								100	00	00	00	05	00	00	00	00	02	00	04
9. Cocoon									100	00	00	04	01	02	01	08	02	00	22
10. Color										100	32	00	00	02	00	46	00	00	00
11. Blue											100	01	02	04	04	00	03	02	02
12. Bees												100	01	02	03	03	04	02	07
13. Summer													100	05	02	00	01	10	00
14. Sunshine														100	02	00	02	15	04
15. Garden															100	00	04	02	02
16. Sky																100	00	01	00
17. Nature																	100	02	03
18. Spring																		100	02
19. Butterfly																			100

SOURCE: J. Deese, On the structure of associative meaning, p. 167.
[a] Decimals omitted.

If we pick words at random from the dictionary and from these words prepare a matrix like those in Tables 3 and 4, the result is a vast sea of zero entries, dotted here and there by some positive values, usually low in magnitude. If such a matrix is prepared from words that are of low frequency of usage in the language, the result will be almost no commonality at all. Even a very large matrix of uncommon words is unlikely to show any intersection. If, however, a large matrix is prepared from a haphazard selection of more common words, there will be a fair number of positive entries. These entries are very un-

TABLE 4: Intersection Coefficients for *Woman, Man, Girl,* and *Boy*[a]

	Woman	Man	Girl	Boy
Woman	1.00	.68	.16	.12
Man		1.00	.08	.04
Girl			1.00	.73
Boy				1.00

[a] $N = 100$ Johns Hopkins University undergraduates.

likely to define structures, however, unless the table is a very large one, and even then the structures will describe the entries for a very small percentage of the cells. It is extremely improbable, therefore, that highly organized matrices, such as those exhibited in Tables 3 and 4, could be arrived at by a process of random selection of even common elements in a language.

Highly organized matrices, like those in Tables 3 and 4, may be generated in any one of several ways. One of these is by the simple expedient of choosing words which are all frequently occurring associates of a given word and then, in turn, finding the associates these words yield. Another way is to consider some structure capable of definition outside of associative terms, such as the sex-age structure implied in Table 4 or the structure that would be implied by a kinship system. Associations obtained from such material will be organized, though the associative organization may not be precisely like the extra-associative structure which generated the table. In short, organized tables of associative meaning may be achieved by almost any method that takes advantage of the relations among concepts and words in a language.

Let us, for a moment, return to Table 2. If we limit Table 2 to the first fifteen words and if we ignore the representational responses, we have a matrix of stimulus-response frequencies. For convenience, such a matrix, with the cell entries given in relative frequencies, has been prepared in Table 5.[16] This matrix, which can be called an interword associative matrix, shows the relative frequencies by which the words

TABLE 5: Interword Associations to the First Fifteen Words in Table 2[a]

	Moth	Insect	Wing	Bird	Fly	Yellow	Net	Pretty	Flowers	Bug	Cocoon	Color	Stomach	Blue	Bees	Average
Moth		2	2	10					2	10						
Insect	4			18						48					2	
Wing				50	24											
Bird			6		30									2		
Fly		10		8						18						
Yellow										3		11		16		
Net	2	2		2												
Pretty																
Flowers						2						2		2	2	
Bug	2	36		2	4										4	
Cocoon	16	6		4						10						
Color														20		
Stomach																
Blue												10				
Bees				15					5							
	24	56	8	81	86	2	0	0	10	86	0	23	0	40	8	28.3

SOURCE: J. Deese, in C. N. Cofer (ed.). *Verbal learning and verbal behavior.* New York: McGraw-Hill, 1961, p. 18.

[a] The numbers presented in the table are percentages.

in the table *elicit each other*. Such a matrix lends itself to a variety of treatments, as Marshall and Cofer have shown in their review. Furthermore, as Pollio[17] has shown, a variant of this matrix can be operated upon to show the possible paths of stimulus-response relationships. Finally, the average of the rows or columns provides a measure of the degree to which there are direct associative connections within the table.

Such a table, or something like it, provides the basic information for experimental studies of the covariation of associative frequency and such processes as free recall, clustering, and the like. These studies, in a great variety of ways, show that stimulus-response frequencies ob-

[16] These data are from J. Deese. Influence of inter-item associative strength upon immediate free recall. *Psychol. Reports,* 1959, **5,** 305–312.

[17] H. R. Pollio. A simple matrix analysis of associative structure. *J. verb. Learn. verb. Behav.,* 1963, **2,** 166–169.

tained from free-association norms predict the probability of recall and ease of learning of the entries in the table when these entries are appropriately combined in some verbal task. Some studies show that the mean of the rows in such a matrix predicts the number of words from the collection that can be correctly recalled after one presentation.[18] Other studies show that the tendency of items to cluster in recall can be predicted from the individual cell entries of matrices like that in Table 5.[19] These and other effects are usually taken to be reflections of the naturally occurring strengths of association between words, as these are revealed in the free-association test. The results of these studies are widely interpreted as being consequences of the laws of classical association theory, particularly the laws of contiguity and frequency.

Measures obtained from arrangements like that in Table 5 differ in principle from the measure of relationship obtained from the index of stimulus intersection. Measures of interword association imply the process of stimulus-response chaining, while measures of stimulus intersection imply stimulus equivalence. Despite this difference, however, measures of equivalence and chaining are highly correlated, particularly when the assumption of the representational response enters into a measure of stimulus equivalence. Therefore, the data presented in Table 6 are not surprising.

Table 6, in part, reproduces some data from one of the studies which relates free-association frequency to availability of words in recall. The first column in Table 6 is the mean number of words correctly recalled out of fifteen words presented in each of eighteen lists. The second column in Table 6 shows indices of interword association frequency (the means of the row totals for matrices like that in Table 5) for the fifteen words in each of these eighteen lists. It is obvious that there is a high correlation (0.89) between the index of interword association frequency and the number of words correctly recalled. The third column of Table 6 presents the averages of all possible stimulus intersection coefficients between the fifteen words in each list. These values are also highly correlated with recall (0.82) and, of course, with interword association frequency.

A simple and straightforward interpretation of the correlation between the interword association index and number of words in recall

---

[18] J. Deese. From the isolated unit to connected discourse. In C. N. Cofer (ed.). *Verbal learning and verbal behavior.*

[19] J. J. Jenkins, W. D. Mink, and W. A. Russell. Associative clustering as a function of verbal association strength. *Psychol. Reports*, 1958, 4, 127–136.

is possible. In recall, the subjects can take advantage of the pre-existing stimulus-response relations in order to recall one word when they have already recalled a good association stimulus for that word. If the list contains few such pre-existing transitions, recall and interword association both will be low, whereas, if the transitions are many, both will be high.

TABLE 6: Mean Number of Words Recalled in Immediate Free Recall for Lists of Words[a] Differing in Interword Associative Frequency and Average Between-Word Associative Intersection

List no.	Mean no. words recalled	Interword assoc. (%)	Mean intersection
1	7.9	28.3	.046
2	6.7	4.3	.016
3	5.6	1.0	.001
4	6.5	15.1	.040
5	5.8	0.2	.018
6	5.8	2.7	.005
7	7.3	22.8	.026
8	5.6	4.0	.019
9	5.4	2.3	.007
10	7.7	20.5	.053
11	6.1	9.3	.021
12	5.1	0.0	.006
13	7.1	13.0	.028
14	5.6	0.7	.005
15	5.2	0.0	.005
16	7.8	17.0	.052
17	6.6	2.0	.010
18	6.1	0.0	.006

[a] Fifteen words in each list.

It is not so easy, as Marshall and Cofer point out, to describe a relationship between the intersection coefficient and recall. From the standpoint of the usual, chaining interpretation of the process of association, the index puts together into a single measure a lot of different aspects of association. Sometimes the index is largely determined by mutual elicitation (*heavy* elicits *light* and *light* elicits *heavy*), and sometimes pairs of words which have responses in common (*heavy* and *lamp* have *light* in common). Furthermore, as Marshall and Cofer point out, sometimes pairs of words which have the same intersection coefficient as other pairs seem to be based upon qualitatively very different relations. For example, the pair *heavy-lamp* and *eagle-crow* have the same index (0.21), yet one relation is based upon a homographic identity between two different morphemes (*light*), while the other relation seems to be conceptual in nature. (Both are instances of the bird category.)

Therefore, while the intersection coefficient, in company with a large number of indices of associative relatedness, is related to measures of recall, a simple interpretation of the measure seems to be difficult. Furthermore, Marshall and Cofer have some evidence to show that categorized pairs and noncategorized pairs with the same intersection coefficient behave differently in recall.[20] Such a result would imply that the intersection coefficient does not exhaust the relation in meaning between two words and that it, in addition, may imply a meaningful relation where none exists. Finally, there seems to be no particular virtue attached to the intersection coefficient, compared with the index of interword association and other measures of relatedness.

The interpretative difficulty that attaches to the intersection coefficient is, however, in no small measure the result of concentration on a limited set of words in making a comparison. The possible relations between individual words are very many, and any given pair may be related for grammatical, semantic reasons or, as in the case of *heavy-lamp*, because of homologous forms. It is only possible to make an intuitive guess, based upon one's own experience with the language, as to the nature of the relation when faced with a single related pair. *In fact, however, the nature of the relationship between members of an isolated pair will be exposed when that pair is embedded in an appropriate matrix.* The intersection coefficients themselves will reveal a good deal of the nature of the relation (though not all) when the pair *heavy-lamp* is placed in a matrix made by the coefficients between *weight, dark, strong,* and *black.* Because the intersection coefficient is based upon all possible associative relations between pairs of words, the specific nature of any given relation cannot be detected without comparison with other possible relations. Thus, it is very likely that the conclusions Marshall and Cofer seem to draw about the extent of clustering in categorized and noncategorized pairs with the same intersection coefficients would have to be modified as those pairs are embedded in different contexts.

It is, as we implied at the outset of this chapter, the very generality of the measure of intersection of associative distributions that is its strength. Associative meaning does describe the most general case of relation between elements in a language as these occur in thought or speech. Specific relations describable as grammatic (through form

[20] G. R. Marshall and C. N. Cofer. Technical Report No. 4. Referred to in Marshall and Cofer, Associative indices.

class) or semantic or in some other way are part of the generalized intersection of associative distributions to two linguistic forms. In order to detect the structures which lie beneath any overt relation between a pair of words, those words must be embedded in a matrix capable of revealing the various possible structures.

By the same token it is also reasonable that two pairs, equal in intersection but different in the nature of the relation, would behave differently in some laboratory test of verbal process. The argument as to why this should be so cannot be made, however, without recourse to the structural analysis of matrices of intersections, a task to be accomplished in later chapters of this book.

The intersection coefficient is not, then, one of a set of equally arbitrary indices of associative relatedness. It is the most general because it includes all possible associative relations between pairs of linguistic forms. Whether or not the intersection coefficient or some derivative of it will predict to a more precise degree verbal processes depends upon the set of verbal elements about which the prediction is made. Therefore, in some particular instance, measures derived from a simple chaining process, as is the interword association index, may more accurately predict data. For example, the ordering of mean recall in data like that in Table 6 may predict more precisely than a measure derived from intersection coefficients. Furthermore, adding some non-associative information, as in the Marshall and Cofer comparison between categorized and noncategorized pairs, may improve the prediction to such processes as recall and clustering. That is because, in adding such information, it is possible to make use of the relations to words other than those in the specific comparison. One knows that *eagle* and *bird* belong to a common category and *heavy* and *lamp* do not because one can draw on other words in the language to make the comparison. It is not so much that *heavy* and *lamp* are less related in the language than *eagle* and *crow* as that they are differently related. How they will behave in any particular laboratory test of verbal processes will depend upon what other words are present and therefore—to speak loosely—what concepts are aroused. Our problem, then, is not to describe the degree of relation between isolated pairs but to describe the patterns of relation among many words.

Relations in associative meaning may be described as a form of stimulus equivalence. Stimulus equivalence is the appropriate psychological description of the nature of concepts. Note, however, that stimulus equivalence based upon associative meaning is not the result of a single response in common between two or more stimuli, as would be the case in some interpretations of concept formation by associative mediation, but it is the result of a distribution of responses in common.

Ordinarily, when a stimulus-response analysis is applied to the problem of the nature of concepts, the concepts themselves are assumed to be discrete. Thus, while a stimulus may belong to several or many concepts, the concepts themselves are not distinct and separated from one another. A particular attribute, present in a number of stimuli, may be said to "elicit" a single response. That response then is the name for that attribute, and it serves to differentiate the attribute from other attributes of the same collection of stimuli. Or alternatively, a collection of stimuli may be divided into different classes on the basis of some purely arbitrary assignment to response classes. In principle, such concepts would not be different from those in which the response is correlated with an attribute, except that a person must either learn such concepts by rote or invent for himself some attributes correlated with responses—attributes that would be appropriate to a larger collection of stimuli.

If, however, we consider stimulus equivalences to be based upon commonality among distributions of responses, we are faced with concepts which are statistically but not absolutely distinct. The boundaries for any given concept must merge more or less indefinitely into those for another concept. There is, however, a "center of density" for a given concept, which, in the notion of associative meaning, would best be represented by that stimulus word which overlaps the most with the other stimuli in the collection comprising the concept.

The highly organized character of words which are closely related (Tables 3 and 4), however, suggests that there is not a continuous distribution of stimuli in some n-dimensional space, such that one could always insert, between any pair of words that resemble one another, a third word that resembles both. Rather, there are relatively sharp boundaries between groups of words in the language. For example, the large classes which define grammatical relations provide examples of such more or less sharp boundaries. The distributions defining associative meaning exist in more or less well-defined clusters. In theory, one should be able to find pairs of words that overlap in associative distributions without overlapping the distributions for any other words—the completely reciprocal case, discussed earlier, provides a theoretical example—though one should not, again in theory, find a completely isolated word.

Highly related words, then, tend to break up into conceptual clusters, clusters that are defined by groups of words mutually high in intersection. If the notion of associative meaning is applied to problems in the analysis of recall and clustering, we are to assume that conceptual clusters emerge within any collection of words that shows some interrelation. These conceptual clusters could, in fact, behave much as Bousfield, in his earlier theorizing, described the process of supraordinate clustering in recall. The concepts implied by associative meaning, however, are not limited by the supraordinate relations. Associative concepts may occur very willy-nilly indeed, so far as any particular logical analysis of conceptual schemes may go.

Though, in theory, we may imagine much the same principle described by Bousfield for category clustering to operate in associative clustering and enhancement of recall, it is more difficult to give a concrete account of the process *in general*. The problem can be put one way by saying that it is not at all obvious that there must always be a readily available concept name to attach to the conceptual clusters defined by intersecting distributions of associations. It is some considerable comfort in this matter, however, to point out that human verbal processes provide many examples of concepts which do not have formal names yet are fundamental to verbal behavior. Everyone makes use of words in such a way as to reveal direct knowledge of form-class membership, even though most people may not be able to apply abstract names properly to these grammatical concepts. Whole languages, indeed, may not possess words in their lexicons to describe the complicated grammatical concepts used by speakers of those languages.

The schemata of concepts, furthermore, may not only serve the traditional roles assigned to concepts in verbal processes but may also serve the role usually assigned to stimulus-response chains. It should be noted that, in the case of single isolated pairs of linguistic elements, the concept and the stimulus-response chain (providing it is reciprocal) are always equivalent. I cannot forbear the comment that, while the usual practice in psychological theory is to derive the concept from the stimulus-response unit, the opposite is implied here—that stimulus-response units are simply relatively isolated concepts.

Therefore, we are to regard both the overlapping distributions of responses in association and the various effects within collections of words observed in verbal learning experiments as the outcome of conceptual equivalences between words. These conceptual equivalences may well be sharp, distinct, and discontinuous for any given person at one moment, but in the general case we suspect that they cannot be. It is a commonplace observation that people are forever using words in new and different ways and that they are not consistent in such use from occasion to occasion. Therefore, any description of verbal schemata based upon data taken from a large number of people or even taken from one person over an extended series of observations should result in blurred, statistically delimited schemata.

The problem before us, then, is twofold. We must find ways of studying the relationship between words within the context of other appropriate words, so that, for example, we can specify in a clear and objective way what it is that enables us to say with certainty that the pair *eagle-crow* is not like the pair *heavy-lamp*. Secondly, we must find ways of reducing the organization inherent within collections of words to underlying patterns—to the equivalences and differences, not among the words themselves, but among the concepts behind the words and collections of words.

It is difficult, not to say impossible, to solve these two problems within any collection of words simply by an inspection of the associative patterns that exist among those words. Fortunately, there exist a variety of techniques, both linguistic and psychological, for solving these problems. The next few chapters will be devoted to applications of these techniques to the data of associative meaning—the intersecting distributions of free associations.

4
The Psychological Structure of Meaning

꽃

It is evident that there are highly organized relations between words; these relations are responsible for the main features of language and the unique character of human language. Some of the organized relations in language are reflected in the distributions of free associations. If two words elicit one another as free associations, the chances are very great that they will also elicit other words in common, other words that, in turn, will elicit the original pair as well as one another. The schematic character of the structure of associations is to be detected in the analysis of patterns of these relations, and it is the thesis of this book that these structures are responsible for whatever generalized and schematic meaning lexical elements can have in isolation.

There are, in general, two approaches to the search for the underlying structures that provide the framework for relations among words. One of these is hypothetico-deductive. It requires that we define the nature of schemata by stating certain propositions. We then look for the empirical evidence which supports the implications derivable from our propositions. The other approach is inductive. It asks us to reduce the statistical relations among words to simple structures which, in turn, allow us to recover the main features of the original statistical relations among words in linguistic usage. Such an approach, for our present problem, would start with the empirical distributions of associations and would make the assumption that the structures discovered by various analyses either consist of or are simply related to the underlying schemata of associative meaning.

In practice, we move back and forth between these two alternative approaches, now electing to examine the structure among associations by purely inductive statistical methods and at some later time examining the relations among associations in the light of certain propositions about the underlying structures—propositions which are themselves derived from psychological or linguistic theory. In this chapter, the primary emphasis will be upon the statistical analysis, a technique, of course, which introduces certain assumptions into the treatment of the data and which is restricted by certain limitations. Before discussing the statistical structure of associative meaning as it is revealed by factor analysis and other techniques, however, certain issues need to be examined. These issues arise out of earlier work and can best be made explicit by a critical discussion of that earlier work. The principal method to date for examining the structural relations among the meanings of words by statistical-empirical treatment is the semantic differential.

The semantic differential[1] is a psychological technique for the investigation of the relationships that exist among words (or, more generally, among concepts, whether verbal or not) by a rating-scale method which is said to define a particular kind of meaning. The meaning discovered by the semantic differential is best explained by a description of the method for obtaining the ratings. Such a description, of course, provides us with an operational definition of the meaning uncovered by the semantic differential. The authors of the semantic differential tell us in addition, however, that this meaning described by the semantic differential is connotative, and they say that it is not only characterized by the techniques of the instrument per se but that it has certain important psychological properties as well. In their words, they contrast *connotative* meaning with *denotative* meaning. In an ultimate analysis, it is very difficult to say what this distinction means in the context of the theory of the semantic differential, but it can be roughly stated by saying that connotative meaning is the emotional or affective meaning of concepts while denotative meaning is their referential meaning.

The semantic differential is both a technique for collecting data and a theory. The technique itself is quite general, and it could be applied to almost any theoretical description of meaning and the processes behind meaning. In many instances, however, the application of the semantic differential purely as a technique is only a trivial exercise. In practice, the generality of the method for the study of meaning depends upon the theory. That theory restricts the kind of verbal

---

[1] The background for the semantic differential was originally presented in C. E. Osgood. The nature and measurement of meaning. *Psychol. Bull.*, 1952, **49**, 197–237, and in C. E. Osgood and G. J. Suci. A measure of relation determined by both mean difference and profile information. *Psychol. Bull.*, 1952, **49**, 251–262. The principal source, however, for the technique is C. E. Osgood, G. J. Suci, and P. H. Tannenbaum. *The measurement of meaning.* Urbana, Ill.: Univ. of Illinois Press, 1957.

68   Structure of Associations in Language and Thought

material used in the rating scales and the resulting structures of meaning to affect and metaphorical extensions of affect. It was such a
restriction that led Osgood, in his original presentation of the semantic
differential, to say that the meaning it reveals is connotative in nature.

The technique of the semantic differential consists in asking an
individual to judge the extent to which any concept (say *socialized
medicine*) can be described by a certain set of rating scales. These
rating scales are defined by end anchors consisting of opposed adjectives, such as *good-bad, strong-weak,* and *hot-cold.* Since the scales are
always bipolar, the adjectives are limited to such antonymic pairs.
The technique, then, at the outset draws upon some *intuitively given
aspect of meaning,* namely, the oppositional or antonymic character
of certain adjectives. Because we must intuitively accept these adjectives as opposite in meaning, the technique in its very foundations
lacks complete objectivity. It is rooted in the process it attempts to
measure; in this respect it is very like many psychological techniques.

In theory, any number of such bipolar scales could be used for the
semantic differential. In practice, a very limited set is generally
employed, and much of the theoretical development of the semantic
differential consists in justification for the selection of a particular
appropriate set. The particular set of bipolar adjectives most frequently used is determined by its usefulness for describing some
underlying bipolar dimensions of connotative meaning. The underlying structure of connotative meaning is supposed to be bipolar in
nature, and such a structure can be discovered by examining the
pattern of relations among the manifest scales. It is, furthermore,
implicit in the semantic differential that the meanings of words or
concepts can be described by unique positions in a semantic space.
The Euclidean co-ordinates of that space provide the framework
for semantic structures. It is, therefore, most important that these
co-ordinates be described. Part of the problem in arriving at the
scales to be used in a semantic differential is to discover the dimensionality of such a semantic space and in so doing identify the
co-ordinates. The positions of words and concepts within the space
define the structure of meaning, as meaning is uncovered by the
semantic differential. Such a structure is said to be evident in the
clusters and families of words that are revealed in some n-dimensional
projection of semantic space.

With the proviso that the meaning defined by the semantic differential is only a limited kind (connotative), the theory behind the
semantic differential implies only that (1) the structure of meaning

can be described within some set of bipolar dimensions and (2) the selection of scales for the semantic differential for all practical purposes exhausts the possible dimensions of semantic space. The argument is further made that only connotative meaning can be studied by such a psychological technique.

The standard form of the semantic differential was obtained from a group of 289 pairs of adjectives selected one each from categories in a thesaurus. This collection of 289 polar pairs (polar on the intuitive assumption noted above) was reduced to 105 by having judges sort the 289 polar terms into seventeen categories on the basis of "similarity of meaning." While this operation is crucial to the generality of the semantic differential, it is not well described in the original source material. However, we need note that the dimensions of semantic space depend not only upon the rating scales but upon this prior sorting operation. One pair represented each of 105 clusters of highly related adjectival meaning. An additional twenty-nine pairs were eliminated by further application of the same technique. This reduced the sample of scales to seventy-six.

Twenty concepts, which consisted of four persons, four physical objects, four abstract words, four "event" concepts, and four institutional concepts, were rated by subjects on each of the seventy-six scales made by using each of the seventy-six polar pairs as anchors on a seven-point rating scale. These twenty concepts were selected to provide some broad sample of the universe of possible concepts. Specifically, these were *foreigner, my mother, me, Adlai Stevenson, knife, boulder, snow, engine, modern art, sin, time, leadership, debate, birth, dawn, symphony, hospital, America, United Nations,* and *family.*

The particular technique of rating, the numerical treatment of the data, and the details of the ultimate factor analysis of the data need not concern us at the moment. A very adequate and detailed critique of these matters, particularly of the factor analysis, is to be found in the review by J. B. Carroll[2] of the book by Osgood and his associates. Suffice it to say that the net result of the treatment of the data obtained from the twenty concepts listed above was to reduce the original seventy-six scales to twenty. Of course, such reduction depended in one way or another upon correlations among the seventy-six pairs. Furthermore, the author of the semantic differential argued that the information in these twenty scales could be, in most cases, summarized by three orthogonal dimensions. The twenty scales, as a

[2] J. B. Carroll. Review of Osgood, Suci, and Tannenbaum. The measurement of meaning. *Language,* 1959, **35**, 58–77.

matter of fact, were said to be as pure as they could be for one or another of the three orthogonal factors. Each scale projected a vector through, or very close to, one of the orthogonal dimensions; therefore, to a greater or lesser extent, each of the scales could be taken as an approximate measure of one of the dimensions. Note that this vast reduction of seventy-six pairs to three basic dimensions depended in the final analysis upon a sample of twenty concepts.

The three dimensions themselves were characterized as evaluation, potency, and activity. For the evaluative dimension, the pure scales were *good-bad, optimistic-pessimistic, positive-negative, complete-incomplete,* and *timely-untimely.* Potency provided for *hard-soft, light-heavy,* and *masculine-feminine,* and activity included *active-passive, excitable-calm,* and *hot-cold.*

The critical reviews by Carroll, Weinreich,[3] and others have already pointed out the deficiencies in method which allowed the discovery of the three dimensions of connotative meaning. These criticisms need not be repeated here. Suffice it to say that the heart of the difficulty (aside from purely technical matters in the application of the factor-analytic techniques) lies in the sample of polar-opposite words used to rate the concepts and in the sample of concepts said to be representative of all possible concepts. Nothing could be more obvious, once we free ourselves of the attempt to make a distinction between connotative and denotative meaning, that the number of possible independent dimensions (and therefore pure scales) should be limited only by our ability to differentiate among objects and events in the world and in our private experience. There would surely be a *green-red* dimension and a *blue-yellow* dimension if the right concepts were chosen to be rated. Such dimensions would not be connotative, in the sense that word is used by the authors of the semantic differential. The existence of synesthesias, to say nothing of ordinary metaphorical usage ("I was green with envy"), however, makes it apparent that one could argue the extension of the concept of connotative meaning even to these cases. In fact, it is extremely difficult to know what the limits of connotative meaning are and how, in some particular application, its use is to be distinguished from that assigned to denotative meaning.

The correlations among the seventy-six scales which enabled the authors of the semantic differential to reduce their scales to twenty and to account for most of the variance among these scales by three

---

[3] U. Weinreich. Travels through semantic space. *Word,* 1958, **14,** 346–366.

factors is clearly the result of the limited sample of concepts listed above. As we shall see later, the dimensions of meaning uncovered in any sample of words (concepts) depend upon that sample. It would be possible to find twenty concepts for which the twenty scales would be inappropriate (and then yield no variance on any of the scales). In addition, it would be possible to find twenty concepts which, for the same scales, would yield three different factors as the dimensions describing most of the variance.

Furthermore, as Carroll pointed out in his review, in order to establish the dimensionality of a space (the number of dimensions required to locate objects with some specified accuracy within the space), it is necessary to have an adequate sample of objects in the space for which one is seeking the dimensions. Such was clearly the intent behind the original sample of concepts used to provide the twenty bipolar scales, though it is very hard to see how the problem of dimensionality could have been solved without a clear and explicit definition of the domain of semantic space (connotative meaning)— something that has never been provided.

Therefore, it cannot be said without risk of argument that the semantic differential is a technique for establishing the basic dimensionality of some specific kind of semantic space, except in the trivial sense that it supplies the dimensions named. It is, however, a useful device. It provides a convenient, standard set of adjectives by which people can indicate how they feel, in certain ways, about objects, events, concepts, and words. It has the merit, in comparing one study with another, of being standard. It is, however, to a large degree arbitrary. The semantic differential should rest on its empirical merits, and it deserves comparison with attitude scales, which it closely resembles.

There is a very close connection between the semantic differential and associations. The nature of the connection will be a topic of discussion both in this and later chapters. For the present, however, we need only point out that the relation is responsible for the fact that ratings derived from the semantic differential predict the ease with which people learn particular associates. Bousfield[4] has presented an analysis largely based upon this fact. Bousfield's analysis views the semantic differential as a particular and somewhat artificially constrained version of an association task in which an individual picks

---

[4] W. A. Bousfield, The problem of meaning in verbal learning. In Cofer (ed.), *Verbal learning and verbal behavior.* In all fairness, it needs to be mentioned that Osgood, in the same source, is able to answer some of Bousfield's arguments.

among two possible associates rather than emits associates. Bousfield implies that the relations between the words or concepts rated on the semantic differential are ultimately derivable from the relations between associations.

While it is certain that the specific nature of the semantic-differential test introduces some unique properties of its own, Bousfield's results are convincing enough to make it profitable to view the process underlying the semantic differential as an associative one. Since the major thesis to be presented in this and later chapters asserts that associations derive from schematic structures, we shall view the results of semantic-differential ratings themselves as so derivable. Therefore, much of what follows applies, in principle, to the semantic differential. We must realize, however, that the rating-scale technique itself forces the data of the semantic differential into a pattern which may obscure the meaning of the concepts rated. It is easy to think of concepts that are, for example, both *good* and *bad*. If a concept is rated on such a bipolar scale, it is not clear whether the obtained position of the concept on the scale is the result of some compromise between the two anchors of the scale or is the result of one side of the scale not applying to the concept. In a word, it is not clear whether vector or scalar addition is at work. Therefore, simply as a matter of technique, the bipolar rating imposes on the data a constraint which is absent in the distribution of free associations.

In short, semantic-differential ratings are constrained by (1) the selection of scales upon which any concept is judged, (2) the applicability of the vector properties implicit in any psychological rating scale with particular anchors, and (3) the bipolar nature of the scales (as opposed to, say, something less than 180 degrees). Analyses of the relationships in distributions of free associations are not constrained by any of these features. If, however, we apply factor-analytic techniques to the study of such relationships, we introduce certain features peculiar to such analyses, and these need to be made explicit.

The most basic and important limitation to the study of relations in associative meaning by factor-analytic techniques is that we cannot obtain the dimensionality of the factor space of associative meaning short of exhausting the linguistic universe. In practice, we cannot establish such dimensionality by any purely empirical technique. If it were desirable to accomplish such an enterprise, it would require, if no theoretical assumptions are introduced, the treatment of matrices of associations in which every linguistic form in a given language occurred as a stimulus. Therefore, a more limited goal must be chosen for the study of associations through factor analysis. Such a goal may be stated as the discovery of the fundamental structure of relations obtaining among the words *within any given collection.*

The factors that result from any factor analysis depend upon the variables entering the factor matrix. In the theory of tests, which has seen the major application of factor-analytic techniques, this restriction is sometimes overlooked, for the reason that a good sampling of tests over some considerable domain of ability is possible. Test theorists are often convinced that the batteries of tests they factor provide representative samples of the entire set of abilities to be tested.

In general, such a restriction is a property of any analysis which seeks to reduce to its schematic essentials any "representative" collection of data. The schematic structure that is obtained will depend upon the selection of the data that make up the collection. If we wish to specify the meanings of words intraverbally, we are limited by the words we chose in order to make the appropriate contrasts in meaning. For example, if we are to give the intraverbal meaning of the word *hot,* we could say (keeping within the spirit of the semantic differential) that "it is the opposite of *cold;* it is close to *warm* and further away from *cold* than is *warm.*" In general, we have great freedom in making such statements; the larger the number of possible relations in meaning any given word has, the richer and more variable our definitions of that word can be. If we are limited to a very few terms in making such a definition (as would be, for example, a pocket dictionary), we cannot exhaust the meaning of the word in question.

In a factor analysis, or, more generally, in any comparison within a matrix of words, we are limited by the collections of words available to us and by the relations between these words in making contrasts in meaning. Conceivably, we could be forced into the position of describing the intraverbal meaning of *hot* by the use of *hard, wet,* and *pretty.* In any general application, that is what the semantic differential would force us to do. In describing the intraverbal meaning of a word when we are not constrained by some special technique, such as the semantic differential, we are free to choose our contrasts from a very large vocabulary. In fact, however, for most cases we actually choose our contrasts from a very limited set; we seldom define a given word in a way that calls upon a vocabulary very different from that employed in defining closely related words. In short, the ordinary meanings of words are structured. For any wide range of words to be defined, however, we need new samples of words in order to make the definitions. It is here that the semantic differential has its greatest weakness.

Once we realize that, in any case whatever, we are limited in the analysis of intraverbal meaning by the collection of words we have available for making appropriate definitions, it is unlikely that we will want to adopt the procrustean strategy of trying to make all concepts fit a limited collection of words, or a limited set of rating scales. Instead, we would like to be free to vary the collection of words providing the description of intraverbal meaning to suit the occasion. That does not mean, however, that any analysis of the intraverbal meaning of words within a language is limited to the production of schematic structures from local samples. It is very possible that there may be very general *structure types* within a language.

A structural analysis of intraverbal meaning, then, should be directed towards finding a simple structure relating the words within any specified collection. We may choose the collections out of linguistic, psychological, anthropological, or statistical considerations. Almost always, however, we shall choose a set that has some structure, for, if we choose words haphazardly, no orderly structure will emerge. A simple structural pattern will only emerge within a collection of words to the extent that the words are related intraverbally.

In any event, it is clear that we cannot use the analysis of any particular sample of words to describe exhaustively the meaning of any one word within a collection. We shall, however, in later chapters describe techniques which may make it possible to exhaust the important or most general meaning of any one word or collection of words. We are interested in an exhaustive description only to the extent that we focus on one word. More generally, we may be interested in the pattern of relations that holds some particular collection together. We may, however, make use of the relations within a collection to predict or extrapolate to relations with other words not in the collection. The sampling of words within a collection will not usually be "representative" in any statistical sense; more usually the "representativeness" will be based upon some linguistic concept or assumed psychological process.

It is characteristic of the relations among words in associative meaning that the values of the intersection coefficients within any matrix produce a skewed distribution. There are, in most collections, a very few high-valued intersections, a large number of low-valued ones, and, perhaps, a majority of zero entries. In general, the amount of skewing is determined by the size of the collection of words, but such skewing is a general property of relations in associative meaning (consider Table 4 in the preceding chapter) and is generally responsible for the kind of simple interpretation that can be given to the structure of most matrices of associative meaning.

The foregoing discussion makes it clear that we do not choose words for analysis at random. We choose words because we suspect that they are related to one another. In later chapters we shall examine various matrices, chosen for a variety of reasons. The matrices presented in this chapter have not been chosen for theoretical or generally important reasons but for the empirical reason that they produce well-defined structures. These are matrices, by and large, generated from associative relations.

Table 3 (p. 56) provides a convenient point of departure. This table is a matrix of intersections in associative meaning for a set of stimuli which themselves are all responses in free association to the word *butterfly*. (*Butterfly* is also contained in the table.) The table may, therefore, be said to illustrate the relations in associative meaning between words which are, themselves, responses to a single stimulus and, as a consequence, themselves comprise a portion of the definition of associative meaning for that stimulus.

Similar tables have been prepared using the words *music* and *slow* as stimuli. All of these tables have been factored by a centroid factor analysis and subjected to a very simple rotation. The rotation, most generally accomplished by rotating pairs of factors through 45 degrees, projects factor axes through the main clusters of words that emerge in analysis. Such a projection has the advantage that one or more of the words in a cluster provides a convenient label for the factor. Since the clusters are always at or near right angles, it is possible to identify orthogonal factors with the clusters. In such an arrangement, all but the first two factors are bipolar, and the scheme provides some readily apparent contrasts in meaning. It has the disadvantage of eliminating an important property of loadings on an unrotated first factor, and in later chapters other schemes are adopted.

TABLE 7: Rotated Centroid Factor Loadings of Intersection Coefficients for Nineteen Words Derived from *Butterfly*[a]

Words	Factors					
	I	II	III	IV	V	VI
Moth	44	03	−27	−01	−03	−32
Insect	50	01	−33	01	−34	11
Wing	52	01	45	01	29	−07
Bird	52	02	46	01	29	−07
Fly	48	03	32	01	−28	−03
Yellow	01	44	−03	34	−32	−02
Flower	01	39	−03	−32	03	44
Bug	41	01	−34	00	−14	37
Cocoon	40	01	−35	00	25	02
Color	−02	42	−04	44	04	−04
Blue	−02	57	−04	52	23	−04
Bees	36	04	34	−02	−30	00
Summer	−01	31	−03	−34	−02	−34
Sunshine	02	37	−04	−33	−03	−35
Garden	00	35	−02	−34	−03	44
Sky	−01	41	−03	43	38	−07
Nature	04	31	29	−02	01	34
Spring	−01	35	−03	−37	−02	−36
Butterfly	48	06	−29	−01	26	01

SOURCE: Deese, On the structure of associative meaning, p. 169.
[a] Decimals omitted.

TABLE 8: Rotated Centroid Factor Loadings of Intersection Coefficients for Seventeen Words Derived from *Music*[a]

Words	Factors					
	I	II	III	IV	V	VI
Tone	19	43	−03	40	02	53
Instrument	43	−01	33	01	−31	01
Symphony	49	06	34	01	43	00
Sing	41	−01	−53	02	−36	−01
Note	43	01	−33	03	37	−01
Song	55	−01	−47	00	−31	01
Sound	04	59	00	−26	41	07
Piano	52	02	37	01	−24	00
Noise	06	59	01	06	02	31
Band	51	08	38	−04	−24	−03
Horn	37	−09	00	−32	00	−43
Loud	00	48	−01	−42	−01	−29
Hear	06	60	−01	49	01	−18
Opera	51	03	−33	01	32	00
Ear	00	41	−01	52	−02	−36
Music	58	08	25	01	37	02
Soft	07	23	−02	−01	00	07

SOURCE: Deese, On the structure of associative meaning, p. 170.
[a] Decimals omitted.

TABLE 9: Rotated Centroid Factor Loadings of Intersection Coefficients of Sixteen Words Derived from *Slow*[a]

Words	Factors					
	I	II	III	IV	V	VI
Slow	67	00	39	—01	20	—01
Walk	41	02	—55	00	—38	03
Speed	49	09	—33	07	47	—04
Quick	61	00	25	—02	—07	—28
Lazy	04	35	05	—38	—05	—36
Drive	10	39	—33	02	00	04
Skid	05	40	—01	36	35	—01
Run	54	01	—52	—01	31	—01
Work	03	33	36	—01	05	—36
Fast	73	01	38	—02	20	—02
Down	01	31	—01	—36	—07	—37
Stop	01	37	05	37	—09	36
Snail	43	02	37	02	—10	33
Sign	00	36	07	07	02	—44
Poke	02	34	05	—37	—05	35
Traffic	04	36	06	33	—04	—36

SOURCE: Deese, On the structure of associative meaning, p. 170.
[a] Decimals omitted.

Figure 2 shows the contrastive nature of the clusters which emerge in analysis. The figure presents the projection of the set based upon *butterfly*; the first two factors are plotted against one another and the third and fourth against one another. A graphic representation of the data in Tables 8 and 9 would show essentially the same features.

An inspection of the loadings on Factor I in Table 7 shows that it contains the words having to do with animate creation (*bees, flies, bug, wing, bird*), whereas the words in the cluster defining Factor II are not animate words (*sky, yellow, spring*). This contrast provides the most basic structure defining the organization of this set of words. Factor III shows zero loadings on the nonanimate words, and, by and large, it splits the animate words into a bipolar contrast. The positive loadings are on *wing, bird, bees*, and *fly*, and the negative loadings are on *bug, cocoon, moth*, and *butterfly*. Factor IV makes a bipolar split of the nonanimate words; *summer, sunshine, garden, flower*, and *spring* are positive, while *blue, sky, yellow*, and *color* are negative.

Such bipolar contrasts are by no means a necessary outcome of the factor analysis, but they occur in such sets of words with great regularity, particularly when the sets consist of words all related to one another in some way. Such a condition is extremely important,

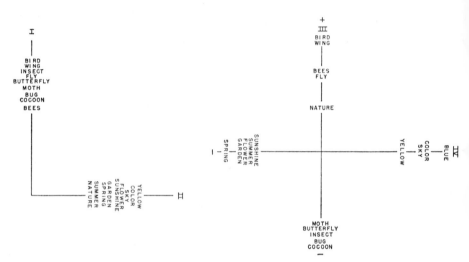

FIGURE 2: A projection of factors I and II and of factors III and IV for the *Butterfly* collection.

for it provides one way of representing the unique choice of a particular word in some context. A word occurs in some particular context because of the contrasts it may provide. Thus, in some metaphorical or poetic context, the word *butterfly* may be chosen rather than *bird* because of some unique cluster in associative meaning in which *butterfly* occurs and *bird* does not.

A similar description may be made of the data in Tables 8 and 9. Thus, the first two factors in Table 8 split the words into a musical and nonmusical cluster. Again, we should remind ourselves, "naming" the factors may add some implications not warranted by the collection of words within the table and should be done only with caution. The contrasts that are provided within any set are determined and limited by the context provided through the words in the set; it is rare that a "name" for a factor does not imply some more general collection or at least one that differs from the named set in some important particulars.

Before going further, it would be well to present some of the evidence for the psychological validity of the results obtained from such factor-analytic studies. Intuitive inspection of the arrangements presented in Tables 7, 8, and 9 yields the impression of psychological validity. Such judgment means little, however, for it is always at least possible that a purely random arrangement of clusters of such factor loadings for highly related words would look "right" on inspection.

In fact, however, the contrasts made by the loadings in these tables can be reconstructed by direct means. If the words comprising the set in Table 7 are given, each on a separate card, to subjects with instructions to sort the words into two piles, the clusters defining Factors I and II will emerge with high reliability. The same is true of the first two factors in Tables 8 and 9, though with considerably less reliability in the case of Table 9.[5] In any event, it is clear that the clusters themselves correspond to some intuitively understood contrast within the sets and that such a contrast easily emerges by direct sorting with minimal instructions.

More detailed evidence for the validity of the analysis comes from examination of the correlations between the structures defined by the factor analysis and the verbal output of subjects. The data for one such comparison come from a study by H. Weingartner.[6]

Weingartner examined the following two hypotheses: (1) The extent to which factor clusters are left intact in a list of words to be learned by rote serial anticipation should determine the ease of learning of the material, and (2) the pattern and distribution of errors should be determined by the arrangements within the list of the factors defining the contrasts among words.

Weingartner used two sets of 16 words. One set came from the factored set in Table 7, while the other came from the factored set

---

[5] I am indebted to Dr. H. Weingartner for making these observations, which he did in connection with the material described in footnote 6, this chapter.

[6] H. Weingartner. Associative structure and serial learning. *J. verb. Learn. verb. Behav.*, 1963, 2, 476–479. These data are also described in somewhat greater detail in a Master's thesis by the same title on deposit in The Johns Hopkins University Library, Baltimore.

in Table 8. The words were chosen so that eight words from each list came from the first factor and the remaining eight from the second factor. The eight words within each of the two primary factors were chosen so that four had loadings of the same size and direction on Factors III and IV, while the remaining four had loadings in the opposite direction. There were, therefore, four clusters of words by factors. The words and the factor arrangement can be seen in Table 10.

TABLE 10: Experimental Arrangement of Weingartner's Words When Associative Structures Are Intact

List I	List II
Moth	Music
Butterfly	Band
Insect	Symphony
Bug	Instrument
Bird	Note
Wing	Song
Bees	Sing
Fly	Opera
Blue	Tone
Color	Hear
Sky	Ear
Yellow	Noise
Sunshine	Loud
Summer	Sound
Garden	Soft
Spring	Horn

SOURCE: H. Weingartner, Associative structure and serial learning, *J. verb. Learn. verb. Behav.,* 1963, **2,** 477.

The resulting lists of words were presented on a memory drum at a three-second rate, and subjects learned them by serial anticipation. Learning was continued to a criterion of two errorless trials. All subjects in Weingartner's experiment learned first one of the arrangements of the *butterfly* list and then learned an arrangement of the *music* list. Ten subjects were tested for each arrangement of each list.

In one arrangement, all of the words within a factor remained together in serial order. In a second arrangement, the middle eight words remained together in intact factor patterns, while the last four words and the first four words were systematically randomized with respect to their factor patterns. The net result was that the arrangement of internal structure[7] within the second set was different than it was in the first. In a third arrangement, the first four and last four words remained in intact factors while the middle eight were randomized. Therefore, this arrangement contained the same kind of internal structure as the second, but it was differently arranged. The well-structured part of the list appeared in the initial and final parts of the list rather than in the middle. It is a well-known fact that the greatest difficulty in learning a list by serial anticipation occurs in the middle of the list. Therefore, there should be a greater advantage in serial learning when the middle is well structurd than when the ends are well structured (since the ends are easy to learn in any case).

Finally, a fourth arrangement produced the least orderly structure. In this arrangement, words from all four factors were in disarranged sequence, so that a word from any factor could follow a word from any other factor. In addition, Weingartner used two control lists, lists that consisted of different words, matched in frequency of occurrence to the words in the factored set but unrelated to one another in associative meaning.

The primary results of Weingartner's experiment are in Table 11. Table 11 shows the mean number of trials required by Weingartner's

TABLE 11: Means and Standard Deviations of the Number of Trials Required to Learn the Experimental Arrangements of Weingartner's Lists

| | Arrangement I | | Arrangement II | | Arrangement III | | Arrangement IV | |
	Mean	SD	Mean	SD	Mean	SD	Mean	SD
Butterfly List	9.0	3.4	11.4	2.5	15.0	2.9	15.2	3.8
Music List	8.2	2.8	6.3	1.7	9.9	3.8	10.9	2.6

SOURCE: Weingartner, Associative structure and serial learning, p. 478.

subjects to reach a criterion of one errorless repetition for each list arrangement. The evidence is quite clear. Subjects learn in fewer trials when the lists are well structured. A comparison of structure in the middle of the list with structure in the ends shows the location of the structure to be important. There is a greater advantage to having the structure in the middle rather than in the ends of the lists.

The shape of the serial position curves is altered in a predictable

[7] Reference here is to the extremely important distinction made between internal and external structure by W. R. Garner. *Uncertainty and structure as psychological concepts.* New York: Wiley, 1962.

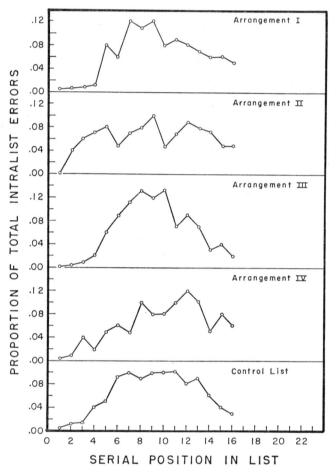

FIGURE 3: Serial position curves for the *Butterfly* list for different arrangements of structure. (Unpublished, by courtesy of H. Weingartner.)

and orderly way by the structuring of the lists. Figure 3 shows the serial position curves, based on proportion of total errors at each position, for each of the four arrangements of the structured lists. The most important alteration in the classical shape of the serial position curve is brought about by the condition in which factors are left intact in the middle. The usual peaking of error frequencies in this region is missing. Detailed examination of the shapes of these curves shows that the amount and arrangement of the structures has produced a very strong effect in the serial position curves.

Weingartner's results confirm the validity of the factor analysis as a technique for uncovering the associative structure within these sets of words. Note that such a result does not imply that the obtained factor structures are the most powerful prediction of these results in verbal learning, but it does imply that the obtained factor structures coincide with the verbal structures of the subjects doing the learning.[8]

For evidence of a different kind, we may turn to some data which concern the relation of measured attitudes to factored associative structures. These data grew out of an unpublished study by R. E. Feldman.[9] Feldman's data show that scores obtained from the Allport-Vernon-Lindzey scale of values correlate with the tendency to cluster, in recall, words derived from a particular value scale. Specifically, Feldman found that individuals who scored high on the religious value scale more readily clustered religious words than did individuals who scored low on such a scale. Such a result suggests the possibility that associative structure for words related to a particular value is more highly organized for individuals who score high in that value than for individuals who score low.

Associations were obtained to the words in Feldman's study that tended to be clustered by students who scored high on the religious value scale. Associations to these words provided the data for a comparison of the associative structure for those high and those low in religious value. The words used in the clustering study had themselves been obtained directly from items of the Allport-Vernon-Lindzey inventory which were keyed for the religious scale.

Separate factor analyses were performed on the associations to these words for fifty Johns Hopkins undergraduates who scored one P.E. below the mean (below the twenty-fifth percentile) on the Allport-Vernon-Lindzey norms and for fifty Johns Hopkins undergraduates who scored one P.E. above the mean (above the twenty-fifth percentile) on these norms. The first two factors from each analysis are presented in Table 12.

The table shows that essentially the same factor structure exists for the first two factors in the two groups of individuals. There are, however, some striking differences in the associative structure for these groups. The first factor for the high scorers is defined by the cluster *religion, worship, reverence, prayer, spirit, divine, faith,* and

[8] For a further analysis of this problem, see G. R. Miller. Extraexperimental transfer in serial recall. *J. verb. Learn. verb. Behav.*, 1963, 2, 494–497.
[9] R. E. Feldman. On the influence of value upon free recall. Master's thesis, The Johns Hopkins University, 1962.

TABLE 12: Factor Loadings of Fifteen Religious-Value Words for Students Who Are High or Low in Religious Value

| | F_1 | | F_2 | |
Word	High	Low	High	Low
Sermon	.03	.36	.43	.05
Clergyman	.11	.45	.42	.07
Religion	.54	.54	.03	.07
Service	−.01	.03	.40	.34
Worship	.57	.51	.04	.03
Reverence	.55	.46	.04	.02
Prayer	.54	.53	.03	.03
Soul	.06	.04	.38	.36
Spirit	.39	.04	.00	.39
Divine	.50	.11	.00	.36
Faith	.52	.49	.08	.05
Inspire	.03	.04	.40	.36
Devotion	.49	.41	.10	.00
Love	.03	.04	.38	.38
Hope	.06	.08	.37	.35

devotion. The first factor for the low scorers is defined by the cluster *sermon, clergyman, religion, worship, reverence, prayer, faith,* and *devotion.* The differences are in the addition of *sermon* and *clergyman* for the low scorers and the absence of the words *divine* and *spirit* for those low in religious value.

Furthermore, the coefficients for the low scorers are almost uniformly lower than those for the high scorers, a fact that indicates these words do not belong together as much for the low scorers as for the high scorers. Table 13 shows the sum of the intersection coefficients for each of the fifteen words for both the high scorers and the low scorers. These sums are consistently higher for the high scorers, a fact which is represented in slightly higher loadings on the first two factors in Table 12 for the high scorers. The differences between these factor structures are not as large in absolute loadings as they might be because of the addition of the diagonal of unity in the original matrices. Such a method for generating the matrices for factor analysis tends to make the loadings on each factor cluster together at some particular value and produces, of course, a unique factor for each word. Therefore, a better indication of the relative cohesiveness of these words for the two groups of individuals is in Table 13. Interestingly enough, the highest sum of intersection coefficients for the high scorers is for the word *religion* itself, while the word *faith* is the highest for the low scorers.

Such a result shows that the structure of attitudes can be discerned

TABLE 13: Sums of the Intersection Coefficients to All Other Words for the Religious-Value Words: High and Low Scorers Compared

Word	Sum for high scorers	Sum for low scorers
Sermon	0.47	0.26
Clergyman	0.78	0.57
Religion	1.78	0.89
Service	0.20	0.02
Worship	1.62	0.87
Reverence	1.57	0.73
Prayer	1.48	0.99
Soul	0.43	0.14
Spirit	0.70	0.22
Divine	1.20	0.40
Faith	1.53	1.05
Inspire	0.37	0.13
Devotion	1.45	0.57
Love	0.28	0.15
Hope	0.40	0.25

from the study of organization in associative meaning. Not only is it fruitful to compare groups of subjects known to differ in attitude with respect to the structure of associative meaning, it is useful to examine the patterns among words. For example, the words *communist* and *American* have some intersection in associative meaning for American undergraduates. The patterns generated by these words within a matrix of appropriate words, however, are very different. The intersection that exists between these two words occurs by way of *Russian, democracy, government, freedom, capitalist,* and similar words. There is a strong polarity between the words underlying the comparison between *Russian* and *American,* a polarity that resembles in many respects the basic polarity of adjectives in general (see Chapter VI). The words which determine the associative meaning of *communist* that make it independent of *American,* include *red, party, socialist, hate, propaganda, spy, bad, traitor, star, Chinese, pinko,* and *bastard.*

The content of the verbal behavior of individuals provides the best and most detailed means for exploring attitudes and opinions. The association test and the analysis of associative meaning provide a means for exploring that content without the usual methodological pitfalls encountered in the traditional rule-of-thumb or impressionistic methods of content analysis.

Another important psychological use of the content of verbal behavior under relatively constrained conditions is found in projective tests. Here less of the burden of interpretation is placed on specific words themselves and their interrelations, because the major results are obtained from the comparison of responses to different ambiguous visual stimuli. Nevertheless, the *content* of test protocols is important, and, more generally, the content of verbal behavior, particularly as it occurs in metaphorical and symbolic interpretation of the stimulus materials in projective tests, is judged to be psychodynamically important. Indeed, from the very beginnings of exploration of personality, the word-association test itself has found an important place.

Therefore, a study of the structure of associative meaning of psychodynamically significant words provides another opportunity for the use and extension of the technique described here. As an example, we may turn to a study of the associative structure of a set of words that was selected because it was alleged to be of general psychodynamic importance.

The words in Table 14 were taken from a study of scoring of the Rorschach test by aggressive content.[10] A few words were added to the collection because they are generally recognized to have aggressive or phallic-aggressive connotations by psychoanalytic theory. These words were presented in an association test having a total of 192 items to a sample of one hundred Johns Hopkins University undergraduates (males). Approximately ninety of the test items were chosen so as to be affectively neutral. Some examples of these are *see, orange, yard, Minnesota,* and *tennis.* The remaining words (the analysis of which is not presented here) were words of metaphorical psychosexual content.

A matrix of overlap coefficients was prepared for the words in Table 14, and this matrix was factored by a program which yields

TABLE 14: Words of Aggressive Meaning by Content Scoring of Rorschach

Ambition	Cut	Force	Pierce	Sneer
Angry	Dart	Gun	Pistol	Spear
Argue	Erupt	Hammer	Pliers	Teeth
Beast	Explosion	Harsh	Poke	Torture
Bore	Fangs	Hate	Punch	Violence
Bull	Fight	Hatred	Rage	Wolf
Bullet	Finger	Hit	Ram	Warrior
Burn	Fire	Knife	Rooster	Wrath
Club	Fireworks	Mob	Shark	Wreck
Crushed	Fist	Nail	Slash	Tiger

[10] G. E. Mackinnon. Unpublished data. The Johns Hopkins University.

a principal-components solution.[11] That the results do not differ materially from the centroid analyses presented earlier can be seen from Figures 4 and 5. The first two factors for each matrix, rotated through approximately 45 degrees, are plotted in Figure 4. Factors III and IV are plotted in Figure 5. The pattern of orthogonality in

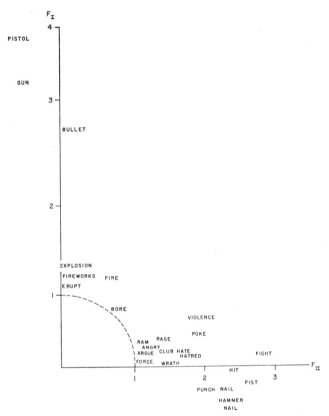

FIGURE 4: A plot of factors I and II (after a rotation of forty-five degrees) for the words in Table 14. (Words with loadings of less than 0.10 are within the dotted line and not plotted.)

these two plots is evident, though it is less clearly marked than in the earlier solutions. That is partly the result of the fact that many of the words in these tables are not highly related to other words in the set. There are clearly a number of words with extremely low

[11] H. F. Kaiser. The varimax criterion for analytic rotation in factor analysis. *Psychometrika,* 1958, **23,** 187–200.

loadings. Nevertheless, distinct and very nearly orthogonal groups emerge.

In Figure 4 it is apparent that one factor is best defined by *gun, pistol,* and *bullet,* though the words *fireworks, explosion,* and *fire* also appear on this factor. The other factor is dominated by *fight, hit, hammer, nail,* and *punch.* These first two factors seem to be dominated by the manifest, denotative meanings of these words. Other factors, however, explore the less obvious groupings of these aggressive words and, therefore, give some indication of the metaphoric and symbolic relations.

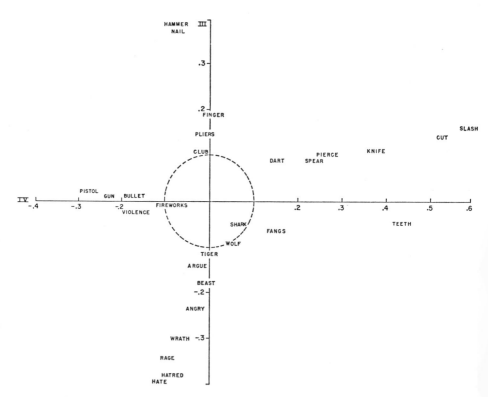

FIGURE 5: A plot of factors III and IV (after a rotation of forty-five degrees) for the words in Table 14. (Words with loadings of less than 0.10 are within the dotted line and not plotted.)

TABLE 15: Factor Loadings after Verimax Rotation[a]

Main Factors

Hatred				*Bull*		*Rooster*	
Rage	.17	Bullet	.13	Argue	.10	Rooster	.85
Wrath	.16	*Club**		Bull	.79	Erupt	.11
Tiger	.12	Punch	.13	Bore	.13	Bore	.11
Fight	.13	Dart	.35	Wolf	.12	*Knife*	
Hatred	.86	Mob	.12	*Warrior*		Rooster	.10
Hate	.13	Bull	.13	Rage	.10	Pierce	.16
Punch	.14	Finger	.18	Gun	.11	Knife	.95
*Ram**		Erupt	.20	Argue	.16	*Explosion*	
Beast	.19	Angry	.20	Wreck	.14	Erupt	.12
Bull	.70	Pierce	.13	Torture	.12	Fireworks	.13
Wreck	.13	Violence	.21	Warrior	.91	Explosion	.93
Torture	.14	Bullet	.10	*Pierce*		*Pliers*	
Erupt	.20	*Torture*		Pierce	.92	Ambition	.14
Angry	.30	Fire	.11	Pliers	.20	Pierce	.21
Force	.10	Torture	.70	Knife	.17	Pliers	.83
Wrath	.11	Force	.10	*Sneer*		Bore	.16
Knife	.11	Warrior	.10	Argue	.13	*Wolf*	
*Hit**		Wrath	.10	Wreck	.14	Beast	.12
Punch	.22	Crushed	.16	Sneer	.83	Tiger	.12
Beast	.11	*Shark**		*Bore*		Wolf	.86
Poke	.19	Force	.13	Bore	.96	*Argue*	
Hatred	.73	Pliers	.25	Knife	.10	Sneer	.11
Fist	.24	Knife	.15	Wolf	.12	Pliers	.12
Angry		Wolf	.46	*Erupt*		Argue	.89
Rage	.10	Fight	.15	Rooster	.11		
Angry	.90	Hatred	.10	Erupt	.85		
Harsh	.13	Fangs	.35	Bore	.10		

Some Isolated Pairs

Gun		*Hammer*		*Cut*		*Rage*	
Pistol	.22	Nail	.27	Slash	.20	Rage	.97
Gun	.94	Hammer	.94	Cut	.95	Hate	.10
Pistol		*Nail*		*Burn*		*Hate*	
Gun	.22	Hammer	.28	Fire	.14	Rage	.10
Pistol	.94	Nail	.94	Burn	.97	Hate	.96
Spear		*Slash*		*Fire*		*Bullet*	
Dart	.12	Cut	.18	Fire	.98	Pistol	.16
Spear	.96	Slash	.96	Burn	.14	Bullet	.95
Dart							
Spear	.11						
Dart	.96						

[a] The words to be interpreted are printed in italics. The factor loadings for these words, on factors on which they have loadings, are given above and identified by the word having highest loading on that factor. The factors are orthogonal and very nearly projected through the vectors for each of the words appearing as factor names, so this is a reasonably accurate interpretation of the loadings. Words indicated by asterisks have relatively low loadings on their unique factors.

TABLE 15 (*Continued*)

Some Single Loading Factors					
Mob	.92	*Violence*	.97	*Fangs*	.99
Poke	.95	*Wrath**	.93	*Finger*	.92
Punch	.99	*Ambition**	.82	*Force*	.93
Tiger	.97	*Beast*	.93		

Table 15 summarizes the main factorial groupings of the words in Table 14. This summary was prepared by an analytic rotation of pairs of factors. There was a complete rotation of the factors by varimax criterion.[12] Such an analytic solution produces too many factors for simple interpretation (there being only four factors which have negligible loadings for all the words in Table 14), but it does make a convenient guide in picking out the important groups or clusters of words. In order to clarify the interpretation of the groupings summarized in Table 15, words are listed only if they have loadings of 0.10 or greater on a particular factor after rotation. Finally, bipolar clusters on a single dimension have been grouped separately.

Certain words in Table 14 do not appear as main factors in Table 15. The most conspicuous example is provided by *ambition* (Table 14). In fact, *ambition* does have loadings on a very large number of factors, but these are all so low as to be eliminated by the criterion used to form Table 15. Such a result is apparent in the intersection coefficients for *ambition*. Table 16 compares the intersection coefficients for *ambition* with those of *fight*. Notice that *ambition* has some overlap with thirty-two out of the possible forty-nine words, but in all these cases, the coefficients are very small. The only coefficient larger than 0.02 is with *force*. The word *fight*, on the other hand, yields a much more skewed distribution of coefficients. There are a few rather high ones (0.21 with *fist*, for example). The distribution to *fight* is characteristic and that to *ambition* the exception within this collection. It is rare, within a collection of related words, to find a word that does not have a pronounced skewed distribution. It is possible that *ambition* has some low but very real relation to nearly all of the possible groupings of words within this set; on the other hand it is possible that it does not belong with these structures any more than any one of a large number of other words.

Some interest attaches to the nature of the responses which provide the basis for the factored structures summarized in Table 15. For all

[12] *Ibid.*

TABLE 16: Comparison of the Intersection Coefficients for *Ambition* and *Fight*

	Ambition	Fight		Ambition	Fight
Ambition	1.00	.00	Hatred	.01	.08
Angry	.02	.03	Hit	.02	.16
Argue	.01	.05	Knife	.00	.02
Beast	.01	.03	Mob	.01	.05
Bore	.02	.02	Nail	.01	.02
Bull	.01	.03	Pierce	.01	.02
Bullet	.01	.04	Pistol	.00	.02
Burn	.01	.02	Pliers	.01	.01
Club	.01	.07	Poke	.01	.09
Crushed	.01	.03	Punch	.00	.10
Cut	.00	.02	Rage	.01	.05
Dart	.02	.04	Ram	.01	.04
Erupt	.00	.01	Rooster	.01	.01
Explosion	.00	.01	Shark	.01	.01
Fangs	.00	.03	Slash	.00	.03
Fight	.00	1.00	Sneer	.00	.02
Finger	.00	.02	Spear	.01	.02
Fire	.00	.01	Teeth	.00	.01
Fireworks	.00	.00	Tiger	.01	.01
Fist	.01	.21	Torture	.00	.05
Force	.04	.06	Violence	.01	.13
Gun	.01	.04	Wolf	.01	.03
Hammer	.00	.04	Warrior	.01	.11
Harsh	.00	.01	Wrath	.01	.06
Hate	.01	.03	Wreck	.01	.02

of the words listed in Table 14, the responses were tabulated by stimuli. There were a total of 1153 types (different responses) out of the possible total of 5000. Of these 1153 different responses, 309 were common between two or more stimuli. Many of these, however, were single instances of responses occurring to only two stimuli. The great majority of the common responses providing the factor structure described in Table 15 are given by the forty-six words in Table 17. These are the words that occur as responses to more than two stimuli. Note that an extraordinary number of the stimulus words themselves provide mediation for the relation in associative meaning among these words. It is equally obvious that the addition of *bad, blood, hard, kill, red, sharp,* and the like, would have enriched the matrix within the structure of aggression. Also, some projective interest can be attached to the role played by the words *mouth, stick, dog, car, death,* and *hand* in providing the relations in associative meaning within this set. By the definition of associative meaning (Chapter III), these words belong within this set. Indeed, this technique of exploring the dis-

TABLE 17: The Forty-six Words Which Occur as Responses to More than Two Stimuli in Table 14[a]

Bad
Bore 1, Burn 1, Fight 1, Force 1, Harsh 2, Hate 2, Hatred 5, Mob 1, Torture 1, Violence 6, Wrath 2.

Bang
Bullet 3, Club 1, Fireworks 8, Explosion 7, Gun 2, Hammer 2, Nail 1, Pistol 1, Ram 2.

Bite
Beast 1, Fangs 1, Finger 1, Pliers 1, Shark 7, Teeth 13, Wolf 2.

Blood
Bullet 1, Crushed 9, Explosion 1, Fangs 1, Fight 1, Knife 1, Slash 3, Spear 3, Wolf 1.

Break
Cut 3, Pierce 6, Ram 2, Torture 1, Wreck 4.

Bullet
(Bullet 100), Dart 1, Gun 22, Pierce 2, Pistol 12.

Car
Ambition 1, Crushed 1, Dart 2, Hit 1, Ram 1, Rooster 1, Wolf 1, Wreck 10.

Cut
Burn 1, (Cut 100), Finger 1, Knife 24, Pierce 17, Pliers 1, Slash 55, Spear 1.

Death
Dart 1, Explosion 4, Pistol 1, Shark 1, Spear 1, Torture 1, Violence 8, Warrior 1.

Dog
Beast 3, Bull 2, Bullet 2, Fangs 13, Fight 3, Gun 1, Rage 1, Sneer 1, Wolf 13.

Fangs
Beast 1, (Fangs 100), Shark 1, Teeth 1, Tiger 6, Wolf 8.

Fear
Angry 2, Bullet 1, Hate 2, Hatred 3, Rage 2, Sneer 1, Warrior 1.

Fight
Angry 3, Ambition 1, Argue 33, Bull 5, Fist 23, Force 3, Gun 2, Hit 1, Mob 1, Pierce 1, Rage 1, Ram 1, Violence 9, Warrior 13.

Finger
Burn 1, Cut 3, (Finger 100), Fist 2, Nail 14, Poke 2.

Fire
Bullet 3, Burn 26, Erupt 1, Explosion 7, (Fire 100), Fireworks 3, Gun 4, Hate 1, Pistol 2, Poke 7, Rage 3, Violence 2.

---

[a] The number after each stimulus is the frequency with which the response to that stimulus occurred.

Fist
  Fight 7, (Fist 100), Hammer 1, Hit 4, Poke 2, Punch 3, Violence 2.

Gun
  Bore 4, Bullet 33, Dart 5, Explosion 1, Fire 3, (Gun 100), Knife 3, Pistol 39, Sneer 1, Spear 2, Wreck 1.

Hammer
  Bullet 2, Club 4, Crushed 1, (Hammer 100), Nail 44, Pliers 4.

Hand
  Burn 1, Cut 1, Finger 20, Fist 24, Gun 1, Hit 1, Knife 1, Pliers 1, Ram 1.

Hard
  Fight 1, Fist 3, Force 1, Harsh 8, Hate 1, Hit 5, Poke 1, Punch 1, Teeth 2.

Hate
  Bore 1, Dart 1, Fight 2, (Hate 100), Hatred 2, Sneer 3, Torture 1, Violence 1.

Hit
  Bull 1, Bullet 2, Club 11, Dart 1, Fight 9, Fist 13, Force 1, Hammer 6, Hate 1, Hatred 1, (Hit 100), Nail 1, Pierce 1, Poke 12, Punch 25, Ram 5, Slash 2, Wrath 1.

Hole
  Bore 14, Bullet 3, Finger 1, Pierce 6, Poke 2, Slash 1.

Hot
  Burn 7, Erupt 1, Fire 10.

Hurt
  Angry 1, Bullet 1, Burn 10, Crushed 3, Cut 6, Dart 1, Fangs 1, Fight 3, Finger 2, Fire 1, First 1, Force 3, Harsh 1, Hit 11, Pierce 2, Poke 3, Slash 2, Torture 25, Violence 3, Wrath 2.

Kill
  Club 1, Fight 5, Fist 1, Gun 2, Hatred 2, Hit 1, Knife 1, Mob 1, Nail 1, Poke 1, Shark 2, Slash 1, Spear 1, Tiger 1, Torture 2, Violence 1, Wolf 1.

Knife
  Bore 1, Cut 18, (Knife 100), Pistol 1, Slash 10, Spear 5.

Lion
  Beast 10, Fangs 1, Tiger 12, Wolf 2.

Mad
  Angry 58, Argue 5, Beast 5, Fight 1, Hate 3, Hatred 3, Rage 16, Violence 2, Wrath 5.

Man
  Angry 4, Ambition 1, Beast 4, Bore 1, Bullet 1, Burn 1, Club 1, Crushed 1, Force 1, Hate 1, Hit 1, Pierce 2, Shark 1, Spear 2, Tiger 1, Violence 1, Wolf 3, Warrior 3, Wrath 1.

Mouth
Hit 1, Punch 6, Shark 2, Sneer 1, Teeth 17.

Nail
Finger 6, Hammer 52, (Nail 100), Pierce 1, Pliers 6.

Noise
Beast 1, Explosion 9, Fireworks 6, Gun 2, Mob 1, Pistol 1, Violence 1.

Point
Argue 1, Cut 1, Dart 9, Finger 14, Gun 1, Pierce 2, Spear 6.

Punch
Fight 6, Fist 3, Hit 5, Nail 1, Pierce 1, Poke 2, (Punch 100).

Red
Angry 1, Argue 1, Burn 2, Erupt 1, Explosion 1, Fire 1, Fireworks 3, Hate 2, Rage 8, Rooster 3, Slash 2.

Run
Dart 6, Fight 7, Gun 1, Hit 13, Pistol 1, Punch 1, Rage 1.

Sharp
Cut 2, Dart 12, Fangs 2, Harsh 1, Knife 15, Nail 1, Pierce 2, Spear 6, Teeth 6, Violence 1.

Shoot
Bullet 4, Erupt 1, Explosion 1, Fire 1, Fireworks 1, Gun 13, Pistol 11.

Shot
Bullet 2, Explosion 1, Gun 6, Pistol 11.

Smash
Club 1, Crushed 13, Fight 1, Fist 4, Force 1, Hammer 1, Hit 2, Punch 4, Ram 2, Wreck 7.

Stick
Club 6, Dart 1, Finger 1, Knife 1, Pierce 4, Poke 5, Spear 4, Violence 2.

Strong
Crushed 1, Fist 1, Force 4, Harsh 3, Pliers 1, Teeth 2, Tiger 1, Warrior 3.

Teeth
Angry 1, Fangs 41, Nail 1, Pliers 1, Punch 1, Shark 15, Sneer 2, (Teeth 100), Tiger 1, Wolf 3.

Throw
Bore 1, Dart 12, Hammer 2, Punch 1, Spear 6, Warrior 1.

Violence
Argue 1, Erupt 2, Explosion 3, Fight 1, Force 4, Knife 1, Mob 5, (Violence 100), Wreck 1.

tribution of common responses between related stimuli provides one of the most powerful techniques for enriching and extending some highly related set of words, a matter that will be touched upon later.

Finally, in this context, a word needs to be said about the very closely related analysis presented by Laffal and Feldman.[13] These authors have also presented factor analyses of relations between associative distributions based upon the overlap method. Their work differs in two important respects from what has been presented here. First of all, they scored responses into categories determined from an earlier analysis. Secondly, they analyzed continuous as well as

TABLE 18: Single Word Association: Rotated Factor Loadings of Intersection Coefficients for Sixteen Words

Words	Factors				
	I	II	III	IV	V
1. Black	89	09	01	—01	03
2. Red	88	08	04	00	—04
3. Dark	85	05	—03	03	07
4. Yellow	85	13	04	—01	—13
5. Light	85	00	—02	00	—02
6. White	83	02	02	05	—04
7. Green	75	03	04	01	—08
8. Blue	71	—07	12	09	—38
9. Butterfly	13	31	00	01	—85
10. Sheep	07	84	17	—08	—15
11. Eagle	05	35	03	—02	—85
12. Spider	06	79	—05	24	—26
13. Lion	06	85	06	04	—21
14. Priest	05	11	06	98	01
15. Woman	04	06	81	05	—01
16. Man	03	08	81	00	—03
Cumulative percentage variance	36	55	63	70	75

SOURCE: J. Laffal and S. Feldman. The structure of single word and continuous word associations. *J. verb. Learn. verb. Behav.*, 1962, 1, 60.

discrete associations. In the continuous-association technique, subjects emit as many associations to a particular stimulus word as they can in some fixed period of time. (In the data reported by Laffal and Feldman, the period was twenty-five seconds.) The use of continuous associations for the study of associative structure is particularly important, since it allows a possible extension of the method to the study of the structure of a single individual.

[13] Laffal and Feldman, Single word and continuous word associations.

Two important points, for present purposes, come out of the various analyses presented by Laffal and Feldman. First of all, their results for single associations are remarkably like those presented here, despite the categorized nature of their data. Table 18 reproduces some of the data from their investigation. As in the analyses presented earlier, the first two factors split the words into two basic clusters. Beyond these two factors, however, the structures in their data seem to differ somewhat from those presented here. Inspection suggests that these differences are largely the result of the choice of words in the matrix. The powerful pair-schema, *man-woman,* dominates and defines the third factor in the Laffal and Feldman data; this pair is essentially unrelated to the other items in the matrix, and it does not appear in the first two factors.

Essentially the same picture is presented by the factors extracted from continuous associations. Laffal and Feldman factored the continuous associations to the stimuli which appear in Table 18, and the results differ from the loadings in that table only in minor detail. Therefore, Laffal and Feldman conclude that there is a basic category structure in vocabulary, one that is reflected in the factors obtained from either continuous or free association. The factor-analysis method provides a very general technique, then, for uncovering the basic structures in a set of words.

The major deficiency in the tables presented so far is that the grammatical structure of the language from which the words are drawn is ignored. There are many reasons for believing that there should be well-defined relations between the associative structures and the grammatical structures of the language. It is to the definition of these relations that the next chapter is addressed.

5 Associative Structure and Grammatical Structure

The various analyses described in the preceding chapter are not altogether satisfactory, particularly from the linguistic point of view. The linguist must feel uncomfortable in the face of any treatment of the structural relations among words which seems to ignore grammatical relations, as do the analyses in the previous chapter. Furthermore, given the impossibility of taking a matrix of the language as a whole, nothing in the preceding chapter suggests a rational method for arriving at some systematic sample of the language for the purpose of a structural analysis, particularly a sample preserving some of the grammatical features which we know to be important. From certain particular psychological points of view, a collection of words need not have any particular grammatical structure; we may choose, as we did in the previous chapter, to examine the structure of some collection of words that has psychodynamic or psychological significance. Any general treatment of relations in intraverbal meaning requires, however, that we consider the grammatical structures of the language. Such structures provide a linguistic basis for systematic sampling.

We have made the point several times in earlier chapters that associative relations should reflect the linguistic organization of the language as a whole. Associative relations in a language have a structure and that structure arises out of the same source as does grammatical structure, namely, the uses of the language. While associative structure need not take the same form or be efficiently described in the same way as grammatical structure, it is difficult to see how these two ways of looking at the patterns in language could be totally independent. Therefore, we are obliged, in the study of associative structure, to examine the relation between associative data and grammatical analyses.

There are several possible approaches to the problem of investigating the relation between associative structure and grammatical structure, and that presented in this chapter will center largely around the empirical relation between associative distributions, associative mean-

97

ing, and grammatical class. The reason for this empirical study is that it will provide us with a deeper understanding of the nature of associative distributions from which the relationships in associative meaning are derived.

Despite the explicit empirical beginning we have made to the problem, our approach is dominated by the point of view that the structures of grammatical class—the relationships which define form class and structure group in English—are among the conditions which give rise to relationships in associative meaning. Form class and structure groups—parts of speech in general—provide large and extremely diffuse classes of lexical elements, though a detailed analysis of any given class (nouns, for example) reveals a finer and more complicated structure than most users or grammarians of the language are willing to recognize. Meaningful structures—associative structures included—are generally less diffuse and more limited in size than these large grammatical classes. In many instances the structure of meaning can be considered as but particular portions of certain grammatical structures, though such a statement hides a complicated picture, for, in most languages, important meaningful relations transcend grammatical class. Such is obviously the case in English, since we can change a stem from defining some meaning within one grammatical class to one defining a closely related meaning in another class simply by changing an appropriate suffix (*beautiful, beautify*).

From the beginning of the empirical investigation of associations it has been clear that associations are not free from the constraint imposed by the grammatical structure of the language. The grammatical relation between stimuli and responses in free association must be described in a special way, however. It cannot be described by any of the phrase or sentence structures of the language. It is not, for example, a subject-predicate relation. In fact, the associative relation can be described only by the internal relations among associations; therefore, the phrase and sentence structures of the language simply do not apply to relations between stimuli and responses in free association. Nevertheless, there are relations between the obtained distributions of free associations and the grammatical organization which emerges from the internal description of ordinary sentences. Specifically, there are systematic and lawful relations between the distributions of free associations and the grammatical classes (defined by the relations in ordinary sentences) of the words used as stimuli in free association and those that occur as responses.

In order to describe these relations we need to specify, as we have already done for associative distributions, the nature of the analysis we are to employ in order to define grammatical class. For theoretical reasons, to be apparent later, as well as for reasons of objectivity, we shall draw upon the analysis of English parts of speech made by Fries.[1] The specific technique used by Fries has a theoretical significance for the views presented later concerning the relations between free associations and the uses of ordinary language, but we can also regard it as something which simply provides us with a kind of grammatical analysis of the English language, the results of which can be correlated with the characteristics of the obtained distributions of free associations.

The essential feature of Fries's method is that it allows grammatical class to be defined by the positions that words occupy in ordinary English utterances. Position is the important property, though Fries is able to show that these positions are partly correlated with certain morphological features of the language. The peculiarities of English in this respect do not lessen the generality of the analysis. In a highly inflected language, a particular grammatical class can be defined entirely by the position of root elements with respect to bound morphemes ("endings"). Such a language is grammatically simpler in theory, since grammatical function is determined by positions of single elements rather than by location of lexical units with respect to a large and often indefinite number of elements within a phrase. In principle, however, definition of class by position within phrase or sentence would not be different for such a language.

In this analysis, all words which can occupy equivalent positions within English utterances are declared to be members of the same grammatical class. These equivalences must be arrived at, in the first instance, inductively. Both in practice and theory, however, a completely inductive description of grammatical classes within a language provides for serious difficulties, for certain of these classes are open-ended. Therefore, it is impossible to provide a complete classification of the total lexicon of a language by an inductive approach. It can be said that such a failure is psychologically realistic, however, because it would be extraordinary to find universal agreement in usage over even a limited portion, much less over the totality of any language's vocabulary. It has further been argued that a purely inductive analysis leads to an endlessly complicated grammar for the description of any

[1] C. C. Fries. *The structure of English.* New York: Harcourt, Brace, 1952.

particular language. As an alternative, students of generative grammar[2] have suggested that a small number of forms may be defined by position within a kernel sentence or a small number of kernel sentences and that all other forms are to be defined by transformation rules. Those who have argued for a generative grammar have done so because of the potentially greater completeness and simplicity of such a grammar in the description of language. Another criterion for preferring a particular grammar is invoked here, however, and it is the criterion which derives from an assumption about the psychological processes behind linguistic usage. For reasons to be argued at length in this and later chapters, we shall find a positional-equivalence notion of grammatical class to be a psychologically useful one. Such a preference is clearly influenced by certain important features of the psychological literature on concept attainment.[3]

For several reasons, the specific analyses by equivalence positions presented by Fries have not resulted in a classification upon which there is universal agreement. That is partly because the sample of the language which Fries uses in arriving at his classification is but a small one, considering the possible sentences in the language. It is also, however, because of the continuity between what is ordinarily described as "grammar" and what is described as "meaning." The structure of the English language is not exhaustively described by the approximately twenty classes into which Fries puts words. One can go on making more elaborate classifications on the basis of equivalences within sentence positions, and, as we shall see, some of these classes can only be described as semantically or associatively structured. There is, in the view presented here, no point at which one can draw a line between grammar and meaning. Both are structured within the language and both have extralinguistic referents. Grammatical classes are, in general, larger than semantically organized classes, but, as we shall see, since grammatical classes have an intraverbal meaning which can be determined from associative structures, no complete distinction can be drawn between grammatical and semantic structures. The intraverbal structure of meaning and grammar is a consequence of the experience people have with particular linguistic and nonlinguistic contexts into which verbal elements are put. The only possible difference between grammar and meaning is that meaning is

---

[2] See, for example, R. B. Lees. The grammar of English nominalizations. *International J. Amer. Linguistics*, 1960, **26**, No. 3.

[3] See E. B. Hunt. *Concept learning: An information processing problem.* New York: Wiley, 1962.

more influenced in its structure by extralinguistic relations (relations in the natural world), but grammar is, to a lesser extent, so structured (by, for example, social relations), so the distinction is one of degree rather than an absolute one.

In establishing an inductive classification of lexical elements in a language, we start with a particular sentence. We delete some one position from that sentence and then examine all the other possible lexical elements which can replace the missing element and still make a grammatical sentence in the language. In theory, we should be able to define equivalences strictly by means of selecting elements from other sentences in a previously defined sample. That is to say, each sentence produced by replacing a deleted element should contain an element occurring in some other sentence and should, even more strictly, generate a sentence which occurs somewhere in the sample of discourse before us. In actual fact, we are forced by the limitations of linguistic sampling to employ further, specially generated samples in order to *judge* that two elements are equivalent. Thus, we start with the sentence, "The concert was good." We delete *concert* and find that we can substitute *food* but not *beautify*; we judge "The food was good" to be an acceptable sentence in the language. All elements which can be so substituted are, to a first approximation, members of a common grammatical class. We also find, of course, that there are many other contexts in which these elements are equivalent. At some point we may find some sentences in which two words, heretofore which had shared a common context, are not equivalent; that is to say, one word belongs in the appropriate position in the sentence while the other does not. Thus, while we may say "The concert was good" and "The weather was good," and while we might conceivably say "A concert was good," we certainly would not say "A weather was good." Therefore, the original class may, on the basis of this and other such sentences, be split into two classes (in this example, into the classes of mass and count nouns). Such subdivision may go on more or less indefinitely as we sample new sentences in the language. It is at least possible that, for every word in the language, there is some unique sentence into which that word will fit and no other will. Grammatical classes are defined by partial, not complete, equivalences of position. There is, therefore, a certain amount of uncertainty about the complete set of elements which comprise a given class. The process implies, however, that a speaker of the language will add a new element to some existing conceptual class inductively, on the basis of the equivalence of that element with some element already taken by him to be a member of the class. There is nothing to prevent a speaker from doing this on the basis of a single instance, and every experience we have with human beings as concept attainers suggests that people occasionally do exactly that.

While in theory the process of substitution within a fixed linguistic environment would be better carried out within the confines of some very large sample of sentences, in reality we need to resort to substitution within specially generated sentences because the fixed sample would have to be impractically large. In order to tell whether two words belong to the same class or classes, we generate contexts in which they may occupy identical positions. Such a procedure can lead to problems. It is very easy to imagine that every sentence so generated is an actual sentence in the language (that is to say, a sentence which might occur outside of the restricted circumstance of asking someone to generate sentences for the purpose of grammatical classification). It is here, however, that we are victims of our own grammatical inventiveness. A word that is extremely unlikely to occur with the singular indefinite article *a/an* may be made to do so. Thus, while the sequence "A helium . . ." may well never occur in ordinary English discourse, if forced to do so, we may assert that a possible sentence could be "A helium was produced in the university laboratory. . . ." Therefore, the use of generated sentences to define grammatical classes leads to the real possibility that we may not define classes as they are properly thought of by people who actually use the language.

The problem is compounded by the fact that, in English, a given word may occupy several positions. Words like *play* or *run* are not only grammatically equivalent to *carry, think,* or *typewrite*; they are equivalent to *carriage, thought,* and *typewriter.* The solution adopted by Fries (and everyone else) is to take the position that different places in sentences define different grammatical classes. Therefore, a word like *play* which can occupy two or more positions in a sentence belongs to two or more classes. The problem cannot be so easily dismissed, for it seems very possible that there are classes of nouns, for example, which readily make verbs and other classes that do not, even when these nouns are not marked as nouns by special bound morphemes. This is a problem of real concern to the characterization of associative structure, as we shall see.

In a grammatical context, then, a particular use of a word, a use which defines its class, can be determined from the position occupied by that word in a sample of sentences. In associations we do not have a phrase or sentence structure which enables us to identify the grammatical class of a word which occurs as a response. We are, therefore, sometimes in the position of saying that we cannot identify the grammatical class of a word that occurs as a response in a free-association test. Our uncertainty about the grammatical class of some associate can be reduced by resorting to some hypotheses about the relations between stimuli and responses, and these hypotheses can be derived from some more easily determined grammatical relations. Such a procedure is the purpose of the balance of this chapter.

The analysis of the relations between the structure of associations and the grammar of the language is conveniently introduced by some observations made by Ervin.[4] Ervin begins with the commonly accepted notion that the responses adults give in free association are usually of the same grammatical class as the stimulus (an overgeneralized notion, as it turns out). She calls our attention to the fact, however, that this result (or even the weaker result that words of the same form class appear as responses in appreciable frequency) challenges an explanation of the learning of associations through simple contiguities in overt speech. That stimuli and their responses in association are often elements which do not appear in successive or even in neighboring positions in speech or the speech-line flow of thought is an altogether remarkable fact, curiously ignored in the history of associationism. In fact, many associations (the majority, for some grammatical classes) are of the same grammatical class as the stimulus.

A convenient way of distinguishing between those associations that can occupy the same position in an utterance as the stimulus (and are, therefore, of the same grammatical class) is provided by Jenkins and Saporta.[5] They classified associations into two modes, *paradigmatic* associations and *syntagmatic* associations. Paradigmatic associations are those in which the stimulus and response fit a common grammatic paradigm and syntagmatic associations are, in general, sequential elements or at least elements which usually occupy different positions within phrases or sentences. Syntagmatic associations are, more often than not, like the transitional frequencies between words in the language itself and are, therefore, in general contiguous. A paradigmatic

[4] S. Ervin. Changes with age in the verbal determinants of word association. *Amer. J. Psychol.*, 1961, 74, 361–372.

[5] J. J. Jenkins, in C. E. Osgood and T. A. Sebeok (eds.). Psycholinguistics supplement. *J. abnorm. soc. Psychol.*, 1954, 52, 114–116. S. Saporta, in J. J. Jenkins (ed.). *Associative processes in verbal behavior: Report of Minnesota conference.* Minneapolis: Univ. of Minnesota, 1959.

association, however, need not be contiguous and usually is not. It is hard to think of the word *hot* as providing the principal or even a moderately frequent linguistic environment for the word *cold*.

Ervin showed that stimulus words which do produce a preponderance of paradigmatic responses in adults tend to produce more, even a preponderance of, syntagmatic responses in children. She obtained free associations to forty-six words from children of school levels ranging from kindergarten to sixth grade. In addition, she obtained some data from a multiple-choice form of an association test in which the subjects chose between a possible paradigmatic and a possible syntagmatic association to a word. The stimuli and responses were grouped into the various English grammatical classes by a generalization of Fries's method. The kind of coding Ervin employed in this study is not without difficulty (to be noted below), but it does make possible a relative comparison of the frequencies of paradigmatic and syntagmatic associations at different age levels.

The results showed a striking increase in paradigmatic responses with an increase in school grade.[6] Thus, the associations of adults and children seem to be qualitatively different, and, as children get older, they become more like adults in associations. Furthermore, an analysis showed that the syntagmatic associations given by younger children seemed to reflect the frequencies of two-word sequences in the language, particularly in samples of language to which young children are likely to be exposed. While Ervin's analysis in this problem is not simple or without difficulties, she does manage to provide some evidence that the syntagmatic associations of young children reflect the frequency with which words of different form classes tend to be adjacent to one another or near neighbors in the kinds of continuous discourse to which children are likely to be exposed.

Not all associations in adults are paradigmatic, however. Furthermore, the tendency towards paradigmatic or syntagmatic association varies with form class. Such a result stems from an investigation by the present author of a wide sample of associations in English. The purpose of the study[7] was to determine, for adult subjects, the relative frequencies of paradigmatic and syntagmatic associations among the form classes of English (nouns, verbs, adjectives, and adverbs).

[6] Since the publication of Ervin's study, there have been many extensive and careful investigations which substantiate this general conclusion. See, for example, D. R. Entwisle, D. F. Forsyth, and R. Muuss. The syntactic-paradigmatic shift in children's word associations. *J. verb. Learn. verb. Behav.*, 1964, 3, 19–29.

[7] J. Deese. Form class and the determinants of association. *J. verb. Learn. verb. Behav.*, 1962, 1, 79–84.

The sample of words used in this study was broad in two respects. It was a large sample, which included a total of over five hundred stimulus words. These words, furthermore, were drawn from a distribution which was approximately rectilinear for frequency of usage of words in the language. The sample included very rare words as well as very common words, and these occurred in about equal frequencies. Such a set of words was important because practically all of the normative data on grammatical class in association come from samples of very common words.

As in Ervin's study, the stimuli and responses were classed into grammatical categories by a generalization of Fries's technique. Stimulus words which could readily fall into two or more grammatical classes were eliminated, so that, so far as form class was concerned, the stimuli were relatively unambiguous. Unfortunately, there is in English a kind of fundamental confusion between certain nouns and adjectives. Many, if not most, nouns in the language can stand in an adjectival position (*an oyster bed*). In the analysis of the data the assumption was made that associations to nouns are determined by nominal use rather than adjectival use, an assumption that is justified by the very different patterns uncovered and described for nouns and adjectives.

Responses to these words were obtained from one hundred male undergraduates. These responses were coded into form classes. Short of eliminating responses, there is no certain way to eliminate the grammatical ambiguity of responses. In the cases in which responses could be coded into either paradigmatic or syntagmatic categories, the responses were coded as (potentially) syntagmatic. Therefore, the data represented the frequency of associations that, in ordinary usage, could be syntagmatic with respect to the stimulus.

Stimuli of different form classes differ markedly in the frequency with which they elicit syntagmatic associations, as Table 19 shows. Adverbs are overwhelmingly syntagmatic in their associations, even within this sample. The adverb *amazingly*, for example, yields *right, new, accurate, true, real, low, strong, deft,* and *built.* These are clearly sequences which could occur in ordinary English. Nouns, on the other hand, are overwhelmingly paradigmatic. That is to say, a word such as *action* yields as its common associates, *words, life, movement, motion, game, war,* and so on. These words are much less likely to make acceptable sequences in ordinary English. Verbs and adjectives fall in between nouns and adverbs with about 50 per cent of the associates to each being syntagmatic.

TABLE 19: Mean Frequency, Standard Deviation of Syntagmatic Associates, and Correlations with Frequency of Usage

	Nouns	Verbs	Adjectives	Adverbs
Mean	21.4	48.1	49.9	72.8
S.D.	16.4	19.7	19.2	20.3
r[a] with frequency of usage	.01	.05	−.40	.13
N[b]	253	101	118	32

SOURCE: J. Deese. Form class and the determinants of association. *J. verb. Learn. verb. Behav.*, 1962, 1, 81.

[a] r = Pearson correlation coefficient.
[b] N = number of words in the sample.

The same table shows that there is no significant correlation between frequency of usage (defined by Thorndike-Lorge L count) and frequency of syntagmatic association, except for adjectives. Nouns are paradigmatic whether they are common nouns or rare nouns, and adverbs tend to be syntagmatic whether they are common or not. However, there is a negative correlation between frequency of usage and frequency of syntagmatic association for adjectives. Common adjectives are somewhat more likely to be paradigmatic than are uncommon adjectives. The adjective *administrative,* for example, yields the syntagmatic associates, *duty, job, control, discipline, power, bureaucrats, position, agency, entity, detail, body, government, school, boss, work, graft,* and *rule* as common associates. These are to be contrasted with the fact that *hot* yields, in large numbers, associates such as *cold, warm,* and *cool,* with only a scattering of syntagmatic associates such as *women, weather,* and the like.

Therefore, the relations between grammatical class and associative distribution are not simple. From Ervin's data we may infer that the tendency to give paradigmatic associations increases with age, but that increase can only occur to any considerable extent among nouns (and common adjectives). Nevertheless, we will do well to consider the process which Ervin believes her data to reveal.

Ervin argues that syntagmatic responses will be frequent when the variety of contexts in which a stimulus word appears in ordinary language is limited. Young children have experienced relatively few contexts for most words. As children grow older, they experience more contexts for any given word, and, Ervin argues, as a result there is a shift away from any particular syntagmatic response. We might expand upon this view and assert that, when a word first occurs in a child's experience, that word has a unique context and cannot be divorced from it. Thus, one might argue, the phrase, "a glass of milk," is a completed unit to the child who has heard the word *glass* for the first time. So there is really no independent meaning for the element *glass;* it is simply part of a larger unit which does have some particular meaning. As new phrases, "a glass of tea," "a glass shelf," occur, the element glass acquires contextual independence, and, therefore, is less likely to be completed in association by the word *milk.* Such an analysis would predict that variations in syntagmatic responses in any large sample of children (or adults, for that matter) would be considerable, since the contexts in which words are first or only occasionally experienced would vary from person to person. It is a fundamental characteristic of syntagmatic associates (with the exception to be noted later in this chapter) that they are more varied than paradigmatic associates.

While there are several persuasive arguments in favor of such a view of the changes in association with age, a view which Ervin manages to adjust to the principle of contiguity, some of the implications that can be derived from it lead to certain awkwardness. For example, the same analysis cannot be extended in any simple way to the associations of adults. It is reasonable to assume that rare words have been experienced by adults in fewer different contexts than common words. Therefore, as words become more common in the experience of adults, there should be a shift from syntagmatic association to paradigmatic association. Yet the data in Table 19 show that there is not a correlation between syntagmatic frequency and frequency of usage, except in the case of adjectives. In fact, if we examine the nonparadigmatic associates to nouns in the original data from which Table 19 was taken, it does not always seem reasonable to suppose that these reflect sequential or environmental occurrences in the language.

For example, one of the nouns that yields many syntagmatic associates is *difficulty.* The responses *hard* and *easy* occur in very high frequencies as associations. It is very difficult to construct an English phrase in which *hard* or *easy* appears as the immediate verbal environment for *difficulty,* and it is almost certain that such sentences would be rare. It must be admitted that some other common nonparadigmatic associates to nouns more readily form common English sequences—for example, *green-grass* or *blue-sky.* Notice, however, that the responses *green* and *blue* occur in normal English syntax before their respective nouns rather than after.

Enough examples occur, however, to make it abundantly clear that not all syntagmatic or potentially syntagmatic associates to nouns appear to be determined by the ordinary contexts in which these nouns appear in English. They are, rather, like the paradigmatic associates to nouns. Such adjectives as *green* in response to *grass* or *hard* in response to *difficulty* define part of the meaningful structure of their nouns. If this is actually the case, the syntagmatic responses to nouns should be more sharply concentrated in just a few types. They should not reflect the variety of contextual situations in which nouns occur but rather reflect the ordinary meaning of those nouns. In brief, they should behave like paradigmatic associations.

One way of investigating such a possibility is to compare the frequencies of the syntagmatic primary responses for the four form classes. Associative distributions, with respect to rank order of occurrences of responses, are, in the main, sharply skewed, and the simplest measure of the extent of this skewing is the extent to which occurrences are concentrated in the most frequently occurring word type. If the frequency of the primary is high, the rank-frequency distribution of associates is steep; there are relatively few types and many tokens of each.

TABLE 20: Mean Frequency of Occurrence and Standard Deviation of Syntagmatic Primaries for Stimuli Yielding 50 Per Cent or More Syntagmatic Responses

	Nouns	Verbs	Adjectives	Adverbs
Mean	44.1	28.4	26.7	18.0
S.D.	27.3	13.4	18.4	9.5
N	34	65	64	29

SOURCE: Deese, Form class and the determinants of association, p. 82.

Table 20 shows a distribution of syntagmatic primaries for all words in the four form classes that produced a total of more than 50 per cent syntagmatic associates. Nearly half of all these syntagmatic associates to nouns are concentrated in the most commonly occurring response, while the syntagmatic associates to adjectives, verbs, and adverbs are considerably more scattered. For adverbs, the form class that seems to yield associations which are most heavily determined by context, only 18 per cent of the syntagmatic associates are concentrated in the primary.

One implication of these data is that the syntagmatic responses to nouns are not like, in origin, the syntagmatic associates to the other form classes. They define paradigms of meaning and do not necessarily, as do the syntagmatic associates for the other form classes, reflect the context in which the stimulus word appears. If this hypothesis is correct, such syntagmatic responses as *green* to *grass* and *blue* to *sky* are not so much representative of the sequential transitions in ordinary language as they are of the most basic and important cognitive characteristics of *grass* and *sky*. The sequence of associations from Hobbes cited in the first chapter—*Peter, stone, foundation, church, people, tumult*—is not so much representative of a real chained linguistic sequence as it is of the paradigms of meanings for these words; by the same token there is nothing so insistently and obviously important about *grass* save the fact that it is *green*.

It is worth pointing out here that the pattern of constraint in simple sentences is related to the paradigmatic structure of nouns. In a study of the way in which people fit words into simple sentences of a given grammatic structure, Clark[8] showed that the greatest constraint among the subject, verb, and object on the distribution of word types chosen is for the subject of simple active and passive sentences. As would be expected from the phrase structure of such sentences (though not from a transformational point of view), there is more contingent uncertainty between the verb and object of simple sentences (in the active form) than between the other possible pairs (subject-verb, subject-object).

Surprisingly, from the point of view of this pattern of constraint, the greatest degree of relation in distribution of associations is between the elements in the two noun positions—that is to say, between the subject and object. This is true both for active and passive sentences. Therefore, even though the object of a simple sentence is more grammatically constrained by the verb than by the subject, its associations are more like those to the subject of the sentence. That, of course, follows from the greater frequency of paradigmatic associations to nouns. Associative relations, as we shall point out later, are much more likely to stem from the paradigmatic portion of associative distributions than from the syntagmatic portion. The important point, however, is the implication that it is from noun-noun relations that sentences are formed. In fact, stimulus-response associative sequences with nouns as stimuli readily form sentences; *man* is the opposite of *woman*, or, the *chair* is beside the *table*. It is this ability of nouns to form sentences in which the associates occupy the predicate position which leads so readily to the sequences described by Hobbes.

[8] H. H. Clark. Some structural properties of simple active and passive sentences. Master's thesis, The Johns Hopkins University, 1964.

Thus, with the exceptions like *grass-green,* nouns do not have associations which readily appear in the immediate environment of the stimulus. They do readily form simple declarative sentences, which, in the long run, describe most of the semantic properties of the nouns in question. The most striking aspect of associations to nouns is this paradigmatic character. The associations to nouns are obviously and intuitively "meaningful"; they do not provide the semantic puzzles given by the paired opposites common among adjectives or in the sequential associations encountered among verbs and adverbs.

This character of nouns makes a strong case for the stimulus-equivalence model for the development of associations. Since this character of nouns, for adult subjects, does not vary with the frequency of usage of nouns, it is not easy to extend Ervin's hypothesis about how it develops to the learning of new nouns in the vocabulary of adults. On the other hand, it is possible that adults have so thoroughly learned the grammatical (sentence position) property of nouns that, without any intervening steps, nouns come to yield nouns, even though only the thinnest of experiential threads may bind a new noun to some old ones.

When we turn to other form classes, we are faced with a different problem, for a large number of the associations to these classes are syntagmatic associates of a clear sequential character. The most puzzling case is that of adjectives, since adjectives do vary in their tendency to produce paradigmatic associations with frequency of usage. Furthermore, there is another striking property of the associations to adjectives which is correlated with frequency of usage.

Paradigmatic associates to adjectives readily divide themselves into two classes with surprisingly few exceptions. (The exceptions form a separate class, to be discussed in a later chapter.) Most paradigmatic associations to adjectives are either in some sense synonymous with the stimulus or the polar opposite (antonym) of the stimulus. Thus, the paradigmatic associates to adjectives are mainly of the type *cold-cool* or *cold-hot.* There is a very high correlation between the frequency of antonymic associates and frequency of usage. After a logarithmic transformation on both distributions (both distributions being, to a first approximation, logarithmic), the correlation between frequency of usage of the stimulus (Thorndike-Lorge L count) and frequency of antonymic association is 0.889. Thus, paradigmatic associates to common adjectives are overwhelmingly opposites. Low-frequency adjectives commonly yield synonymic associates (and, of course, very uncommon adjectives most often yield syntagmatic sequences).

A simple pattern of organization, then, emerges for common English adjectives. The pattern is one of contrast. This property makes possible the obvious face validity of the semantic differential; the polar-opposite scales defined by adjectival anchors make intuitive sense. The existence of such a strong pattern among the most basic adjectives suggests that the structure of adjectives is fundamentally different from that of nouns. In order to make a more complete description of the structure of English adjectives, however, we shall have to treat in some way the considerable number of adjectives which do not show the contrastive pattern; that treatment is accomplished in the next chapter. At this point, however, we shall have to consider the fact that the basic meaning of many words can transcend form class. Characteristically, words that are formed of some basic, semantically definite morpheme plus an affix which signals form class are not the most common words in the language. Such words may not have their associative structure determined primarily by the schema appropriate to a particular form class; indeed, there may be some conflict between the associative meaning aroused by the semantically definite morpheme (such as the *continent* in *continental*) and the structure aroused by the affix which signals form class (*-al*). Such may well be the case for uncommon adjectives, for which the root morphemes take nominal form. If that is the case, nouns are more fundamental from an associative point of view than the other classes. Not only are nouns more likely to be completely paradigmatic in the associations of adults but they provide the basic structures for many words that appear in other form classes. This whole matter of the relations between form class and associative structure can be illustrated by reference to adverbs.

Most adverbs yield, in association, their verbal environments. Furthermore, the response is more likely to be the right-hand than the left-hand environment of an adverb; stimulus and response produce adverbial phrases or parts of them in their normal sequence. For example, *mainly* yields *because* as its highest frequency associate; *blissfully* yields *happy* and *greedily, hungry* (though the latter does not seem to be a very probable combination). The point is that adverbs yield possible and, most often, probable sequences in English.

Adverbs, in the majority, are marked by a single affix, *-ly*. Some are marked by a prefix (*abroad, away*) and a few by the suffix (*-ward*). It is rare, however, to find a new adverb or one newly made from an adjective to be marked by anything other than the *-ly* suffix. While *-ly* also marks a class of adjectives, that ending is overwhelmingly taken to signal adverbial position. Furthermore, when the associations to adjectives are examined in detail, it is clear that the adjectives formally marked by *-ly* are in the majority syntagmatic. Therefore, it seems reasonable to suppose that, when people respond associatively to words containing *-ly* as a suffix, they are responding to it as the signal for a grammatical position and, as a consequence, complete a phrase. In short, associates to adverbs are primarily grammatical and tend to generate adverbial phrases. If this is so, adverbs do not yield so readily in associative distributions the semantic meaning of the root morpheme or morphemes. They yield the grammatic or positional meaning of the *-ly* element.

An important exception occurs among certain adverbs which characteristically modify adjectives in some quasi-quantitative way; these constitute the so-called quantifiers (*very, slightly, probably,* and so on). They have been thoroughly studied by Cliff[9] and by Howe,[10] and they form psychological scales with arithmetic properties. What is particularly important from the present point of view is that these scales assert themselves in the factorial structure of associations to these adverbs, as Howe[11] has demonstrated. This extremely important matter will be more thoroughly explored in the next chapter; for now we need only note that the well-defined semantic structures that arise from the associative intersections of these words demonstrate that this claim of adverbs does have important paradigmatic characteristics.

Therefore, adverbs, with some important exceptions, tend to yield the grammatical or positional meaning of the *-ly* element. Since paradigmatic associates do sometimes occur, the situation is a mixed one. In one sense associations to adverbs containing a familiar suffix are very like associations to compounds; at one time the response is determined by one part of the compound, at another time by the other, and occasionally by both. The small number of adverbs that are not marked by adverbial suffixes constitute well-defined and limited associative classes, rather like the structure groups discussed in the balance of this chapter.

The structure groups in English provide an interesting and special

---

[9] N. Cliff. Adverbs as multipliers. *Psychol. Rev.*, 1959, 66, 27–44.

[10] E. S. Howe. Probabilistic adverbial qualifications of adjectives. *J. verb. Learn. verb. Behav.*, 1962, 1, 225–242.

[11] E. S. Howe. Associative structure of non-evaluative adverbs. *J. verb. Learn. verb. Behav.* (in press).

case for the analysis of associative meaning. It is asserted by linguists[12] that the meaning of structural words is entirely intralinguistic; these words serve only to connect other words and have no external referents in experience. Both common sense and the associative analyses to be presented here suggest that this notion is not entirely correct. However, these classes do comprise small and essentially closed groups of related words. New words are only very rarely added to these groups.

For treatment of the associative structure of these groups we may turn to the data collected by Jones and Fillenbaum,[13] which are the only extensive associative norms obtained to words comprising well-defined structure groups. These data were collected from 466 male respondents at the University of North Carolina. Stimuli provided examples of all main form classes and structure groups in English, and both stimuli and responses were coded into grammatical class by a program derived from principles described by Jones, Goodman, and Wepman.[14] In the analyses which follow, we have maintained the stimulus classification used by Jones and Fillenbaum with only slight occasional modifications, but the response classifications have not been used. The classification differs in certain particulars from one that would have been derived from the grammatical principles discussed earlier in this chapter, but the differences are, for our purposes, slight.

Intersection coefficients were computed between all words within a class and for a random sample of all structural words in the Jones and Fillenbaum sample. The values of these coefficients are slightly smaller in some instances than they should be, since intersections due to single common responses could not be counted. Jones and Fillenbaum did not list single occurrences.

The most important characteristic of matrices formed by the various structure groups in English is that they are highly organized, even more highly organized than the associatively related sets presented in the last chapter. Table 21 shows the matrix for the verbal auxiliaries, and the highly organized nature of the relations among these words is evident from a casual inspection of the table. Furthermore, the

[12] See, for example, Roberts, *Patterns of English.*

[13] L. V. Jones and S. Fillenbaum. Grammatically classified word-associations. Research memo. no. 15, Psychometric Laboratory. Chapel Hill, N.C.: North Carolina, 1964.

[14] L. V. Jones, M. F. Goodman, and J. M. Wepman. The classification of parts of speech for the characterization of aphasia. *Language & Speech,* 1963, **6,** 94–107.

TABLE 21: Intersection Coefficients for Verbal Auxiliaries[a]

	Be	Are	Was	Been	Has	Have	Had	Does	Do	Can	Could	Would	Will	Might
Is	.18	.32	.27	.13	.11	.08	.08	.13	.12	.04	.07	.05	.07	.06
Be		.17	.14	.14	.08	.06	.08	.05	.03	.04	.07	.04	.04	.06
Are			.19	.06	.06	.07	.05	.05	.06	.06	.07	.10	.08	.05
Was				.20	.12	.07	.10	.08	.05	.05	.04	.04	.05	.04
Been					.22	.11	.16	.03	.01	.02	.04	.03	.02	.03
Has						.30	.33	.11	.10	.04	.07	.05	.05	.05
Have							.32	.09	.10	.05	.08	.07	.09	.05
Had								.08	.08	.04	.06	.05	.05	.05
Does									.27	.11	.09	.09	.14	.08
Do										.17	.09	.09	.14	.08
Can											.20	.15	.20	.11
Could												.48	.16	.19
Would													.17	.17
Will														.14

SOURCE: These coefficients were calculated from data presented by L. V. Jones and S. Fillenbaum. Grammatically classified word-associations. Research memo. no. 15, Psychometric Laboratory. Chapel Hill, N. C.: Univ. of North Carolina, 1964.

[a] The table has been arranged in a rough order of grammatical relatedness. Notice that such an arrangement produces well-defined clusters.

kinds of relations evident in this table are, in most instances, limited to within groups defined by Jones, Goodman, and Wepman or to closely related groups. We cannot say that the associative organization of these words occurs entirely within a traditional grammatical category, but certainly the magnitude of intersections shown in Table 21 would not be likely to occur, say, in a sample of verbs at large.

The structure underlying the coefficients in Table 21 is portrayed, through the first four factors, in Figure 6. The first two factors in this analysis define clusters of the auxiliaries primarily used in tense and voice—*is, be, has,* and the like—and of auxiliaries which are chiefly modal or aspectual in use—*could, would, might.* This separation is evident in the break between *had* and *do* in the supradiagonal coefficients in Table 21.

Factor III splits the second class of auxiliaries into a cluster consisting of *do, does, can,* and *will,* which is contrasted with a cluster consisting of *might, would,* and *could.* The fourth factor provides for the contrast of the forms of *to be* with the forms of *to have—been, be, is, was,* and *are* with *has, have,* and *had.* It would be difficult to imagine a better parallel between grammatical and associative structure than that yielded by this analysis.

This remarkable parallel demonstrates several important points. For one, it shows that associative data yield meaningful structures for the nonsemantic classes of functional words as well as for seman-

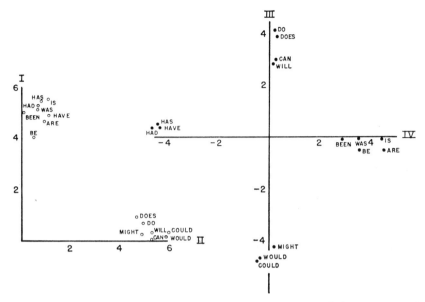

FIGURE 6: Plots of rotated factors I and II and factors III and IV of the intersections for verbal auxiliaries in Table 21.

tically meaningful form-class words. It also demonstrates that grammatical concepts derived from orderly linguistic usage reveal themselves in associative processes. Finally, it provides additional validity for the use of factor analysis in the study of associative structure.

Figure 7 shows a similar plotting of the first four factors derived from the sample of personal pronouns in the Jones and Fillenbaum data. The results are only a little less satisfactory. The greatest anomaly from the grammatical point of view is provided by the location of the word *it*. The position of this word suggests that it may have some grammatical characteristics not shared by the other personal pronouns. Otherwise, the pronouns organize themselves in a way that can be described by ordinary grammatical statements. Factor III splits the nominative use of the third person from other uses of the third person, and Factor IV provides a similar break for singular and plural. Additional factors, beyond those presented in the figure, show splits between first and second person, and so on. In general, the organization is a simple one, quite similar to those presented in the last chapter and correlated with grammatical features in a satisfactory way.

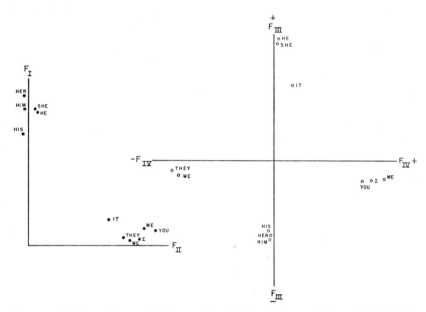

FIGURE 7: Plots of rotated factors I and II and factors III and IV of the intersections for personal pronouns. (Data from L. V. Jones and S. Fillenbaum. Grammatically classified word-associations. Research memo. no. 15, Psychometric Laboratory. Chapel Hill, N.C.: Univ. of North Carolina, 1964.)

The class of words consisting of *out, in, on, up, down, to, from, away, with, of, at, about, for, like,* and *by* does not provide for so simple a structure. Table 22 shows the intersection coefficients for these words. It is apparent that, while the words in this table are highly related, they do not show the simple organization evident in Table 21. There seem to be two basic patterns combined here. One pattern is defined by the strong polar-opposite pairs, *out-in* and *up-down*. The remaining words are related, but no simple pattern emerges (except possibly for the weak polar pair, *to-from*).

As might be supposed, a factor analysis of this table does not yield a readily characterizable structure. If the view of the conceptual nature of associative structure presented in this book is correct, we are left with the strong possibility that the class of prepositions is not, for the users of English who generated these associative data, well organized conceptually. This possibility appears to be even stronger when the data in Table 23 are examined. This table lists the prepositions and the relative frequencies of occurrence of paradigmatic associates to each. The frequencies vary from more than 80 per cent

Table 22: Intersection Coefficients for Associations to Prepositions

	In	On	Up	Down	To	From	Away	With	Of	At	About	For	Like	By
Out	.61	.05	.02	.04	.03	.05	.03	.08	.06	.06	.02	.02	.00	.03
In		.09	.02	.04	.05	.05	.03	.10	.06	.11	.05	.04	.02	.02
On			.02	.04	.07	.05	.02	.06	.13	.11	.08	.06	.04	.06
Up				.66	.02	.02	.02	.01	.01	.03	.02	.00	.00	.01
Down					.03	.06	.03	.03	.01	.05	.03	.01	.01	.02
To						.26	.06	.11	.15	.13	.07	.15	.07	.11
From							.12	.08	.11	.17	.09	.11	.05	.11
Away								.02	.01	.07	.05	.01	.01	.07
With									.10	.07	.09	.19	.11	.10
Of										.11	.13	.18	.07	.11
At											.11	.09	.04	.11
About												.11	.06	.06
For													.11	.12
Like														.07

Source: Data from Jones and Fillenbaum, Grammatically classified word-associations (see Table 21).

to nearly 0 per cent. The words *for, by, at,* and *like* only infrequently yield other prepositions as associates. Nevertheless, Table 22 shows that these words are related to one another. These occupy other functional positions in the language, and their interrelations with one another may define classes other than that of prepositions. If this is so, some members of the class of prepositions should lead to confusion. The ordinary user of English may know that *out, in, down, up,* and *on* are prepositions, but he may be uncertain about *for, by,* and *like.*

Table 23: Percentage of Paradigmatic Associates to Various Prepositions

Preposition	Percentage paradigmatic
Up	81
In	73
Out	70
Down	69
On	51
From	41
With	41
About	37
Away	34
Of	33
To	31
For	22
At	21
By	18
Like	4

Source: Data from Jones and Fillenbaum, Grammatically classified word-associations.

We would expect then, that children would have difficulty learning the membership of the total class, more difficulty than they would have, say, with verbal auxiliaries or personal pronouns.

Finally, Figure 8 shows that the sample of conjunctions studied by Jones and Fillenbaum organizes itself into a simple hierarchical structure. This figure is based upon the unrotated first three factors.

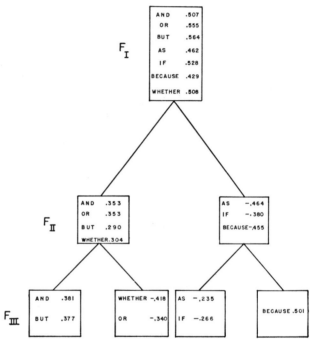

FIGURE 8: Unrotated factor loadings for factors I, II, and III defining conjunctions. (Data from Jones and Fillenbaum, Grammatically classified word-associations.)

The profiles for these factors define a simple branching tree of relations. The loadings on Factor I are all close together, a fact which testifies to the unity of the class. The positive and negative loadings on successive factors split the words into subsets of the next higher set. This simple pattern implies that, unlike prepositions, the class of conjunctions is one of which users of English have a good working conception.

In conclusion, then, we may say that grammatical patterns are as readily revealed by the structure of associative relations as are semantic patterns. So far as intraverbal meaning is concerned, the differences between grammatical organization and semantic organization are minor and subordinate to the similarities in conceptual organization. These similarities reinforce the view that it is the pattern of relations—not what leads to what in stimulus and response—which reveals the intellectual processes behind the use of language and those intellectual processes which result from patterns of linguistic context, a matter more throughly treated in the next chapter.[15]

[15] Certain grammatical theorists have argued that the "substitution-in-frames" technique is inadequate to produce a descriptive grammar of a language. That this may be so does not argue that people do not acquire grammatic equivalences through inductive generalization of substitutions. The arguments presented in this chapter have been meant to apply to linguistic usage, not to the description of language. For a criticism of the equivalence-in-frames notion, see R. B. Lees. On the so-called "substitution in frames" technique. *General Linguistics*, 1964, 6, 11–20.

6

The Analysis of a
Form Class—Adjectives

At this point we are ready to consider the characteristic structure of an English form class, that of adjectives. The object of the analysis will be to determine the basic type of associative structure which provides the meaning of the class itself.

Adjectives are the obvious words with which to begin such an analysis, since we have already determined that they have some unique features which suggest a basic structural type. The schema for adjectives implied by the analysis presented in the preceding chapter is, of course, one of contrast. In that chapter, we saw that they show a negative correlation between the frequency of syntagmatic associations and frequency of usage. This correlation implies that the paradigmatic meaning for adjectives is concentrated in the frequently used ones. To some extent, the meaning of rare adjectives derives from the meaning of underlying roots borrowed from other form classes, mainly from the class of nouns, and that condition accounts for the syntagmatic distributions to rare adjectives. There is, therefore, some reason to restrict our search for the underlying structure of adjectives to commonly occurring adjectives. Furthermore, as the analysis of the preceding chapter showed, the common adjectives are overwhelmingly contrastive in nature. Finally, inspection of the distribution of obtained associations to common adjectives which were not fundamentally contrastive gave some reason to believe that these adjectives, in associative meaning, could be reduced to the meaning defined by contrastive pairs.

We start, then, with the hypothesis that the larger part of adjectival meaning can be very well described by a comparatively limited set of common adjectives which contrast with polar opposites in meaning. If the viewpoint developed by the authors of the semantic differential was correct, these contrasts themselves might well be correlated, so that the associative meaning of many English adjectives could be reduced to a very small number of fundamental contrasts. The critical examination of the semantic differential, reviewed in Chapters IV and V, would not encourage us to expect to find such a result for associative meaning. We might reasonably expect, however, that the dimensionality of the fundamental contrasts in English might be, say, on the order of one-half the number of contrasting pairs of words.

The semantic differential also makes the assumption that contrasting pairs define verbal anchors for scales; such an assumption is implicit in the rating-scale technique that is the tool of the semantic differential. The readiness with which people scale concepts on the semantic differential might lead us to expect that those adjectives which themselves were not part of a fundamental contrast would easily find locations within the semantic space defined by the polar opposites as anchors. All in all, there was reason to expect some large and systematic reduction of many adjectives to a smaller number, all of which are of the same basic type.

With these considerations in mind, the author has studied the associative distributions to a large sample of English adjectives.[1] In order to make the results as general as possible, an attempt was made to study all the very common adjectives in the language. Common adjectives are defined here as those which occur with a frequency of fifty instances per million words or more in the Thorndike-Lorge count. The sample was complete so far as could be determined by a visual search of the total Thorndike-Lorge vocabulary (though the results of the study pointed up several serious omissions). If the sample is deficient in any general respect, it is most so in the exclusion of some participles. Some common participles were included, but others were excluded, and the decision was subjective. The count itself does not distinguish between verbal, nominal, and adjectival use of such words. If, however, the arguments presented here are correct, the omission of participles may not be so serious, since these words are, by their formal characteristics, derived from another form class. As such, many of them may have the semantic features determined by the schematic characteristics of verbs and not those of adjectives (see p. 100).

As in the case of most of the data discussed in earlier chapters, the 278 adjectives which made up the sample were administered to one hundred Johns Hopkins University undergraduates as a free-association test. A program generated the associative distributions and the 38,503 intersection coefficients among these adjectives. The

---

[1] J. Deese. The associative structure of some common English adjectives. *J. verb. Learn. verb. Behav.*, 1964, 3, 347–357.

size of the matrix of coefficients itself gives evidence for the
need to reduce the relations so described to some more basic pattern.
The material presented in the preceding chapter provides the rationale
for such a reduction.

One of the difficulties with the notion of contrast is that everything
to which it has been applied—including the semantic differential—has
depended upon a subjective judgment as to when contrast or antinomy
exists. This fact produces considerable embarrassment, because the
structure by which we hope to describe intraverbal relationships is
itself only defined by subjective judgment. If, however, the contrastive
property of adjectives is semantically important and if the characteristics of associative meaning are as they have been described, this
property should be directly revealed by some aspect of the associative
distributions themselves. Instead of relying on judgment (which,
itself, should be one of the features of verbal behavior described by
associative meaning) to decide whether or not we have a fundamental contrast, we should be able to discover the existence of such
a pattern in some unique aspect of the relations between associative
distributions.

Such is provided by one of the basic properties of associative
meaning (see Chapter III). The notion of contrast implies that one
member of a pair of words should have its associative meaning most
strongly determined by the other member of the pair and that the
relation should be reciprocal. Contrasting words, in brief, are words
that are defined by each other. Notice that such an idea implies that
synonyms are not so defined. The general relationship defining
synonymity in associative meaning is one in which the associative
distribution of one word is determined primarily by some other word
but in which the relationship is not reciprocal.

By this notion, all pairs of words in which the stimulus to one is
the most frequently occurring response to the other are the best
candidates for being reciprocal pairs. Table 24 lists all of the adjectives
from the sample of 278 that obey this rule. The most important aspect
of this table is the extent to which the principle which generated it
produces pairs which do not violate intuitive expectation. There are
no false positives, that is to say, pairs which are not by ordinary
usage antonyms. By intuitive judgment there are, perhaps, some pairs
which we think ought to be there. For example, we might expect
brave and *cowardly* (both of which were in the sample) to appear.
As we shall see, however, we would expect that not all formally
defined contrasts would appear in the list of fundamental sets, and

TABLE 24: Words That Form Contrasting Pairs by Eliciting One Another as Primaries[a]

Words		Response frequencies		Words		Response frequencies	
Alone	Together	10	6	Hard	Soft	28	15
Active	Passive	17	21	Heavy	Light*	18	5
Alive	Dead	44	22	High	Low	17	31
Back	Front	22	25	Inside	Outside	40	40
Bad	Good	43	29	Large	Small	23	13
Big	Little	14	15	Left	Right*	51	19
Black	White	39	23	Long	Short*	21	11
Bottom	Top	25	28	Married	Single	21	20
Clean	Dirty	15	21	Narrow	Wide	15	12
Cold	Hot	20	41	New	Old	13	20
Dark	Light	16	16	Old*	Young	7	25
Deep	Shallow	10	19	Poor	Rich	19	26
Dry	Wet	19	25	Pretty	Ugly	13	18
Easy	Hard*	17	5	Right	Wrong	39	41
Empty	Full	17	23	Rough	Smooth	10	16
Far	Near	17	35	Short	Tall	14	15
Fast	Slow	19	27	Sour	Sweet	18	12
Few	Many	41	21	Strong	Weak	13	26
First	Last	28	21	Thick	Thin	21	13
Happy	Sad	16	19				

SOURCE: J. Deese. The associative structure of some common English adjectives. *J. verb. Learn. verb. Behav.*, 1964, 3, 350.

[a] For those words marked by an asterisk, the primary has been pre-empted by another contrast. In these cases, the word marked elicits the other member of the pair as its second highest frequency response. The numbers are response frequencies ($N = 100$); the first number is the association from left to right, while the second number is the association from right to left.

those that do not appear are, in general, the right ones. There are practically no words in Table 24 which are formally marked as adjectives by one of the suffixes available in English (*-ly, -able, -ive*). Furthermore, these words are practically all of old English rather than French or Latin origin and are inflected in the comparative and superlative rather than being modified by *more* or *most*. Finally, among this set of very common adjectives, these are among the most common.

It is very possible that those antonyms not appearing by the criterion—allowing for the possibility of sampling error—are not in the cognitive sense defined by each other. We do not think of *brave* as being the opposite of *cowardly*; we think of *brave* as being *strong* and *cowardly* as being *afraid*. *Cowardly*, *brave*, and *afraid* are all related in a basic way to the pair, *strong-weak*.

In any event, it was not possible to find a single instance of a reciprocal pair in the collection of adjectives which did not conform to the notion of contrast as defined by a dictionary. It is also worth noting that most of the words a good dictionary lists as having antonyms are adjectives (and their adverbial derivatives). Polar pairs do appear in other form classes in English, as is testified to by the heroic efforts exerted by Roget in his arrangement for a thesaurus. Yet, as we page through a thesaurus arranged according to Roget, we are struck by the dubiousness of many of the listings. We are willing to accept *existence* and *inexistence* as antonymic nominal pairs, but we are less happy about *state* and *circumstance* or *circularity* and *convolution*. Most of the words listed in parallel by Roget's method are not to be found as antonyms in a dictionary, though the ingenuity of the arrangement suggests that some contrast can be found for every word. The difficulty in finding altogether sensible ones, however, is a profound fact about the nature of meaning and one that we shall have occasion to refer to in contrasting the basic pattern best exemplified by adjectives and that pattern exemplified most characteristically by nouns.

Certain nominal contrasts are associatively strong and obvious, as, for example, *mother-father* and *hand-foot*. If we examine the associations to enough nouns, however, we can find what we cannot find with adjectives—false contrasts. Two examples are *house-home* and *clock-time*. These pairs are strongly reciprocal in association but they are not contrastive in the ordinary sense (though perhaps "A house is not a home" does qualify). Paired contrast is not an ordinary property of nouns, and reciprocal pairs are rare; when they are found, they are not always, by intuitive meaning, contrastive.

Of the 278 common adjectives sampled in this study, the basic contrast pairs account for about 29 per cent. They are concentrated in the most commonly occurring words in the set. It is very likely that there are some basic contrast adjectives in English not represented here because one or both members of the pair are lower in frequency of usage than the criterion set in selection. Nevertheless, the data presented in the preceding chapter make it likely that the majority of such contrasts are represented.

Granted the fundamental nature of adjectival contrast, the question arises as to whether the pairs in Table 24 could be reduced to a smaller number of linguistically or cognitively intelligible dimensions. In one attempt to answer this question the pairs in Table 24 were subjected to a principal-components factor analysis with diagonals of unity and a varimax criterion of rotation. All factors were extracted and all variables determined in the rotation. Such a technique projects

TABLE 25: Correlations between Factor Loadings of a Selected Sample of Pair Contrasts

	Large–small	Bad–good	Pretty–ugly	Soft–loud[a]	Soft–hard	Easy–hard	Light–dark	Tall–short	White–black	High–low	Clean–dirty
Big–little	.43	.09	.03	.09	.06	.05	.02	.09	.02	.03	.03
Large–small		.06	.04	.01	.05	.02	.02	.08	.00	.06	.02
Bad–good			.07	.00	.03	.02	.06	.02	.02	.03	.06
Pretty–ugly				.04	.05	.00	.03	.00	.04	.00	.04
Soft–loud[a]					.09	.05	.03	.01	.01	.04	.00
Soft–hard						.14	.02	.00	.04	.03	.03
Easy–hard							.06	.00	.03	.02	.03
Light–dark								.00	.12	.04	.08
Tall–short									.00	.08	.00
White–black										.04	.05
High–low											.02

SOURCE: Deese, Associative structure of English adjectives, p. 350.
[a] Soft–loud is not a fundamental contrast by the reciprocal primary criterion. It conforms, however, to the general pattern of adjective contrast, and it is included here because of the interest in the series easy–hard–soft–loud.

125

a unique vector for each word. The polar opposite for a given word emerges clearly since it is the only other word from the entire set which has any appreciable loading on the factor for that word. This result suggests that all pairs are very nearly orthogonal.

Table 25 presents correlations between factor loadings for the first and second factors in a pair-by-pair analysis. In this treatment the four words defining any two pairs were entered in a matrix 4 by 4 and the complete set of factors extracted. The first two factors in such an analysis always defined the polar pairs, and the third factor always separated the members of the pairs into positive and negative loadings. The particular pairs in Table 25 were picked, by inspection, to produce a sample of pairs more highly intercorrelated than would be the entire set. For example, intuition would lead us to expect that the pairs *big-little* and *large-small* would be correlated with one another.

The correlations between the contrasting pairs were computed from the angles made by the vectors for sets of pairs in two dimensions. Figure 9 shows an example of the first two factors so plotted. Notice that the loadings for the members of each pair are almost identical,

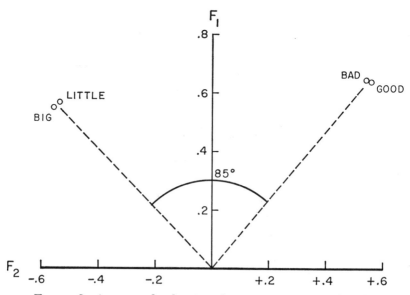

FIGURE 9: An example showing the vectors projected by the factor loadings in F_1 and F_2 of fundamental contrasts. (Data from J. Deese. The associative structure of some English adjectives. *J. verb. Learn. verb. Behav.*, 1964, 3, 347–357.)

a fact which makes it extremely easy to determine the angle from single vectors plotted through both members of the pair. The cosines of the factor-loading vectors are the numbers listed in Table 25.

The correlations in Table 25 are all remarkably low. Only three exceed 0.10. The correlation for the *big-little, large-small* pairs is 0.43, that for the *soft-hard* and *easy-hard* set 0.14 (the partial correlation between *soft* and *easy* holding *hard* constant), and that for the *white-black, light-dark* sets 0.12. In a word, most of the vectors defined by the pair factor loadings are very nearly at right angles; the loadings on the first two factors are very nearly equal. Therefore, a model of completely orthogonal contrasting pairs is one that is not too far in error.

Independence of the basic pairs is not so unparsimonious as it first appears. These pairs all occur with very high frequency in the language at large, and presumably they are among the most functional words in the language. If a smaller number of linguistically viable distinctions is to be made—allowing for three, four, or even ten dimensions—one would suppose that common contrasting pairs would exist to define them. The fact is that any scheme designed to reduce these contrasting pairs to a smaller number of dimensions produces dimensions which must be named with linguistically improbable words (consider *potency* or even *activity-inactivity* in the results of the semantic differential). When we consider how relatively poor a language with a very small number of adjectival dimensions would be in making necessary distinctions without confusion among attributes in the real world, the possibility of forty-four or more orthogonal contrasts appears not to be quite so unparsimonious.

Even the apparently synonymous pairs, *big-little* and *large-small*, have different uses in the language, so that the rather modest correlation of 0.43 between these "identical" pairs is not too surprising. Consider the meanings of the two sentences: "That's a small thing to do," and "That's a little thing to do." It is very easy to find many such examples. Think of the difficulty, for example, of substituting *large* for *big* in "He opened his big mouth." Therefore, it is not surprising that much of the meaning of one of these pairs, as that meaning is described by linguistic context, cannot be determined from the other.[2]

If these pairs define almost orthogonal, namable concepts in English, what of the remaining common adjectives, to say nothing of the vast

---

[2] Staats, Staats, and Crawford (*J. gen. Psychol.*, 1962, **67**, 159–167), much to their surprise, found that a conditioned response attached to *Large* as a stimulus did not generalize to *Big*.

sea of uncommon ones? Some adjectives at least owe their meaning, in part, to the fact that scalar properties exist for the majority, though not all, of the contrasts. The fact that distances between the polar opposites are psychologically meaningful is to be expected from a number of facts. Adverbial qualification can scale the intensity of adjectival meaning, as both Cliff and Howe have shown.[3] Furthermore, inflected series (*big, bigger, biggest*) suggest at least an ordering along a single semantic dimension. Finally, ordinary usage suggests that adjectives such as *huge* express a position more extreme but on the same dimension as an adjective such as *big*. These words occupy, then, a more ambiguous position than do the fundamental contrasts. They can and do project more than one contrast.

If any given adjective is to define some position on a scale the direction of which is given by the polar-opposite terms, it must have some appreciable intersections with both members of the contrasting pair or with one member and one other word related to one or both of the members of the pair. Therefore, the entire set of adjectives was explored for those words which had this property. The rule was applied with an arbitrary value of 0.10, after some preliminary investigation of other cutoffs. This value seems to be able to produce unidimensional semantic scales, as we shall see, though it does so at the expense of eliminating some words which would have been appropriate to the dimensions.

Table 26 shows the unrotated factor loadings for the first three factors extracted from the collection of words centering around *big-little*. The fact that all three of these unrotated factors produce psychologically meaningful results is an accident, but it is not an accident that the first unrotated factor does so. There is, in fact, a unique and psychologically important interpretation to the unrotated first factor loadings for any such collection.

The F_1 loadings in any matrix of unrotated factors are proportional to the column sum of the intercorrelations in the original matrix from which the factors were derived. For the data on associative distributions presented here, such intercorrelations reflect the extent to which the word defining any particular column shares its associative distributions with the other words in the same set. We have asserted at several places in the preceding chapters that the extent to which words share associative distributions is determined by the extent to which they share contexts in ordinary discourse. In a word, associative inter-

[3] N. Cliff. Adverbs as multipliers. *Psychol. Rev.*, 1959, 66, 27–44. Also, Howe, Probabilistic adverbial qualifications of adjectives.

sections are the outcome of shared contexts—of partial equivalences. Such an assertion provides us both with a psychological interpretation of unrotated F_1 loadings and a method for establishing the validity of the implication that associative intersections and shared context should be positively related.

TABLE 26: Factor Loadings and Validation Data[a] for the Collection of Words Centering around *Big-Little*

Words	F_1	Context ratings	F_2	L count	F_3	Size ratings
Tiny	.460	1.71	−.301	527	−.446	0.8
Slight	.360	1.42	−.345	419	−.424	1.5
Little	.490	3.22	.413	8659	−.338	1.8
Small	.519	3.53	.382	1818	−.333	1.9
Big	.556	3.59	.335	1773	.308	4.3
Large	.544	3.56	.353	1697	.323	4.5
Great	.399	2.15	−.363	3834	.342	5.1
Grand	.372	1.39	−.330	429	.347	4.6
Vast	.406	1.93	−.380	241	.365	5.5
Huge	.473	2.11	−.315	311	.381	5.6

SOURCE: Deese, Associative structure of English adjectives, p. 352.
[a] The nature of the validation data is explained in text.

In principle, we should like to correlate these F_1 loadings with the frequency with which each of the adjectives in the set occurs in contexts common to all the other adjectives in some extended sample of the language. In fact, it would be difficult, not to say impossible, to obtain data which would make such a correlation feasible. Therefore, we have simply extended the technique of using judgments to determine the appropriateness of certain contexts to particular adjectives.

The second column in Table 26 provides a measure of the extent to which each adjective in the set is judged to share the nominal contexts obtained from all the other adjectives. These judgments were obtained in the following way. For each of the ten adjectives in Table 26, ten students were asked to produce ten nouns that might reasonably follow those adjectives in ordinary discourse. The result was a sample of one hundred nouns for each adjective. The adjective-noun sequences produced by the students were for the most part very commonplace, as, for example, *big dog, little car, grand canyon,* and so on. The ten most frequently occurring nouns for each adjective were selected (eliminating between-adjective duplications) and assembled together on a single sheet. Ten of these sheets, listing the one hundred nouns obtained from all the adjectives, were presented to each of ten new students. At the top of each sheet was listed one of the original adjectives. The subjects were asked to place a check mark opposite each noun which would be expected to go with that adjective in ordinary discourse. One would expect the students to check *man* for *slight* but not *canyon*, and so on. In general, these expectations were borne out.

The second column in Table 26 shows the mean number of subjects per noun who checked a context to be appropriate. The measure reflects the extent to which each particular adjective is judged to be an appropriate modifier for contexts generated from all the other adjectives—that is, the extent to which it shares contexts with the other adjectives.

The adjective *big* has the highest value (with 3.59 subjects judging it to be appropriate for an average of all the nouns), and the adjective *grand* has the least. The mean values in column two produce a rank-difference correlation with the F_1 loadings of 0.903. Therefore, the first factor is closely identified with a measure of shared context.

The second factor in Table 26 is correlated with the frequency of usage. The numbers in the fourth column are L-count frequencies from the Thorndike-Lorge count. Again, there is a significant rank-order correlation (0.612) between word frequency and F_2 loadings. The single anomalous case is provided by the adjective *great*. It is possible, however, that the frequency count, which is very high for this word, reflects more the usage in other than simple adjectival positions (as, for example, an adverbial qualifier in the phrase, "a great big lie").

F_3 provides the principal semantic dimension relating this collection of words. Column five shows that the F_3 loadings define a bipolar factor which clearly separates the large words from the small words. This factor is highly correlated ($p = 0.988$) with ratings of these words on a size dimension. The numbers in column six are mean ratings, obtained from ten subjects who rated each adjective according to the size of an object that adjective might describe. The anchors of the scale were the largest thing imaginable and the smallest thing imaginable. The words *huge* and *tiny* were rated as closer to these anchors than any other words.

These data show us that this collection defines a common semantic dimension and that the words in it are related to one another through shared contexts. The structure underlying associative distributions are partly semantic and partly the result of more general linguistic features.

Another set that is of interest is provided by the series of inflected adjectives, *worst, worse, bad, good, better,* and *best.* If the analysis

TABLE 27: Factor Loadings for the First Two Factors in the Inflected *Good-Bad* Series

Words	F_1	F_2
Best	.524	.403
Better	.530	.374
Good	.565	.278
Bad	.562	—.279
Worse	.553	—.382
Worst	.559	—.392

SOURCE: Deese, Associative structure of English adjectives, p. 353.

of associative structure by the extraction of factors is valid, we would expect to uncover a single semantic dimension which orders these words in the same way as does inflection. Table 27 lists the first two factors for these words. If we accept the interpretation of the F_1 loadings as the product of partial equivalence in context, we would conclude that these words are almost identical in context, since the F_1 loadings are very close together. Given the grammatical structure of the series, this result is very reasonable. The second factor is perfectly ordered with respect to the formal definitions of the inflected series. Therefore, it can be said to be validated directly by linguistic usage.

The size series presented in Table 26 was one of the two largest collections of related words obtained in the present data by application of the criterion described earlier. The other sizable series could be described as a numerosity or quantity set, and the analysis of it is presented in Table 28. If we again identify the first factor as a contextual one, we are faced with a somewhat lower correlation between it and context ratings than in the case of the size adjectives. The context ratings listed in the second column were obtained in the same way as those given in Table 26. The correlation in this case, however, is only 0.552, which is just significant at the 0.05 level. Some problems encountered with the numerosity series make it altogether reasonable that the correlation be lower in this case. The contextual equivalences within this set must be subject to some grammatical modification, since some of these adjectives take plural nouns while others take the singular (for example, *all* and *total*). Restricting the study of context to nominal contexts is less satisfactory for these words than it was in the case of the size adjectives. Furthermore, in making the ratings the subjects were required, in some cases, to change the nouns from singular to plural and vice versa. For example, the sequence *many times* would have to be changed to *entire time*. Because of this additional task one would expect the ratings to be less reliable, and in fact there was greater intersubject variability in the ratings. Nevertheless, the correlation does show, despite these inadequacies, that the context ratings and F_1 loadings are related.

The F_2 (rotated) loadings in this case reflect a dimension of numerosity. This assertion is validated by the correlation of 0.903 between F_2 loadings and the fourth column of Table 28, labeled "mean numerosity choice."

TABLE 28: Factor Loadings and Validation Data for Words Describing Numerosity

Words	F_1	Context ratings	F_2	Mean numerosity choice
Entire	.305	4.45	.511	86.0
Total	.314	3.89	.502	71.4
All	.416	6.13	.452	85.5
Various	.451	5.24	.044	28.9
Numerous	.525	5.23	—.042	36.7
Considerable	.329	3.00	—.063	34.9
Some	.483	6.43	—.159	36.5
Many	.629	5.84	—.398	27.5
Several	.564	5.97	—.405	13.1
Few	.581	5.69	—.434	9.3

SOURCE: Deese, Associative structure of English adjectives, p. 353.

The data in the fourth column were obtained by presenting to fifty students a series of statements about (1) an audience of one hundred individuals attending a lecture and (2) an objective examination consisting of one hundred questions. Each statement contained one of the adjectives from the numerosity set. The subjects were asked to circle the approximate number described in the statement from among the following alternatives: 100, 95, 75, 50, 25, 5, 0. The statements themselves were of the following sort: "A few questions were ambiguous"; "the entire examination consisted of numerical examples"; "some people interrupted the speech with applause"; "many people fell asleep because of the heat in the room." The content of the questions was balanced over the adjectives by suitably modifying each sentence, and all the subjects answered both sets of statements.

The nature of the relation between the numerosity choices and F_2 can better be seen in Figure 10. The significant feature of these data is that both the F_2 loadings and the reactions of subjects to these adjectives, when embedded in sentences, do not conform to the logical or dictionary definitions of the words. The most remarkable aspect of this result is that *many* seems to mean less than half of the total

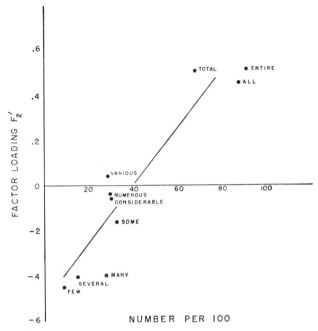

FIGURE 10: F'$_2$ (rotated F$_2$) loadings and mean number per hundred chosen by subjects for the numerosity words. (Data from Deese, The associative structure of some English adjectives.)

and is closer to *few* and *several* than to *considerable* and *numerous*. Furthermore, the numerosity choices show that the words *total, entire,* and *all* apparently do not always mean what they should. "The entire audience was bored," as an assertion, apparently means that well over half of those present but not really 100 per cent were bored. In fact, the whole numerosity scale seems depressed downward, and one cannot help but speculate that such a result reflects the overuse of numerical exaggeration in American English. Even the term "100 per cent" is sometimes misused to indicate a large majority.

Indirect evidence suggests that not all contrasting pairs readily produce scales. Some contrasting adjectives do not easily appear with the class of adverbial modifiers usually described as intensifiers or quantifiers. Some examples of these are *former-latter, outside-inside, front-back, first-last,* and *married-single.* Furthermore, only under very unusual circumstances would these words appear in the comparative or superlative form. Therefore, while scaling is a major characteristic of contrasting pairs, it does not appear to be a necessary one.

Many of the adjectives which do not appear among the contrast pairs themselves own their intraverbal meaning to combinations of underlying pairs. These are the words which provide the various scale positions exhibited on the semantic scales in Tables 26 and 28. Some of these words appear on several semantic scales, and, if the viewpoint presented here is correct, these words are fundamentally more ambiguous than the basic contrasts themselves. The word *great*, for example, is likely to appear in a context for which the unique meaning in context would be closer to *good* than to *big*. The near independence of the fundamental contrasts makes us suspect, however, that we would not find any particularly orderly pattern in the relations between the contrasting pairs to which a particular word is related. That suspicion is confirmed by a consideration of the two analyses presented in Table 29. This table presents the first three factors for matrices of, respectively, *good, bad, big, little*, and *great*, and *good, bad, pretty*,

TABLE 29: Three Factors from Small Sets Made by Combining Two Contrasting Pairs with a Single Word Common to Both

	F_1	F_2	F_3
Bad	.576	.620	—.306
Big	.533	—.436	—.323
Good	.595	.602	.307
Great	.489	—.373	.658
Little	.545	—.412	—.333
Bad	.598	.597	.307
Good	.595	.600	—.306
Nice	.531	—.370	—.340
Pretty	.518	—.424	—.297
Ugly	.489	—.403	.638

ugly, and *nice*. The second factor in both cases divides the words according to the contrasts represented. The single odd word goes, on this factor, with the pair with which it has the closer relation (*nice* with *pretty-ugly* and *great* with *big-little*). In the case of the words associated with *nice*, the third factor defines a semantically orderly scale. The order of words on the scale is from *ugly* to *bad, pretty, good*, and *nice*. No such orderly relation emerges in the case of the words associated with *great*. Because of the general absence of correlation between contrasting pairs, we would not expect orderly relations on a single dimension (though the matrix itself is quite orderly). In fact, the great matrix is more the rule, and the *nice* matrix, the exception.

Certainly, the relationship between *big-little* and *good-bad* is an ambiguous one. An incautious generalization from the notion of single ordering in cognitive processes[4] would lead us to think, perhaps, that *big* should be associated with *good*, and *little* with *bad*. But even a very limited sample of linguistic examples easily shows independence in linguistic context is the rule. Surely a *big mistake* is a *worse mistake* than a simple *mistake* and a *big success* is a *better success* than just a *success*. Thus, while we may expect isolated cases of semantically reasonable dimensions like that of F_3 for the words grouped with *nice*, we would not expect such dimensions to occur all the time or even very frequently.

Many adjectives which do not appear as polar opposites in Table 24 or in the sets in Tables 26, 27, and 28 combine to form other closely related sets defining single dimensions. For example, there is a group centering around *old-new* consisting of *ancient, modern, young,* and *recent.* Another set consists of *light, dark, dim, bright,* and *dull. Happy* and *sad* scale from *merry* to *happy, contented,* and *sad.* There are also probably many missing contrasting pairs, either because of deficiencies in the original sampling among adjectives or because of sampling error in the application of the reciprocity rule. All in all, a large majority— 64 per cent—of the words in the sample consist of either polar opposites or words that fall on one or more polar scales by application of the 0.10 rule.

An important exception to groups of adjectives which easily fit into the polar opposite scheme is the class of color names (*black-white* excluded). Color names do not form polar pairs by the associative reciprocity criterion. For reasons to be discussed more thoroughly in the next chapter, they tend to resolve themselves into multidimensional clusters much like those presented in Chapter IV. These clusters might reasonably be expected to form an arrangement resembling that of the familiar color space, but they do not. Neither are the clusters entirely satisfactory from an intuitive view of linguistic usage. Suffice it to say here it is possible that the color matrix is so unusual because it is the result of the imposition of an abstract dimensional scheme (color space) upon the kind of categorical system characteristic of English nouns (not adjectives). Color words are anomalous indeed, for there is no other collection of common words the relations among which can be described by an abstract dimensional system having wide popular circulation. Physicists have abstract systems for discussing the

---

[4] C. B. De Soto. The predilection for single orderings. *J. abnorm. soc. Psychol.,* 1961, **62,** 16–23.

relations among physical variables and measurements, and various other linguistically unusual systems exist for special groups. But the color-space system, in a rough form at least, is well known among people of relatively little formal education. Elementary school children receive instruction in the color circle and the complementary principle. It is not surprising that at least some the characteristics of this system may influence associations to color names. It is to be noted, however, that the complementary principle in color space is not represented in a polar-opposite scheme among the color names. This is altogether reasonable, for, as we shall see, no polar-opposite scheme should exist among words which have a multidimensional structure of meaning.

If color names are to be considered as adjectives, they are adjectives of a special kind. That fact can be appreciated from the absence of any tendency towards contrast in associative criteria and by the fact that color names do not readily take the prefixes which grammatically invent polar opposites. The negation prefixes for adjectives (for example, *-un, -in, -im*) do not have the effect of undoing the sense of the adjective which follows them. They have the force of creating polar opposites where none existed before. Thus, *incomplete* can be made from *complete,* and *immoral* from *moral.* Even the element *not,* which in most logical or grammatical analyses is described as canceling (nullifying) the effect of that which it modifies, does not produce a true negation when it precedes an adjective. As Howe[5] shows, *not* before an adjective has the effect of converting that adjective to its polar opposite, though in a somewhat less intense state. Thus, "That's not bad" can best be taken to mean "That's mildly good." The implication is that *not bad* is *good.*

This peculiar property of negation applied to adjectives does not in general apply to nouns, save for those which have quasi-contrast properties. Nor does it apply to color names. To say that something is *not red* does not imply, as perhaps color space would lead a psychologist to expect, that it is *blue-green.* Color names do not obey any of the usual rules for adjectives because they are, in certain essential respects, more like nouns than like adjectives. They are essentially words which describe multidimensional relations, not unidimensional

[5] Howe, Associative structure of non-evaluative adverbs. Also, E. S. Howe. Verb tense, negatives and other determinants of the intensity of connotative meaning. *J. verb. Learn. verb. Behav.* (in press). Howe also points out that the relation between evaluative words and quantifiers is complicated. *Big* can be a pure quantifier *only* if it is evaluatively neutral.

relations. They fail of most of the usual criteria for adjectives both on the associative measures and in ordinary linguistic usage.

The remaining adjectives in this set do not, on inspection, appear to be unusual. For some of them the data do not exist which could test their conformity to the polar-opposite scheme, but a number of considerations, including the existence of the negation prefixes, tend to argue for their conformity to the scheme. Certain words were missing from the present sample, either through oversight or failure of the general validity of the Thorndike-Lorge count. For example, the word *late* does not appear in the sample, though *early* does. It is very probable that *early-late* constitute a fundamental contrasting pair. An earlier sample of fifty Johns Hopkins undergraduates yielded *early* as the primary to *late*, and the sample from which most of the data discussed in this chapter were obtained yielded *late* as the primary to *early*.

Some less common adjectives undoubtedly do not conform to the pattern. These owe their paradigmatic meaning to root morphemes associatively defined within other form classes. The participles constitute an interesting group in this respect, since there is already ample evidence to show that their adjectival status is ambiguous. Chomsky[6] tries to differentiate between the participles which are true adjectives and those which are not by application of adverbial modifiers. He points out that the word *smoking* is not usually preceded by *very* while the word *interesting* often is. *Interesting* is regularly an adjective; *smoking* rarely is. Yet this rule fails of generality, for we have already seen that certain important polar adjectives (such as *former-latter* and *married-single*) as well as some derived adjectives (*viable*, for example) do not readily take *very*. The more fundamental principle of contrast may provide the necessary distinction, however, once we understand that color words are not ordinary adjectives. Thus, participles which readily function as ordinary adjectives are participles which take negation prefixes; we easily say *uninteresting*, but not *unsmoking* or *nonsmoking*.

Available evidence suggests that the contrasting scheme for English adjectives also occurs in the closely related languages, French and German. Russell and Meseck[7] drew upon their own data in German,

---

[6] Chomsky, *Syntactic structures*.

[7] W. A. Russell and O. R. Meseck. Der Einfluss der Assoziation auf das Erinnern von Worten in des Deutschen, Französischen und Englischen Sprache. *Zeitschrift für Experimentelle und Angewandte Psychologie*, 1959, 6, 191–211.

the data of Rosenzweig[8] for French, and those of Russell and Jenkins[9] for English (American) to make a comparison between languages for the one hundred words in the usual Kent-Rosanoff list. Many of these words in English are polar-opposite adjectives, and in almost every instance the corresponding adjectives in French and German are also polar opposites. For example, *dark-light* in English is paralleled by *dunkel-hell(e)* in German and *sombre-clair* in French. Another example is provided by the pairs *black-white, schwarz-weiss,* and *noir-blanc.* The pairs *smooth-rough* and *lisse-rugueux* are polar opposites in English and French but not in German; German subjects give *Eis* as the primary associate to *glatt.* The parallels are striking enough to provide evidence for comparable adjectival structures in French and German. It is to be noted that the position of adjectives in French is after the noun, and a naïve interpretation of the stimulus-response or sequential view of associative processes would lead us to expect a very different pattern for French speakers.

In a number of respects, then, the contrast scheme seems basic to the class of adjectives. The polar-opposite form of the semantic differential is satisfactory, though we must recognize that not all adjectives are sensibly scalable. As a measuring device, however, the semantic differential is linguistically more natural than the adjective check list or the adjective circle. The number of adjectival dimensions in English is very large and, in fact, may be extended to infinity by the grammatical device of the negation prefix. The basic dimensions, corresponding to those aspects of things we talk about most, are very nearly independent, and it is even very likely that the number of these dimensions is large and growing within the language.

We have argued that the schemata underlying associative distributions grow out of equivalences within linguistic contexts. If this notion is correct and if the relations between contrasting pairs of adjectives are as they have been described here, there is implied a particular pattern to the contexts in which these adjectives appear in ordinary discourse. An idealized version of that scheme is presented in Table 30. Arranged across the top and down the side of the table are polar pairs. The top of the table represents adjectives which occurred in sentences on Occasion A. The side represents the same adjectives occurring in

---

[8] M. R. Rosenzweig. Études sur l'association des mots. *L'Année Psychologique,* 1957, **57,** 23–32.

[9] W. A. Russell and J. J. Jenkins. The complete Minnesota norms for responses to 100 words from the Kent-Rosanoff word-association test. Technical Report No. 11. Minneapolis: Univ. of Minnesota, 1954.

TABLE 30: Theoretical Table of Equivalences among Adjectives

		Occasion A: Hot	Cold	Good	Bad	Big	Little	Etc.	—	Total
Occasion B:	Hot	50	25	1	0	1	2	—	—	100
	Cold	25	50	1	1	0	1	—	—	100
	Good	0	1	50	25	0	0	—	—	100
	Bad	0	0	25	50	1	0	—	—	100
	Big	1	1	2	0	50	25	—	—	100
	Little	0	1	0	0	25	50	—	—	100
	Etc.	—	—	—	—	—	—	—	—	
		—	—	—	—	—	—	—	—	
	Total	100	100	100	100	100	100			

the identical sentences on Occasion B. The cell entries are the frequencies of occurrence. Thus, we read that, of one hundred sentences containing *hot* on Occasion A (the column total for *hot*), fifty of the same sentences contained *hot* on Occasion B. The word *cold* appeared in twenty-five instances on Occasion B, and the remainder of occurrences were scattered among all possible adjectives. The consistency with which a given adjective occurs in the same sentence from occasion to occasion helps to establish (and, indeed, may be the major factor in establishing) the basic meaning for the adjective. The occasions on which the same sentence also contains the polar opposite must be correlated with a discriminative difference in nature in order to establish the contrast. ("That dog is big; this dog is little.") The lack of relation to other adjectives is given, in part, by the failure of any other adjectives to enter these sentences in great frequency. If we can imagine this process to continue through Occasion C, and so on, with the occurrences of adjectives other than the polar opposites uncorrelated with sentences, we have a model for the pattern of contextual equivalences responsible for the basic scheme of adjectives.

An approximation to such a table is shown in Table 31. Table 31 presents some data for the two polar pairs, *hot-cold* and *good-bad*. For each of these four words a single subject generated fifteen

TABLE 31: Percentage of Adjectives Occurring in Original Sentences and in Sentences Reconstructed by Subjects

		Original sentences: Hot	Cold	Good	Bad
Reconstructed sentences:	Hot	54.7	5.8	0.2	0.0
	Cold	10.5	54.1	0.0	0.0
	Good	1.3	0.3	57.4	1.2
	Bad	1.9	0.2	4.1	55.6

sentences. These sentences were like the following: "A bad apple spoils the lot"; "the coffee is too hot to drink." These sentences, with the adjectival position blank, were presented to fifty undergraduates who were instructed to guess at the missing adjective. Table 31 shows the relative frequency with which *good, bad, hot,* and *cold* were replaced in the sentences which came from each of these words. The general pattern of Table 31 conforms to that in Table 30. The extremely high frequency (above 50 per cent) with which the subjects replaced the original adjectives with the same word suggests that these sentences more strongly determined the original adjective than would, perhaps, sentences at large. Three out of four of the polar opposites were higher in frequency than the frequencies in the eight cross-pair cells. A Mann-Whitney U-test applied to a comparison of the polar-opposite cells and the nonpaired cells in Table 31 yields a U value significant beyond the 0.01 level.

There is, then, considerable evidence for the correspondence between associative patterns and the contextual patterns of underlying sentences. The referential meaning of the contrasting members of pairs must be the outcome of some contingencies between events in the natural world and these words. It is to be noted, however, that a twofold state exists in such contingencies. *Big* is contrasted with *little,* not with *little, soft,* and *bad.* Some psychological reasons for the twofold nature of such contingencies will be advanced in the next chapter.

7

Nouns and Some General Properties of Associative Structures

We have just examined in some detail the characteristic structure of English adjectives. Earlier, we saw that most adverbs (particularly those marked by affixes) have their associative distributions largely determined by the structural relations of the root morpheme within other form classes. Those adverbs that do not conform to this pattern have been shown, by the analyses of Cliff[1] and Howe,[2] to be semantically described by various scales—such as intensity, probability, closeness in space and time—which modify the meaning of adjectives. Furthermore, as Howe[3] has demonstrated for such adverbs, these scales can be recovered by a factor-analytic treatment of the intersections derived from the associative distributions of the adverbs.

There remain, among the content words, the classes of nouns and verbs. Verbs, as they are ordinarily described, are a mixed group. The class consists of both content words and verbal auxiliaries. In addition, there is the class of verbs commonly described as linking verbs—*be* and *seem*, for example. We have already seen, in Chapter V, that the verbal auxiliaries organize themselves into groups much as do other classes of functional words and that there is a close correspondence between the descriptive analysis which comes from a structural grammar and the analysis which comes from the treatment of associative intersections among the members of the classes. The remaining verbs—those which have some referential meaning—we shall treat much as nouns, and it will be our purpose to show in this and the next chapter that semantically, if not grammatically, verbs

[1] N. Cliff. Adverbs as multipliers. *Psychol. Rev.*, 1959, **66**, 27–44.

[2] Howe, Probabilistic adverbial qualifications of adjectives.

[3] Howe, Associative structure of non-evaluative adverbs. Also, Howe, Verb tense, negatives and other determinants.

are very much like nouns. Even grammatically there is, in Indo-European languages, a close relation between nouns and verbs, as is illustrated by the importance of gerundive constructions and the readiness with which nouns may be formed from verb stems.

Because of the grammatical position nouns occupy in sentences, however, it is easier to see the structural relations between the meaning of nouns than between the meaning of verbs. Therefore, in this chapter, we shall devote the major portion of the exposition to the case of nouns and only very briefly extend the analysis to verbs.

The basic distinction between the types of associative meaning for the content-carrying classes is best exemplified by the differences between nouns and adjectives. We have just seen that adjectives are characterized by a fundamental polar-opposite structure. The contrast between adjectival pairs refers to qualities in experience which are essentially twofold and which, in ordinary human experience, vary independently of other possible qualities. Over some considerable range of events, we do not expect *warm* things to be either *big, little, good,* or *bad.* While the accuracy of our expectation can only be attested to by a general ecological survey of human experience, the data presented in previous chapters make the hypothesis reasonable so far as linguistic environments or the distributions of words within sentences are concerned. We have seen that the various pairs of adjectives are not likely to be correlated in their nominal distributions. *Good* and *bad* are no more nor less, in the long run, likely to modify the nouns modified by *big-little* than modified by *hot-cold.* Furthermore, there is not likely to be a correlation between particular sides of polar dimensions. A *warm fire* is surely *good,* but so is a *cold Martini.*

If, however, we examine the adjectival environment of any particular noun, a very different pattern emerges. That pattern reveals at least one of the important characteristics of nouns. Any particular noun selects a group of adjectives and rejects others. Therefore, for that noun and its associatively related nouns, there is a correlation among the adjectival modifiers. A *puppy* is *warm, furry,* and *lively,* not the opposites of these terms. Nouns, except for certain unusual cases, do not contrast with one another in meaning. They cannot, for if they did, we would not know what was being contrasted. Rather, it seems intuitively obvious that we group nouns and that this grouping is, in part, determined by the correlated sets of adjectives which modify or describe the nouns. For example, we think of *kittens* and *puppies* together. As Hobbes would have it, the mind runs naturally from one to the other. Both *kittens* and *puppies* are *young, warm, furry,* and so on.

If we consider nouns to name concepts, we realize that these concepts may be characterized by their *descriptions*. These descriptions are mainly adjectival (though perhaps not always formally so). Hovland[4] and Hunt[5] have pointed out that the basic system for specifying descriptions is a notation in which objects can be characterized by values with respect to basic attributes. These attributes themselves should, for efficiency of description, be unidimensional and uncorrelated, as are the basic adjectives of the language. Therefore, we might suppose that a particular noun (those which require the use of color names to characterize them aside) could be uniquely described by some combination of fundamental unidimensional adjectives. Certainly, concrete objects readily lend themselves to such a description. Thus, we may characterize a particular individual as being *tall, thin, happy,* and *smart*. That characterization may serve to differentiate him from a large number of individuals. Of course, such a limited set of adjectives would not permit a unique specification of an individual. The more such adjectival descriptions we add, the more differentiations we can make and the more likely we are to specify uniquely some concept.

Yet, a moment of searching through one's own associative processes makes it abundantly evident that we do not think of nouns in this way. Our most common associations to nouns are not adjectives which characterize the nouns in question but other nouns. We do occasionally think of adjectives in response to particular nouns, and these adjectives are appropriately descriptive. Nevertheless, for most nouns, the main content of our associations to them consists of other nouns. Therefore, our primary task in describing the associative structure of nouns is not to specify the logically descriptive attributes for nouns but to describe the way in which nouns group themselves with other nouns.

We have already seen that there is a negative correlation between frequency of usage and frequency of syntagmatic responses in association for adjectives. That is to say, rare adjectives, more often than not, yield their verbal environments (usually nouns) rather than other adjectives. No such relation exists in the case of nouns, however.

[4] C. I. Hovland. A "communication analysis" of concept learning. *Psychol. Rev.*, 1952, **59**, 461–472.

[5] E. B. Hunt. *Concept learning: An information process problem.* New York: Wiley, 1962.

Irrespective of frequency of usage, the associations to nouns are paradigmatic. The paradigmatic character of nominal associations would lead us to expect no difference between common and unusual nouns in their associative structures, though there is in the case of adjectives. In general, as we shall see, this expectation is confirmed. The associative structures for uncommon nouns are not different from those for common nouns, except for the fact that the uncertainty of meaning of unusual nouns for ordinary people may lead to a statistically more diffuse or less precise structure when that structure is defined by populations of individuals.

However, this characteristic paradigmatic responding to nouns is not so simple when it is examined closely. Not all of the responses to any given noun are nouns of the same type as the stimulus. Often they do not fit the linguistic distribution of the nominal stimulus. For example, the noun, *basket,* elicits *paper, bread, food,* and *waste* in high frequency. Or, again, *bedtime* elicits *sleep* and *music.* The rare word, *academician,* yields, among other nominal associates, *academy, school,* and *diploma.* Therefore, while we may characterize the majority of responses to nouns as nouns, the responses are not always the same kinds of nouns as the stimuli, and often they may be fitted into common environments only in unusual and awkward constructions.

The implications of this fact are several and important. For one thing, it becomes immediately obvious that we cannot completely describe the paradigmatic associates to nouns within a supraordinate, subordinate, co-ordinate scheme. For another, it is certain that grouping nouns on the basis of their associative intersections does not sort these nouns according to the nature of the events and objects to which they refer. An *academician* and a *school* certainly cannot be said to be similar in their natures, though they clearly "belong together." It would seem that some nouns are thought of not only in connection with other concepts which share descriptive attributes but with concepts that are merely present with or related to the noun in question. Furthermore, it is at least a reasonable hypothesis that such words would more likely occur at different positions within the same sentences than as substitutes for one another within the same sentence.

Because the possible kinds of relations between a noun and its various associates is central to the analysis of the possible patterns of relations between nouns in associative meaning, it will be useful to provide some concrete examples of the types of responses which can occur to a nominal stimulus. Table 32 presents a classification of

TABLE 32: Associations to Nouns Classified by Type and Listed in Order of Frequency[a]

Stimuli	Responses

1. Academician
   Nominal of Same Type
   Scholar, Student, Professor, Teacher, Scientist, Magician, Midshipman.
   Nominal of Different Type
   Academy, Study, School, University, College, Diploma, Building, Albany, Robe, Law, Navy, Book, Report, Hopkins.
   Attributive
   Smart, American.
   Other
   Agree.

2. Action
   Nominal of Same Type
   Movement, Motion, Fight, Game, War, Excitement, Happening, Trouble, Detention, Drama, Inaction, Reaction.
   Nominal of Different Type
   Artist, Mud, Police, Speed, Football.
   Attributive
   Fast, Sedentary, Small, Direct, Quick.
   Other
   Do, Go, Stop, Run, Hurry.

3. Alibi
   Nominal of Same Type
   Excuse, Story, Lie, Crime, Reason, Falsehood, Suspicion, Truth, Fib.
   Nominal of Different Type
   Witness, Thieves, Sheik, Perry Mason, Man, Place, Ali Baba, Murderer, Relay.
   Attributive
   Guilty, Good, Arabian.
   Other
   Standing, Pretend.

4. Animal
   Nominal of Same Type
   Dog, Man, Cat, Creature, Rat, Plant, Free, Deer, Lion, Fly, Person, Primate, Fish, Bear, Clown.

[a] Data from fifty Johns Hopkins undergraduates.

TABLE 32 (*Continued*)

Stimuli	Responses

Nominal of Different Type
Farm, Fur, Instinct, Husbandry, Tendency, Skin, Lust, Drive, Book, Body.
Attributive
Carnal, Lower, Brutish, Strong, Alive, Unhuman, Animate, Male.
Other
None.

5. Announcer
Nominal of Same Type
Man, Speaker, Host, Lowell Thomas, Killer, Parr.
Nominal of Different Type
Radio, Talk, Commercial, Program, Product, Sport, News, Microphone, Show, Station, Mistake.
Attributive
Gaudy.
Other
Read, Munch, Sing, Tell, Call, Raid, Begin.

6. Apprentice
Nominal of Same Type
Boy, Seaman, Understudy, Sorcerer, Beginner, Magician, Craftsman, Journeyman, Layman, Actor, Butcher, Carpenter, Man, Blacksmith.
Nominal of Different Type
Shop, Trade, Guild, Union, Franklin.
Attributive
New, Young.
Other
Learn, Work, Help, Paint, Start, Of.

7. Asparagus
Nominal of Same Type
Food, Vegetable, Fruit, Lettuce, Legume, Plant.
Nominal of Different Type
Esophagus, Can, Shute, Caesar.
Attributive
Green, Stringy, Thin.
Other
Echh, Hate.
8. Attorney
Nominal of Same Type
Lawyer, General, Perry Mason.

TABLE 32 (*Continued*)

Stimuli	Responses

Nominal of Different Type
　　Law, Trial, Court, Money.
Attributive
　　Legal.
Other
　　Argue.

9. Bedtime
　　Nominal of Same Type
　　　　Night, Dawn, Dinnertime.
　　Nominal of Different Type
　　　　Sleep, Story, Sheet, Bed, Joke, T.V., Music, Covers.
　　Attributive
　　　　Late.
　　Other
　　　　Go.

10. Certainty
　　Nominal of Same Type
　　　　Sureness, Uncertainty, Confidence.
　　Nominal of Different Type
　　　　Mark, Equation, Choice, Heisenberg, Idea.
　　Attributive
　　　　Surely, Right, Certain, Positive, Quaintly, False, True, Soon,
　　　　Complete, Always, Maybe.
　　Other
　　　　Not, Must, Again, Of What, Yes.

11. Cigarette
　　Nominal of Same Type
　　　　Cigar, Weed, Butt, Winston, Pipe.
　　Nominal of Different Type
　　　　Cancer, Machine, Lighter, Holder, Case, Tax, Pleasure, Store,
　　　　Match, Girl, Rings, Tobacco.
　　Attributive
　　　　Bad, Sick, Round.
　　Other
　　　　None.

12. Clemency
　　Nominal of Same Type
　　　　Mercy, Leniency, Easiness, Forgiveness, Kindness.

TABLE 32 (*Continued*)

Stimuli	Responses

Nominal of Different Type
Governor, Pardon, People, Prisoner, Clementine, Judge,
Arithmetic, Reprieve, Peace, Pity, Clemenceau, Leadway.
Attributive
Merciful, Lenient, Free, Easy, Capital.
Other
What, Allow, Save, Plea, Toward, Beg, Believe.

associates to a sample of nouns. The sample serves to illustrate the
various kinds of associates one finds to nouns. The responses are
grouped into four classes. One class consists of the nominal responses
that are of the same type as the nominal stimulus. If, for example,
both the stimulus and the response are animate nouns, they are both
of the same type. A second class consists of the nominal responses
which are not of the same type as the nominal stimulus. A third type
consists of responses which are mainly attributive or descriptive in
character. These are, of course, overwhelmingly adjectives. The fourth
class consists of words of other kinds, mainly verbs and functional
elements. Some words belong to two or more classes, but in Table 32
these words are assigned to only one class.

The classification in the table is not meant to be anything other
than intuitive. It does reveal, however, the possible kinds of associative relations nouns can have with one another. First of all, nouns can
be related by being grouped together. Such a relation would depend
upon the responses being of the same type as the stimulus. Secondly,
nouns can be related by conceptual or physical environment. The
response *shop* or *trade* to *apprentice* illustrates such a relation, and
an inspection of the second type of responses in Table 32 reveals
many such possibilities. Thirdly, nouns can be related because the
objects or concepts they describe have attributes in common. This
mode of relation is most clearly illustrated by the third class of words
in Table 32.

It is clear, however, that the three modes by which nouns may be
related are not independent. Things or concepts which are grouped
together in the main share the same conceptual or physical environments, and, of course, the attributes which describe them are likely
to be correlated. These relations may be illustrated by the analysis of
a group of closely related nouns. Such nouns may be obtained in the

TABLE 33: Intersection Coefficients for Animal Names

	Bear	Beaver	Buffalo	Cat	Cow	Deer	Dog	Fox	Goat	Gorilla	Hamster	Horse	Lion	Moose	Mouse	Muskrat	Pig	Pony	Rabbit	Rat	Sheep	Sloth
Antelope	.14	.07	.09	.01	.04	.26	.02	.08	.11	.03	.12	.03	.06	.15	.04	.12	.06	.03	.12	.03	.06	.12
Bear		.10	.08	.02	.04	.14	.03	.11	.12	.08	.14	.03	.10	.11	.04	.18	.07	.04	.14	.04	.06	.16
Beaver			.07	.02	.03	.10	.02	.10	.07	.03	.09	.03	.06	.07	.04	.18	.08	.06	.10	.04	.05	.08
Buffalo				.01	.04	.07	.02	.05	.09	.06	.07	.03	.07	.09	.04	.08	.08	.04	.06	.03	.08	.06
Cat					.02	.00	.79	.03	.17	.01	.04	.02	.03	.01	.13	.03	.02	.08	.03	.10	.07	.01
Cow						.04	.02	.04	.20	.02	.04	.16	.04	.08	.04	.04	.06	.04	.04	.02	.01	.04
Deer							.03	.12	.09	.03	.08	.04	.06	.16	.04	.11	.07	.01	.12	.03	.06	.10
Dog								.04	.02	.01	.04	.02	.04	.02	.12	.02	.02	.08	.04	.08	.08	.02
Fox									.05	.04	.07	.05	.05	.10	.05	.13	.06	.05	.13	.06	.07	.06
Goat										.03	.10	.06	.04	.10	.04	.10	.10	.05	.10	.03	.21	.10
Gorilla											.03	.03	.09	.07	.03	.03	.03	.03	.03	.03	.03	.05
Hamster												.04	.04	.06	.20	.17	.09	.04	.10	.21	.05	.15
Horse													.04	.05	.04	.04	.05	.38	.05	.05	.08	.03
Lion															.06	.03	.05	.04	.05	.05	.05	.06
Moose															.03	.09	.07	.04	.07	.03	.08	.07
Mouse																.12	.04	.04	.05	.02	.04	.04
Muskrat																	.08	.05	.13	.38	.05	.04
Pig																		.05	.08	.07	.08	.13
Pony																			.04	.09	.04	.12
Rabbit																				.03	.06	.04
Rat																					.03	.09
Sheep																						.05

SOURCE: B. H. Cohen, W. A. Bousfield, and G. A. Whitmarsh. *The Connecticut free associational norms.* Technical Report No. 35. Storrs, Conn.: Univ. of Conn., 1961.

data supplied by Bousfield and his colleagues,[6] who gathered associations to a number of words which belong to the same conceptual category. Table 33 presents some intersections in associative distributions between words which themselves, by the Connecticut norms,[7] are examples of the class of *animals*. Necessarily, then, all the words in Table 33 are of the same type.

An inspection of the table shows that these words are highly related in associative meaning (though the structure is not a simple one). It is not the case, however, that these words are related only because they tend to elicit one another as associates. The pair, *cow* and *goat*, for example, are highly related, not only because they tend to elicit one another and animal names in common, but because they also elicit, in common, words such as *milk, farm, meat, grass*, and so on.

Very few of the associates to these words consist of adjectives or other purely attributive or descriptive words. Therefore, we can assert that associatively we tend to think of these words together because they elicit one another and environmental objects and concepts which they share. Nevertheless, descriptive relations lie beneath the associative surface. That can be illustrated in the following analysis.

Since the attributive characteristics of these words do not readily occur in association, it is necessary to go outside the purely associative process in order to show the attributive relations. Ten subjects were asked to list as many adjectives as they could which would describe specific animals. These subjects were given ten minutes to list the adjectives, and during that period of time the words in Table 33 were before them. The kinds of adjectives they produced are exemplified by *tame, wild, furry, domestic, friendly, strong*, and *big*. Those listed by more than two subjects were arranged in pairs (after some necessary alterations), excluding those, such as *furry*, which would seem to apply to all the names in the collection. There were twenty-five such pairs (listed in Table 34). Three additional subjects were asked to judge each of the animal names in Table 33 against the adjective pairs in Table 34. A force-choice method was used, even though some of the pairs do not seem particularly appropriate for some of the animal names. Two of the subjects were naïve, and the third was the author.

For each of the three subjects a matrix of descriptive agreement

[6] W. A. Bousfield, B. H. Cohen, G. A. Whitmarsh, and W. D. Kincaid. The Connecticut free associational norms. Technical Report No. 35. Storrs, Conn.: Univ. of Conn., 1961.

[7] Bousfield, Cohen, and Whitmarsh, Cultural norms for verbal items in 43 categories.

TABLE 34: Descriptive Attributes Used to Determine Agreement in Descriptions for the Words in Table 33[a]

Large-small	Strong-weak
Tame-wild	Friendly-unfriendly
Herbivorous-carnivorous	Light-heavy
Unfamiliar-familiar	Stupid-smart
Fast-slow	Native-foreign
Ugly-attractive	Good-bad
Clean-dirty	Placid-excitable
Solitary-social	Troublesome-useful
Lazy-spirited	Alert-dull
Awkward-graceful	Gross-delicate
Admirable-detestable	Common-rare
Safe-dangerous	Low-noble
Meek-dominant	

[a] Subjects were asked to check one member of each pair for each animal name.

was prepared. The matrices were obtained by finding the number of pairs checked in the same way for two animals. A subject, for example, might say that both *cats* and *dogs* are *tame, small, carnivorous,* and the like. The descriptive agreement between *cat* and *dog* would be determined by the number of adjectives checked for both by that subject. For each of the three subjects the matrix of agreements was correlated with the matrix of intersection coefficients. The product-moment correlations between log intersection (the logarithmic transformation being due to the markedly skewed distributions found within matrices of intersections between related words) and agreements are, for the three subjects, 0.41, 0.38, and 0.32. (The last is for the author.) With $N = 253$, these are all highly significant.

There is, then, a correlation between the associative intersections and the extent to which a set of related concepts share descriptive attributes in common. The set of animal names is the largest categorical set available in the Connecticut free associational norms, but the same relation holds for the smaller sets of flower names, sports, foods, and so on. It must be repeated, however, that the descriptive attributes themselves only infrequently occur as associates to the nominal concepts. When they do occur, they are quite clearly appropriate. Thus, *friendly* occurs to *dog, big* to *gorilla*. Yet, we do not think of the relations between nominal concepts by way of their descriptive attributes in common; we think of the concepts as simply grouped and occurring in common contexts. Such is a more efficient cognitive process for detecting relationships and making analogies than is a process which would encode the nominal concepts by their principal descriptors. It is easier to think that a *cat* is like a *dog* than to think that a *cat* is *small, furry, tame, domestic,* and *carnivorous,* and so is a *dog.* The noun-noun relation in association is a very convenient and efficient way of dealing with the problem of multidimensional similarity in thought processes.

The factor structure of categorical sets like that in Table 33 is usually quite complicated. The highest loadings on the first unrotated factor for the animal set do not occur, as we might at first have expected, to the most familiar of the animal names. Instead, these loadings seem to define the most representative members of the set. These are *bear, goat, hamster,* and *muskrat.* These names share the greatest number of descriptive adjectives in common with the other members of the set. The lowest loadings on the first factor are for *gorilla, lion,* and *pony.* Not surprisingly, *gorilla* and *lion* are the lowest in total number of descriptive attributes in common.

A number of comparatively loosely defined clusters occur within the set. A representative example of these is to be seen in the group, *antelope, deer, rabbit, fox,* and *muskrat.* It is clear that clusters such as this one are not defined by single attributes or by a single contextual condition in common, but represent the nexus of several. In a word, it is possible to say that *antelope, deer, rabbit,* and so on are similar, but it is less easy to specify exactly in what way or ways they are similar.

The fundamental scheme relating such sets of nouns, then, is one of grouping. The grouping is correlated with the descriptive attributes in common possessed by the individual concepts and by the correlated set of contextual elements. What, however, can be said for the generality of such a scheme for nouns? The animal set is clearly a categorical set, one in which all the concepts themselves are particular instances of a more general concept (*animal*). Not all nominal concepts lend themselves so readily to so simple a categorical treatment. Furthermore, there is the problem of the relation between the category name and the particular instances of the category. That defines the classical associative problem of the subordinate-supraordinate relation, and it implies that there is a branching-tree structure to at least some nominal concepts. How are the levels in such a tree represented in the associative process?

First of all, let us repeat that all nominal concepts are organized as groups. The groups do not always correspond to logical classes, and they do not always have simple names or supraordinate labels. It is only the group structure itself which seems to be universal among nouns. We shall briefly examine some of the varieties of group structure shortly. First, however, it would be wise to dispose of the problem of categorical structures and the branching-tree relation.

Wherever a common category name exists in common use within the language, it will reveal its presence by a particular pattern of associative intersection that it has with a large and representative sample of instances of the category. That pattern can be described by two characteristics: (1) The category name will have the largest summed intersection with all the instances found in the matrix, and (2) the intersections of the category name with the instances will be more or less evenly distributed. The result is that, in any general factor solution of the matrix, the category name will generally have loadings on all or the majority of the factors.

These two conditions hold for the word *animal* and its categorical set. In a matrix composed of that word plus all the instances in Table 33, the highest summed intersection in the matrix is 3.312, and that is for the word *animal*. The highest summed intersection of any of the instances with all the other instances plus *animal* is 2.142. The intersections of *animal* with the instances are more evenly distributed than any other subset within the matrix. Note, however, that the concept name will not, in general, have the highest single intersection within a set. In the *animal* set, the highest single intersection is between the words *cat* and *dog* (0.79).

This same pattern holds for the category names *flower* (Connecticut norms), *tree* (Hopkins norms), *vegetable* (Hopkins norms), *insect* (Hopkins norms), and *country* (Hopkins norms). It does not hold for all of the category names which are to be found in the Connecticut categorical norms. For example, the category (parts of the) *body* does not yield this pattern, despite the fact that the specific instances listed in the norms (*arms, legs, eyes, head, neck, hands, feet*) form a well-organized associative group. Neither does the category *vehicle*, though here the matter is complicated by the fact that the associative group does not completely correspond with the instances yielded by the categorical norms. Hence, we might suppose that a category *vehicles* is not one which occurs naturally in the thought processes of the subjects used in these various normative studies. Where the category name does not obey the pattern described by *animal*, its intersections with the category instances tend to be very low, and it neither yields the category instances in association in great frequency nor does it occur often as an associate to those category instances. Thus, *body* has very low intersections with *arms* and *legs*.

It tends to locate itself best in a group consisting, among others, of the concepts *mind, person, soul,* and *man.* These concepts form some group that itself is, perhaps, not readily namable in the language but which might be described by the phrase, *entire man.*

There is some evidence which shows that more than one level of a branching tree of concepts may exhibit itself in association. One example that is readily available in the extant associative data is the concept *country.* This concept readily splits into groups clearly defined and named by the terms, *Europe, South America,* and so on (or more likely, in association, *European, South American,* and the like). The appropriate specific instances are grouped under each set category. As a general rule, however, associative processes are more local, and extended structures are not strong. Furthermore, genuine cognitive concepts are seldom cleanly organized. For example, people tend to think of *Spain* and various *Latin American* countries together, with the result that the categorical structure of associations for the concept *country* is not simple.

Furthermore, of course, individual nominal concepts may belong to two or more sets. There seems to be no necessary pattern of relation between these sets. Two sets may share but a single instance in common, or they may share many in common. The groups, defined by associative structures, are statistical and not sharply delimited, a fact that is reflected in the commonly observed flexibility of (and concomitant occasional contradictions in) human thought.

These structures, like all associative structures, are best thought of as statistically defined. There is considerable variation from individual to individual in the composition of a given structure, and there is probably also variation from time to time in the same individual. In any event, there is ample reason to suppose that there will be statistical uncertainty in the structure of any associatively related group of words when that structure is defined over a sample of individuals. Therefore, class membership in a categorical or hierarchical structure, considered over the language at large, cannot be a fixed and all-or-nothing matter.

Despite the fact that such categorical structures are often socially determined by systematic principles (as is the case in the classification of living organisms), not everyone understands these systematic principles and thinks in accordance with them. The associative data for the class *animals* make it quite obvious, for example, that most American college students think of it much of the time as coextensive with the biological class *mammals* (though these students may not have a clear idea of the criteria for membership in the class *mam-*

mals). *Birds, snakes,* and *insects* are not instances of the class *animals* for these individuals. Instead, these are comembers of some larger associative category.

We must remember that the reasonably well-informed college student can reconstruct a better picture of the systematic biological classification of living organisms than his associative structures would suggest. There is, then, temporary variation in the structures which generates manifest results of thought. However, most of the time, thinking will not be under any constraint of this sort, and the associative structures we obtain from the "free" testing situation are more general than those we would obtain under any given conditions of constraint. Temporary variations in the nature of nominal concepts are more likely than in the nature of adjectival or attributive concepts. While we may add new words to underlying attributive dimensions, the nature of the dimesions themselves changes very slowly with adult experience. However, our nominal concepts are probably continuously undergoing change, and some of these changes may be radical. The result is that it is possible to discuss only in a general and statistical way the nature of particular nominal structures.

Two different types of nominal structures will help illustrate the principles which organize all nominal structures. In a categorical or hierarchically organized structure, each member will possess some characteristic or characteristics shared with all members of the group. Furthermore, each member will also be described by some unique set of attributes. In the simplest kind of nominal organization, no subset of instances shares attributes not shared by all the members of the group. An example of such a simple categorical structure is to be seen in Table 35. If the matrix of associative intersections is determined by the pattern of underlying descriptors, one would expect

TABLE 35: A Hypothetical Example of a Categorical Structure[a]

				Concepts			
	A	B	C	D	E	F	G
Attributes							
1	X	X	X	X	X	X	X
2	X						
3		X					
4			X				
5				X			
6					X		
7						X	
8							X

[a] The letters represent nominal concepts and the numbers attributes. "X" indicates that a given concept is described by a given attribute.

the arrangement in Table 35 to lead to uniform associative intersections among members of the set and a resulting single general factor. Such a simple case would never occur in practice. It is clear that associative relations are determined not only by the minimal common descriptors organizing the set but are determined by local descriptors or contextual factors in common between subsets of the entire category. Thus, the local set *cat* and *dog* forms a structure within the general class of *animals*, a structure that is heavily determined by contextual or environmental relations these concepts share in experience. In general, however, we would expect any simple categorical set (such as the class *animals*) to show a less sharply skewed distribution of intersection coefficients than a noncategorical set. There would be, therefore, fewer zero entries in the matrix of intersections for such a set. It so happens that in Table 33 (the intersections of the *animal* concepts), there are no zero entries. Any representative matrix of non-categorically but highly interrelated concepts shows many zero entries. There are, for example, fifty zero entries in Table 3, a number which is almost a third of the total entries in the table.

A loosely organized set of noncategorically related concepts would best be illustrated by a set in which there are relations between each member and two other members but no others. That would be the case in a set in which each member is described by two attributes and in which each attribute is shared by only one pair of concepts. This situation is illustrated in Table 36. While again, we would hardly expect so uniformly simple a structure to occur naturally, approximations to it do occur, and when they do they produce the matrices of intersections which are highly skewed.

There appear to be a large number of specific types of group struc-

TABLE 36: A Hypothetical Example of a Noncategorical Structure[a]

				Concepts			
	A	B	C	D	E	F	G
Attributes							
1	X						
2	X	X					
3		X	X				
4			X	X			
5				X	X		
6					X	X	
7						X	X
8							X

[a] Concepts and attributes are presented as in Table 35.

tures, and these types are systematically related to the underlying patterns of descriptors and contextual circumstances shared by the concepts defining the structures. The structures will all exhibit a common feature of similarity. The underlying attributes responsible for that similarity, however, will seldom intrude themselves directly into the associative structures, and they will not be directly represented in most of our thought processes in which those structures occur. People find it natural to think of *birds, butterflies,* and *flowers* together, as well as to think of *bears, antelopes,* and *lions* together. We are usually not aware, however, of the structural differences underlying the relations within these two sets. These structural differences will only be revealed by the differing patterns of relations within the associative matrices (data not directly available to us as we think about these concepts) or by some conditions which constrain people to look for the structural differences in terms of attributes and contextual conditions. So far as our immediate thought processes are concerned, the associative relations between pairs of concepts differ only in one respect—the extent of the intersection.

Since we have taken a radically different approach in this chapter than in the last in describing the conditions underlying matrices of associative relations, a word needs to be said about the relations between the two approaches. In the previous chapter we emphasized the relations between common linguistic contexts as the determiners of the structures among adjectives. That is a situation not original to adjectives but particularly important for them.

We can put the matter in the framework of the discussion found in the present chapter by asserting that adjectives are related by means of the subsets of nouns they appropriately modify. To the extent that there are differences in the nouns described by adjectives, there will be differences in their associative distributions. Because adjectives as a class provide most of the underlying descriptors for nouns and because they are grammatically linked with nouns, either as modifiers or in the predicate position following a linking verb (verbs of the class *to be, seems,* and so on), there is a close correspondence between linguistic contextual patterns and the semantic properties of the adjectives. We should expect, then, a correlation between the adjectival environments of nouns and their intersections. While grammatically different classes of adjectives do exist—some adjectives can only occur as nominal modifiers, not in the predicate position—these different classes are fewer and less rich than nominal classes. Further-more, the analysis of associative structures itself reveals some hitherto ignored grammatical properties of adjectives (for example, the failure of color adjectives to take affixes indicating antonomy, a failure based upon the multidimensional relations of color adjectives).

It is difficult to find a general correlation between linguistic environ-ments and associative relations among nouns in general, though subsets of nouns may well exhibit such a correlation. The difficulty is that not all nouns easily fit into common grammatical paradigms. Because the associative relations among nouns are often very close when these same nouns do not share many common contexts, we must accept the fact that there is a lesser relation between associative structures and usage within ordinary discourse for nouns as a whole than for adjectives, a fact which is based on the fundamental attribute —concept or dimension—group difference.

Nouns which are highly related to one another in association may only infrequently and with difficulty be fitted into common linguistic contexts. The words *religion* and *clergyman* are related associatively, but they have fundamentally different functions in sentences. There-fore, the equivalences that exist between nominal concepts are not always simply represented in linguistic usage. As we have noted before,[8] however, these words that are closely related but of funda-mentally different linguistic structure will tend to co-occur in sentences. That is true of certain strong adjective-noun pairs, such as *green-grass* and *blue-sky*. (Note that these pairs, more often than not, are combinations of color adjectives and nouns.) Such a lack of correspondence between equivalences within possible sentences and associative equivalences is a necessary consequence of the dependence of one or the other on small subsets of the properties of concepts. The large and diffuse class of animate nouns is based upon a relatively small subset of the total possible descriptors for that collection of nouns. A particularly important cognitive relation between a noun from this set and some other noun may completely ignore this subset and be based upon some other subset ignored in the grammatical classification.

We would expect much the same condition to hold for verbs. The verbs *run* and *hit* or *eat* and *sleep* are closely related associatively despite the fact that *run* is most often intransitive, *hit* transitive, *eat* often transitive, and *sleep* never transitive. (Furthermore, *run, hit,*

---

[8] Deese, On the structure of associative meaning.

and *sleep* function as nouns, while *eat* does not.) As with nouns, there will be correspondence between the associative relations among verbs and the grammatical relations only so far as these are based upon common properties. Furthermore, associative relations commonly occur between words of different form classes, and to the extent that the concept of form class depends upon equivalences within phrases and sentences, these relations cannot possibly correspond to grammatical relations.

Thus, while there is sometimes a correspondence between the local contexts within ordinary sentences that words may take and their associative relations, the correspondence is by no means necessary. It is uniquely strong in the case of adjectives, though it will also occur within particular subclasses of nouns and verbs. Linguistic equivalences provide only part of the general experience which gives rise to associative relations. Of course, we must view the associative relations among the purely structural elements of a language as determined by purely linguistic considerations, for these elements, by definition, have no consistent relation to experience outside language.

Finally, we must remember that we actively operate upon both our linguistic and nonlinguistic experiences in such a way that there can be only a moderate correlation between the various describable characteristics of that experience (for example, its frequency) and the consequences in associative and other verbal processes. In a word, our cognitive structures are the outcome of the operation of hypotheses upon our experience.

8

꧁

The New Laws
of Association

The first chapter pointed out that almost all comment or theory—philosophical or psychological—about association is based upon but a single property of manifest associations, that of temporal succession. A succeeding idea is seen as caused by the first or at least connected to it in some direct way. If for no other reason than that it fits so well with stimulus-response theory—which has dominated American psychology for fifty years or more—investigations of the associative process have concentrated on the single paired unit or upon chains consisting of successive paired units. Later chapters in this book argue that the basic laws of association are to be found in the relations between the distributions of potential associates to particular occasions or stimuli. Associations are structural; they are to be described by the relations which obtain between them. The manifest and particular associations we find in ordinary thought and language are derived from and can be described by fundamental structural types. These structural types are defined by contrasting relations and grouping relations. These, then, provide the new laws of association.

More generally, however, the later chapters show that relations between distributions of association provide a new and powerful means for the analysis of cognition, particularly as it is manifested in language. The distributions of associations to individual stimuli are highly organized, and they are related to a whole array of psychological processes evident in attitudes, the structure of human language, and the use of human concepts. Throughout this book we have examined data which hint at the richness of such relationships, and in the current psychological literature are to be found many other examples of the correlations between associative structures and the varieties of cognitive processes. Part of the purpose of this chapter is to discuss, in a more general way, some of the issues at stake in the study of the relation between associative structures and the manifest products of cognition.

In addition, we have left many questions about the measurement and evaluation of associative distributions unanswered. The basic measure of relation in the study of associative structures is the intersection between distributions of associations. There are many ways in which a measure of such intersections may be taken, and there are many ways in which the associative data can be gathered in the first place. A brief word of comment about these is required.

The data described in this book almost entirely have been obtained in a situation in which (1) single words are used as stimuli, (2) subjects are constrained to give single words as responses, (3) associations are otherwise free or unconstrained, and (4) the intersections are based upon distributions in which only one response per stimulus comes from the same individual. These conditions are reasonably satisfactory, since our major task has been to describe the most general features of associative structures. Each one of them, however, contains at least a measure of arbitrariness. There are, then, theoretical and practical reasons for examining some of the alternatives to these conditions.

The word, for example, has most ambivalent linguistic status, and it is possible that our fundamental structures could be more precisely described by some analysis of or restriction upon the morphemic combinations in associative stimuli and responses. Also, it is psychologically of great importance that we be able to describe the associative structures as they exist within a single individual. In order to accomplish such a description we need to obtain intersections of associative distributions for single individuals. Methods for accomplishing such a treatment of data have been proposed,[1] and we need to comment upon and extend such proposals within the present account.

Finally, something needs to be said about the way in which associative relations are learned. While there is no intention of developing here a general theory of associative learning, it should be obvious that the matter requires some comment. The emphasis upon structural relations makes much of the existing analysis of associative learning simply inappropriate, and some possible alternatives should be at least alluded to. We can point out what is wrong with the existing theories and analyses from the vantage provided by the data presented here, and we can state the kinds of relations which need to be incorporated into a theory of associative learning that would take its point of departure, not from individual stimulus-response units, but from matrices of associative interrelations.

[1] Garskof and Houston, Measurement of verbal relatedness.

It has not often enough been commented that the really enduring contributions to psychological theory seem not to come so much from the formal and abstract issues in learning theory as from applied and particular problems in measurement and evaluation. More often than should be the case, useful and deep psychological theory has been dismissed as being merely methodological or procedural. We have not paid sufficient attention to the psychological theory that is implicit in multiple factor analysis, multidimensional scaling, or uncertainty analysis. These provide us not only with ways of doing things, they provide us with fundamental hypotheses about the nature of abilities, judgment, and perception. This book has been written from the point of view that useful psychological theories come naturally out of descriptions of ways of doing things in gathering psychological data. There is less room, in the study of traditional verbal learning, for the description of some particular way of gathering and analyzing data in which the primary emphasis is upon relation than in almost any other large area of psychological investigation. Therefore, we are not yet ready to develop a new associative theory of learning; we need to wait for further work in the descriptive analysis of manifest associations to provide the framework for such a theory. Nevertheless, we cannot escape the need to make some comments about learning, and these are to be found in this chapter. These comments are directed towards problems in the analysis of associative structures, and they are only tangentially related to traditional laboratory problems in the study of learning.

First of all, we need to remind ourselves of something that has been slighted in our earlier discussion. Structural cognitive relations grow out of experience that is, for the most part, piecemeal. We do not acquire all of the information that goes into any given structural relation all at once (at least as a general rule); we acquire it in bits and pieces. It is not so certain, however, how to describe these bits and pieces. Traditional association theory and the laboratory techniques that have developed for the study of associative learning are based upon the principle of contiguity. The elements of thought and language are glued together by contingencies in experience, and these contingencies are modified only by the simple structural principle of stimulus generalization. If, however, we take as a possibility, an existing structure to which bits of experience are assimilated, then contiguous contingencies may be irrelevant in any situation save that in which the only possible structure which can be learned is based upon paired contingency.

In general, the acquisition of or an alteration in particular associative structures depends upon the structures existing for the individual at the time of learning and the relations between those structures and the organization in the information presented to the individual. It is possible to present information in which the only possible organization is in the frequency with which various elements are presented in temporal and spatial contiguity. It is not surprising that the behavior of an individual required to learn such information will in very large part be determined by this pattern of organization. Such a fact, however, tells us nothing about the more general organizations which exist in the individual as the result of prior experience and/or inherent, biologically determined patterns.

Characteristically, the experimental tradition in the study of association has been to keep to a minimum the possible influence of pre-existing structures, though it has become increasingly apparent from the correlational nature of much of modern experimental work that this is an all but hopeless task. In any event, the usual procedure in the laboratory has been to present information to a subject in such a way that the organization is limited to that provided by classical association theory. As we have noted before, this restriction leads to the attempt to reduce all contingencies to simple stimulus-response pairs. The structures have an asymmetric directional property only partially enforced by the mode of presentation (the only partial success of the enforcement being attested to by the volume of recent work on reverse associations) and the careful counterbalancing of material on successive presentations, a counterbalancing which limits all relations to single pairs. In the presentation of material, all other contingencies are made to be zero or so close to zero that they have no detectable influence.

In recent years a number of investigators have begun to examine the properties in the learning experiment of a wider variety of abstract structures.[2] It is at least possible that we shall shortly see the laboratory study of associations turn to the comparative study of the learning of various kinds of structures. The study of structural learning in the laboratory by the classical technique of introducing independent variables is undeniably difficult. We must deal with materials which, for human subjects, have structure already, either by previous experi-

---

[2] See, for example, L. M. Horowitz, Z. M. Brown, and S. Weissbluth. Availability and direction of associations. *J. exp. Psychol.*, 1964, **68**, 541–549.

ence or by the capacity of the human nervous system. Even at the phonetic level there are complicated structural relations, relations which must influence the learning of languages by very young children and which may very well be part of the innate perceptual-motor organization of speech.

In this connection, it should be pointed out that the literature on concept-learning has provided us with a rich literature important to structural analysis. The problems in the study of concept attainment have forced experimenters to determine certain kinds of structural relations among the materials to be learned. We may reiterate at this point that the literature on concept attainment provides a much more satisfactory starting point for the consideration of associative structures than does the literature on classical associative learning. As a final point, concept attainment emphasizes not only structural relations among materials but the existence of particular kinds of operations which subjects perform upon the material, operations generally called hypotheses.

A great deal of the older literature was based upon the assumption of particular operations of a very simple sort. Thus, the principle of frequency assumes that subjects tally and score each repeated experience with some material in accordance with some simple rule based upon the order of the experience. In a more general way, however, we can say that all experience is operated upon in some way by individuals. It is not the purpose of this book to attempt to present in a detailed account the possible operations people perform upon material they learn, but we do need the open-minded assumption that there are such operations and that we can discover something of their nature by observation. Perhaps the typical concept-attainment experiment provides more information about this matter because it is closer to the level of unconstrained observation than the associative-learning experiment.

The data on associative distributions suggest that the two fundamental operations we have for sorting out meaningful—that is, logical and syntactical relations among words—are contrast and grouping. We can establish the position of any given element in a language within the larger vocabulary of the language by contrasting it with some element or elements and/or by grouping it with respect to some other element or elements. Which of these two processes operates at any given moment depends upon conditions at least partly dependent upon the nonverbal experience to which the verbal elements refer or are related.

There are two ways in which we can examine the structure of the external world by this view. We can isolate attributes so that everything in the world can either be ordered with respect to this attribute or is irrelevant to the attribute. Or, alternately, we can ignore the individual attributes and describe things in terms of collections or nexuses of attributes. In this case, we lose the possibility of describing in any articulate way the logic of the structure we impose upon the world, but we can quickly and efficiently characterize an astounding number of things in the world simply by placing them with some more familiar things which share an (indeterminate) number of attributes in common. An automobile is cognitively within particular groups (most things being multiply grouped) because it represents a unique collection of experiences which remain stable in the face of a shifting perceptual world, and we can characterize its stability by reference to the other things that share, in their stable way, many of the same attributes. Grouping, then, is a way of bringing order into those aspects of the world that are stable (have "thing constancy"). The words that refer to these stable aspects of experience become grouped together, and this grouping is based upon the undifferentiated (with respect to attributes) similarity among the objects and events to which they refer.

We need not emphasize the perceptual aspects upon which such grouping depends, but it is clear that there is another whole area of structural study based upon these aspects. The perceptual unities which stable things in the world make cannot be efficiently studied by a simple extension of the associative technique. Nevertheless, the implication is clear that some details of the associative process must be related to or correlated with the perceptual laws which describe the organization of things in experience.

The two associative laws may be stated as follows: (1) Elements are associatively related when they may be contrasted in some unique and unambiguous way, and (2) elements are associatively related when they may be grouped because they can be described by two or more characteristics in common. Contrast must always be unique, and grouping reveals the underlying concordance only upon analysis. A unique and particular associative sequence reveals one or another of these, but which it is can only be seen when (1) we have a reasonable sample of the potential distribution of associates and (2) we have some other appropriate terms with which to compare that distribution.

In learning new elements we assimilate them to existing groups or establish them with reference to some fundamental attributive contrast.

New groups may emerge when there are a sufficient number of objects in experience and memory to establish some new and unique collection of attributes. Our learning is socially determined, but the structures for any particular individual are only correlated with, not completely determined by, the abstraction we may term "social usage." Variations in meaning from person to person and from group to group, as well as from time to time within the same individual, are related to and fundamentally determined by the shifts in grouping and contrast as we establish new relations among verbal elements. Words and concepts do not uniquely belong to any given group or any given contrast but may, as the occasion demands, be thought of with respect to first one and then the other group and/or contrast. Furthermore, there may be organization among groups, organization determined by more general grouping characteristics or by the intrusion of logical and other systems of linguistic organization. Therefore, the problem of describing the nature of particular relations among associative structures is an empirical one, one which becomes ever richer as refinements of method and data allow.

Finally, in this connection, we need to point out that the patterns of grouping and contrast which are revealed in our associative structures, and which are coincident with patterns in linguistic usage and order in thought, evaluation, judgment, and attitude, must be determined in part by the patterns of relations implied by sentences within the language. We have had little to say in this book on the subject of grammatical analysis at the level of the sentence. Yet it is clear that the growth of particular associative structures is modified by sentence relations. Indeed, the new secondary laws of association would appropriately describe the influence of sentence forms on associative structures. So elementary and obvious an example as the sentence "Cats and dogs are both animals" shows that the form of sentences influences relations in associative structures.

Most of the work on the growth of associative relations has ignored the forms and nature of sentences. Yet it is clear that the ordinary forms of (English) sentences intrude on such psychological relations. It has been pointed out elsewhere[3] that mediational transfer experiments can be properly described by attributing to the individual stimulus-response pairs the properties of ordinary linking sentences. By this description each paired-associate term would consist of a sentence of the form "A is B," where A is the stimulus term and B,

[3] See discussion in J. Deese and S. H. Hulse. *Psychology of learning.* Third ed.; New York: McGraw-Hill (in press).

the response term. While no one has suggested that all paired-associate experiments must be immediately reinterpreted as if the individual pairs consisted only of linking statements, we must grant the possibility that subjects in such experiments cast these pairs in sentence or phrase forms. If that is the case, the traditional experimental method is paradoxically less well controlled than an experiment in which ordinary English sentences are used as the experimental materials. By actually presenting the subject with "A is B" rather than simply "A_____B" we may more successfully restrict his associative processes.

Associations, then, are modified by the nature of sentences. They become detached from particular sentences (save, perhaps, in rare instances), so that almost any attempt to relate stimulus and response to a small group of sentences or sentence types fails. We think directly in associations, and it is not necessary for sentences to appear in the process. So much is readily apparent from the ease with which even unsophisticated individuals and children are willing to play the free-association game by giving single-word responses divorced from ordinary syntactic settings.

A more difficult question, however, is whether or not these same associations have any influence upon the generation of sentences. It is certain that sentences are not merely concatenations of associations. Sentences are composed of syntactic structures, though it is less certain at what level these structures are generated. Class membership which makes assignment of words of different syntactic value possible, however, may well be determined by the same functional properties, namely, contrast and grouping, that determine the patterns among manifest associations. We can imagine sentences, then, in which the structural properties are syntactic but for which the choice of the particular elements that fit into various positions is determined by associative processes. Such sentences, of course, would assert very unlikely things. While such sentences do occur in poetry and in similar kinds of writing, they are not ordinary sentences.

What about the role of associations in sentences? Ordinary sentences are formed under both syntactical and referential constraints. We may, however, for experimental purposes eliminate referential constraints. When that is done, there is evidence that the morphemic elements generated within the syntactic constraints provided by functional elements are like those which would be expected from associations.

One investigation[4] determined the relation between associations and substitutions within sentences in which there was semantic constraint

---

[4] The data reported here were gathered and analyzed by Marie Mottram.

provided by only a single word. The sentences contained nonsense words, functional elements, and a single English word, as, for example, "The cef gaxed the slow zuc." In this study, there were two types of sentences: D–Adj–N–V–D–N and D–N–V–D–Adj–N. In some sentences the subject nouns were underlined, and in other sentences the adjectives or predicate nouns were underlined. The task of the subject was to replace the underlined element with an English word. Sometimes the underlined element was a nonsense word, and sometimes it was a common English word. The English word, in various sentences, occurred in nominal, verbal, and adjectival position. The subjects were one hundred Hopkins undergraduates.

The results were tabulated in the form of a frequency distribution of the words placed in each sentence. These frequencies were then correlated with the size of the intersection between the single English word and each of the substituted words. The total correlation of the intersections and the frequency with which these words were used in sentences was 0.485 for the case in which one English word was substituted for another and 0.464 for the case in which the English word substituted for a nonsense word. These correlations are not high, but nearly all of the responses used by the subjects had some appreciable intersection with the English words in the sentences—a condition that is remarkable. Some of the actual frequencies of substitution of associatively related words were not high. For example, the word *cocoon* rarely occurred in substitution for *butterfly*, but its intersection with *butterfly* is high. Because nouns do belong to different classes, the low correlation for such words is not unexpected. Also not unexpected is the fact that the highest individual correlations occurred for substitutions of common adjectives. The highest correlation occurred with the substitutes for *slow*, 0.865. Also, the correlations of substitutes in the adjectival position with English context, nominal or verbal, were low and, in some instances, negative. That is to say, there was in these cases a negative correlation between the frequency of substitution and magnitude of intersection coefficient.

Furthermore, the same pattern of results holds when the substitution is for entire sentences. Data[5] are available in which subjects generated simple sentences by associating to them under the constraint that the responses be sentences of exactly the same form. Thus, to the sentence "The wide road spoiled the park" a typical response might be "The narrow path hid the beauty." Despite the considerable contraint intro-

---

[5] The author is indebted to H. H. Clark, who provided the data.

duced into this situation, the distribution of individual words substituted for particular words in these sentences are remarkably like the distributions of free associations (once the grammatical constraint is considered). This fact can be seen by the examples in Table 37,

TABLE 37: Some Sample Words Occurring in Substitution to Stimulus Words[a]

1. Stimulus: *Dark* in "The dark room scared the child."
   Responses: 11 Bright.
   8 Light(ed).
   5 Frightened, Haunted.
   3 Unlighted, Dim.
   2 Big, Black, Horror, Little, Night, Old, Red, Small, Young.
   1 Beautiful, Bleak, Compassionate, Concerned, Dangerous, Desolated, Drab, Empty, Feared, Ghost, Gloomy, Glowing, Horrified, Illuminated, Kind, Long, Loud, Loving, New, Nightmare, Nuclear, Obscure, Odd, Quiet, Scared, Scary, Smoky, Stark, Sudden, Terrible, Understanding, Weird, White, Yellow.
2. Stimulus: *Room* in "The dark room scared the child."
   Responses: 14 House.
   7 Hall.
   4 Boy, Mother.
   3 Sun, Girl, Light, Movie(s).
   2 Car, Chamber, Child, Ghost, Kid, Moon, Room, Wallpaper.
   1 Air, Apartment, Baby, Bomb, Candle, Children, Class, Concept, Den, Dog, Irony, Laughter, Man, Nightmare, Night, Noise, Parents, Place, Shadow, Shelter, Snake, Staircase, Story, Study, Surroundings, Theory, Thunder, Walls.
3. Stimulus: *Young* in "The young policeman stopped the speeder."
   Responses: 34 Old.
   9 New.
   4 Cute.
   3 Angry, Inexperienced, Traffic, Young.
   2 Fast, Mad.
   1 Agitated, Cold, Cranky, Cruise, Drunken, Elderly, Experienced, Five, Indignant, Irresponsible, Little, Mean, Pretty, Red, Small, Speeding, Terrified, Unhappy, Warning, Woman, Wreckless.
4. Stimulus: *Boy* in "The difficult problem distressed the boy."
   Responses: 18 Girl.
   17 Student(s).
   8 Child.
   4 Test.
   3 Teacher.
   2 Answer, Boy, Citizens, Hardest, Homework, Man, Pupil, Woman.
   1 Example, Extras, Formula, Kid, Lab, Mirror, Mother, Nuisance, People, Person, Policeman, Room, Scooter, Situation, Voters, Youngster, Youth.

[a] The stimulus words are part of complete sentences and the response words are part of complete sentences of the same form. Data obtained by H. H. Clark.

which present the substitutions within the sentences generated in response to sentences including the words *dark, room, young,* and *boy.*

The point is that, despite semantic constraint, the distribution of verbal elements is very much like what one would expect from simple associative processes. Thus, syntactic and semantic constraint provided by words in ordinary sentences do not eliminate or replace associative processes.

Many, if not most, ordinary sentences, however, are under some referential constraint. We need to talk about particular things, irrespective of whether or not those things are associatively related. We can, nevertheless, regard that constraint much in the way the problem of set is viewed in the classical associative literature. That is to say, it places narrower limits on the associative process but does not replace or eliminate it. If that is the case, we may ask whether or not there is some coincidence between the kinds of vocabulary retrieval that seem to characterize the associative process and the conditions by which ordinary sentences are formed. Indeed, we may consider the possibility that sentences are formed by calling upon a small number of syntactic elements, transformations, or particular functional units. It may be that sentences are formed from locally determined processes, no larger than phrases, and that these are patched into sentences (not always well-formed ones) by a secondary process. We do not have the data available to investigate such a possibility, but it is by no means certain that ordinary speech consists of well-formed sentences, that is to say, of sentences capable of being generated from some linguistically general rules. We do not, in any detailed or accurate way, really know what people say when they talk, and until we have some better ideas about the range of possibilities in human language, we should not seriously commit ourselves to any fixed ideas about how speech is generated. The richness of associations in referentially unconstrained material, such as that found in the psycholinguistic laboratory, and the extensive associative analyses of poetic and metaphoric writing[6] lead us to believe, however, that associative relations may be firmly embedded in all linguistic usage.

We too readily assume, when we discuss language as communication, that "something" is communicated. The ordinary requirements of the world are such as to put very little stress on the precision of language, however. Language need only have a rough and schematic

---

[6] The classical example, of course, is provided by the analysis of Coleridge in J. L. Lowes. *The road to Xanadu.* Boston: Houghton-Mifflin, 1930.

correspondence with the real world. I may give someone verbal directions about how to get to my home, but the information I supply is referentially related to the geographic environment only in a very sketchy way. I rely upon the well-understood and highly organized spatial regions into which a city is divided (streets, blocks, and so on) to provide the appropriate guides. So, even with my vague account, I have reasonable expectation that my visitor will arrive. When we consider the physical distances involved and the comparatively small spatial area that must be found, that expectation seems to be staggeringly inappropriate.[7]

It is also possible that what we take for communication or the transfer of information is in large part the result of activation of correlated but not identical structures in two or more individuals. A great deal of linguistic communication is never subjected to external test (as in the giving of directions, making of commands, or asking of questions), and it is always possible that two people talking to one another understand different things by the content of speech. Here the analysis of associative structures has a particular value, since we may arrive, through such an analysis, at some characterization of what it is each person understands by a given segment of language.

The use of associative structures to characterize the nature of linguistic understanding is not well developed, but some data do exist, and they hold considerable promise for future development. P. E. Johnson[8] has, in a series of investigations, studied the associative structures for words defining key concepts in classical mechanics. He has examined the structures that exist among these words in (1) high-school students who were taking physics, (2) high-school students who had taken physics, and (3) students who intended to take physics but as yet had not. Johnson was able to show that associations to the critical words were more highly organized for those taking physics than for those who had taken physics a year previously, and those who had previously taken physics showed a higher degree of organization among the concepts than those who intended to take physics.

---

[7] It is hardly necessary to remind the reader that this is an issue about which writers in philosophic analysis have had much to say.

[8] P. E. Johnson. Associative meaning of concepts in physics. *J. educ. Psychol.*, 1964, **55**, 84–88; also, P. E. Johnson. The associative structure of schemata in science and their relationship to problem solving behavior. Doctoral dissertation, The Johns Hopkins University, 1964. In addition, W. S. Verplanck has investigated the psychometric possibilities inherent in associative analysis (personal communication).

More to the point, however, is the fact that the specific structures for those who were taking or who had taken physics were correlated with and apparently determined by the relationships defined in basic equations in mechanics. Force, work, mass, and acceleration were not only structured in a group for these individuals, but the fine organization among the concepts revealed the relationships implied by the underlying physical equations.

These data show, then, that associative information may be used to study the kinds of understanding people have of particular sets of concepts. Associations are immediate and direct, and they reflect a more general semantic or meaningful organization than do the same elements cast into the particular sentences of a language. What is critical to the use of associations in the assessment of understanding, however, is the fact that they do predict linguistic and, more generally, conceptual usage. Johnson was able to show that there is a correlation between the extent to which individuals exhibit appropriate associative structures for mechanical concepts and the accuracy these same individuals show in solving simple mechanical problems. In a word, the associative structures are revealed in the objective and traditional measures of achievement. Associations are more direct than the usual measures of achievement, and they are less likely to be contaminated by other considerations (arithmetic computation in solving physical equations, for example). Furthermore, anyone who has ever been a teacher has lingering doubts about problem solution as a measure of understanding. Often, particular problems can be solved by slavish imitation of examples found in a textbook (for example, the traditional exercises in algebra). The student who gives a particular pattern of associations to critical words cannot "see" the organization apparent in his associations; that can be seen only when these are put down together in a matrix or some similar form. Therefore, the student cannot easily produce the "correct" pattern of associations by rote. Furthermore, the associations themselves are but a by-product of the teaching; few teachers coach students in relevant associations as they may coach them in solving problems.

Here, then, is an example of the use of associative structures in the study of conceptual understanding. Such an analysis can, of course, be readily extended to other situations, social communication among them. We may, by extension of the techniques we have already examined, obtain some grasp of that great problem of how and what people understand by one another's linguistic usage.

Finally, we must deal once again with the problem of measurement. The distribution of obtained associations which serves as the measure of associative meaning for any concept is characterized by an average uncertainty determined by the form of the distribution. Most distributions are heavily weighted by large frequencies of occurrence of a few responses. Therefore, the uncertainty for most associative distributions is considerably less than the maximum possible. The assumption implicit in nearly all of the foregoing analysis has been that this average uncertainty is an important component in the structure of associative meaning, at least as it is defined for a population of individuals. It is important to the analysis that some responses occur more frequently than others. For example, in the recovery of the unidimensional character of basic adjectives, the assumption was made that the primary responses served to define the basic contrast. The existence of primaries, defined in frequency, implies something less than maximal uncertainty in the distribution of associates.

In order to obtain these distributions in which frequency of particular responses is an important characteristic, it is desirable to obtain but a single response to each stimulus from each individual. That condition is required in order to prevent the associations to a particular stimulus from being contaminated by other responses made by the same individual to that stimulus. Because of this requirement, it is impossible to obtain a measure of associative meaning defined in precisely the same way from a single individual. We are led, therefore, to at least consider the possibility that associative meaning is to be somewhat differently defined for the individual.

The problem of finding a measure of the associative distribution and eventually of associative intersection can be solved empirically by resort to several assumptions. Garskof and Houston[9] have discussed the application of the concept of associative meaning to the "idiographic" case, and much of what follows here is a critical account stimulated by their argument.

First of all, it is necessary to assume that one can obtain a distribution of responses to a single stimulus from a single individual without introducing contingencies among the responses. That means that each response must be contingent upon the stimulus only and not upon the preceding or some earlier response as it would be in the chained-association case. In practice, even when great care is introduced into

---

[9] Garskof and Houston, Measurement of verbal relatedness.

the testing situation, some influence of the earlier responses cannot be avoided. Nevertheless, comparisons with distributions obtained by the more usual technique show that there is good agreement.[10] There is a moderately high correlation between the frequency of responses in which each subject contributes one response and the order of responses to a single stimulus from a single individual. Therefore, while we must accept some contamination due to chaining, it may not be serious, particularly when we perform the data reduction necessary to obtain schematic structures. Furthermore, the chaining is always contingent upon the stimulus.

Unfortunately, however, a decision to accept multiple responses to the same stimulus only partly solves the problem. For, in order to apply the technique outlined here, we need some measure of the uncertainty of a single individual's distribution, and it is almost impossible to obtain any reasonable data in which subjects are allowed to repeat responses.[11] Several alternatives are available to us, however. In the main, these alternatives fall into two classes: (1) attempts to obtain an estimate of the form of the frequency distribution latent in the associates by resort to some judgmental process on the part of the subjects (ratings, for example), and (2) attempts to approximate the form of the frequency distribution by subjecting the rank order of emission of responses to some transformation. The latter alternative entails the assumption that the strongest responses are given first and the weakest last. This assumption is in accord with Bousfield's[12] extension of Marbe's law, an extension that seems to be justified by a wide variety of data.

So far as the author knows, no one has applied the first alternative to associative meaning, though C. E. Noble[13] has studied the correlation between associative meaningfulness (number of associates per unit time) and ratings of familiarity. Garskof and Houston, however,

---

[10] C. N. Cofer. Comparison of word associations obtained by the methods of discrete single word and continued association. *Psychol. Rep.*, 1958, 4, 507–510.

[11] The author gathered extensive associative data on a single individual over a period of four months. Under some conditions, repeated occurrence of a response to a given stimulus was allowed. The results of such a procedure are almost uninterpretable. In one instance, repetitions of a particular stimulus, under different conditions at different times, elicited the same response. In other cases, a reasonable distribution occurred and in still others, no repetition at all occurred. It is clear that the tendency to repeat a response is under some as yet little-understood internal control.

[12] See W. A. Bousfield, B. H. Cohen, and J. G. Silva. The extension of Marbe's law to the recall of stimulus-words. *Amer. J. Psychol.*, 1956, 69, 429–433.

[13] C. E. Noble. Verbal learning and individual differences. In Cofer (ed.). *Verbal learning and verbal behavior*.

do discuss alternative transformations applied to the rank order of associates, transformations which have the effect of markedly altering the nominal uncertainty of the distributions. They were able to show that some subjects showed a higher correlation between their judgments of relatedness of words and the intersection coefficient based upon multiple responses to these words when the distributions of associates were weighted to give greater emphasis to the initial responses, while other subjects showed a higher correlation when the weighting was essentially linear with rank order of association. The fact is, however, that these correlations did not differ greatly, and, therefore, there is little to recommend going beyond the simple procedure of weighting the distributions linearly by rank order. That would seem to be particularly true since we do not have any really well-grounded ideas about the metric of the rating scales.

An alternative not explored by Garskof and Houston would be to weight the order of associates according to Marbe's law. Such a procedure would stem naturally from Bousfield's extension of that principle. In fact, however, any weighting, either within the limits suggested by Garskof and Houston or by Marbe's law, accomplishes only minor changes in associative structure. The magnitude of individual intersection coefficients can be changed by weighting, but in any matrix of such coefficients the over-all pattern remains the same. Some reasonable approximation to a frequency distribution can be obtained, if that is desired, by the assumption that rank order of emission is some monotonic function of strength.

Garskof and Houston seem not to have considered the alternative of abandoning any dependence on rank order of emission. Yet, the concept of associative strength seems misapplied to structures of meaning for individuals. Strength, or more precisely, frequency, has an important meaning when one considers populations of individuals and when one wishes to characterize the general meanings of words existing within that population. A meaning possessed by a single individual ought to have less influence in the description of the generalized meaning for the population than a meaning shared by a number of individuals. For a single individual, however, either a word is part of the associative meaning for another word or it is not. To be sure, meanings will fluctuate both systematically and quasi-randomly in time, but in the determination at any given time either a meaning is there or it is not.

Viewed in this way, a far more fundamental question than that of what weighting to apply to the rank order of associates is the problem of how many responses to a stimulus to obtain from a single individual. In one example, the present author was able to obtain over three hundred associates to a single word from a verbally gifted English major. A casual inspection of the distribution suggested that the later responses were just as "meaningful" as the first and that the potential had not yet been exhausted when the testing stopped. One cannot obtain generalized structures without frequency distributions, but then one would hardly expect to find structures characteristic of an entire population within an individual. The structures that exist within an individual may be studied directly by examination of the intersections in occurrence of single forms as responses to related stimuli. No weighting by frequency is required; only a sufficiently extended series of responses must be elicited to ensure that the salient features defining relations to other words are obtained.

The particular problems encountered in the description of associative structures for particular individuals go beyond the scope of this book. Suffice it to say that any investigator must cope with the problems of response contingencies, editing or suppression, and amount of testing. The problems are almost identical with those of the clinician who would make use of free-associational material in obtaining information from a patient. These are problems associated with managing individual personalities and not problems in the general nature of associative structures. Therefore, it is only necessary in the present context to assert that the appropriate application of techniques for the investigation of associative structures in individuals does not make use of frequency. The structures are to be defined simply by the occurrence of particular responses. The whole notion of the nature of and development of associations presented in this book argues against the application of the concept of strength to individual associations, particularly as that concept may enter into the investigations of meaningful structures. Marbe's law is an associative law, but it describes only the comparative availability or order of responses in association. Availability or order enters into problems such as rate of acquisition, but not into the description of the nature of associative structures themselves.

Associative structures provide but one way of looking at the highly organized group of processes that make up human cognitive activity. Perceptual organization and operational organizations of the grammatical or logical sort are other aspects of that activity. Associative relations influence other cognitive functions and are influenced by these in turn. We cannot, however, characterize all cognitive organization as associative in nature, and the various distinctions we like to make between semantics and grammar, between meaning and form, and between morphology and process testify to this state of affairs. Observers of human thought processes were aware of associative structures at least as early as they were aware of grammatical relations, so the topic of associative organization runs through the whole of the history of psychology and epistemology. However, the persistent stress through that history upon contiguity both as description of the nature of any given associative sequence and as the cause of the sequence itself has obscured the structural nature of the events underlying association.

If we accept the structural description of association, there are several tasks before us. The lesser tasks include the refinement of treatment of associative data, the new methods and approach that new problems require, and the expansion and generalization of structural methods for treating data. The greater problems require us to look for ways in which the varieties of cognitive activity interact. We have evidence that associative structures do enter into ordinary linguistic processes, but we are unable to say just how they interact with other processes to produce sentences, phrases, and entire sequences of thought in discourse. We do not know how these structures enter into concept formation and problem-solving, though, again, a very large experimental literature testifies to the fact that they do.[14]

While we do not know how associative processes relate to these other functions in cognition, we find that at least the solution of this problem becomes feasible when we abandon the view of associations as laboriously learned sequences in the language and view them as generated from structural types or schemata. We have suggested, in this book, that at least two such types exist. These types depend very heavily upon the linguistic properties of English and closely related languages, and it is at least possible that very different languages yield very different schematic types in associative processes. While

[14] The present work was completed before the author had read J. Lyons. *Structural semantics: an analysis of part of the vocabulary of Plato.* Oxford: Philological Society, 1963. The views expressed by Lyons concerning the structure of meaning are remarkably close to those presented in this volume, despite the radically different problem, method, and subject matter behind the two books. The similarities in results achieved by such different approaches give considerable comfort to those who would like to think that associative processes are fundamental to language and thought.

a psychologist would tend to think of cognitive activity as linguistically general or universal, the arguments that have been made in favor of linguistic relativism make us at least conscious of the possibility that the schemata of associations may be very different in different languages.

In any event, we have seen that the organization existing among associations demands an investigation that is structural and correlational in approach. Parsimony need not come in the form of an assumption of a few elementary processes, such as contiguity and stimulus generalization; it may come in the assumption of a relatively small number of general structures from which a wide range of associative relations may be generated. Such an assumption demands that we look for the underlying generalities in associative relations, and that has been the purpose of this book. We have looked for these underlying generalities in terms of the associative processes themselves, and not in the form of imposed or invented schemes which come from logical or perceptual modes of organization. For that reason we have tended to stress associative organization. One of the fundamental mistakes made by the classical theorists in association was that they thought associative relations provided the general scheme for organization, in perception and in everything else. Fortunately, the work of Gestalt psychology and the recent experimental work in concept-learning and problem-solving has dispelled the effects of that mistake. We can now go ahead to examine associative processes in their own right and for their own intrinsic importance.

✽ *An Associative Dictionary*

The word list which follows is a dictionary of associative meaning. It is based upon norms available from American college students, and it embodies the principles described in this book. Since the normative samples (see sources below) are of college students and, by and large, male college students, factors idiosyncratic to this group intrude themselves. Therefore, the dictionary cannot be taken as ideally representative of general usage, though serious departures from general usage are probably isolated and in particular entries.

The entries are descriptions based upon intersections that particular words have with other words. Some entries consist merely of lists of words, with an indication of the schematic type. Other entries contain more detailed explanations. The entries, except where noted, are not descriptions of response distributions. They are based upon intersections which the particular entry has with other words.

The important intersections were estimated from a response listing. In the response listing, each stimulus which elicited a particular response is listed under that response. Frequencies of less than approximately 6 per cent are ignored in this tabulation. It is possible, however, to obtain a good idea of the important intersections characteristic of each entry by working back and forth between the response listing and the various stimulus listings. Since certain critical responses do not occur as stimuli in the original norms, it was necessary, while preparing the dictionary, to obtain additional norms. Stimuli for these norms are not included in the dictionary save where they could be defined by words already contained in the various norms.

The associative structural type and the form class or form classes are indicated for each entry. The form classes were arrived at by inspection of the response distributions, though in some cases it is necessary to comment on the decisions in particular entries because of the kinds of intersections characteristic of that entry. It is important to note, however, that form class will not always agree with ordinary dictionary entry or with structural grammar. The most important form-class membership is lisited first. Entries marked *environmental* are markedly asymmetric cases in which a very frequently occurring response to the entry is otherwise unrelated to the meaningful structure for that entry. These cases appear to come from common sequences in the language, or from descriptions.

Sources

1. Norms obtained by the author from samples of Johns Hopkins University undergraduates during the years 1957–1964. The *N*'s for the norms varied from 50 to 200 (men).

2. W. A. Bousfield, B. H. Cohen, G. A. Whitmarsh, and W. D. Kincaid. *The Connecticut free associational norms.* Technical report no. 35, Storrs, Conn.: Univ. of Conn., 1961. *N* = 150 (men and women).

3. V. Biase and G. H. Marshall. *Single response free word association norms to 122 abstract words or phrases.* Mimeo. 1962. *N* = 182 (87 women and 95 men).

4. L. V. Jones and S. Fillenbaum. *Grammatically classified word-associations.* Research memo. no. 15, Psychometric Laboratory. Chapel Hill, N.C.: Univ. of North Carolina, 1964. *N* = 466 (men).

5. W. F. Battig. *Single response free word-associations for 300 most frequent four-letter English words.* Mimeo (undated). N = 50 (men).

6. W. A. Russell and J. J. Jenkins. *The complete Minnesota norms for responses to 100 words from the Kent-Rosanoff word association test.* Tech. report no. 11. Minneapolis, Minn.: Univ. of Minnesota, 1954. *N* = 1008 (men and women).

Abbreviations

Adj. = Adjective
Adv. = Adverb
C.i. = Concept instance
Con. = Contrast
Env. = Environment
Gr. = Group
N. = Noun
Opp. = Opposite
Str. = Structure
V. = Verb

A

A, *Str. gr.* An, The.

Abandon, *V. gr.* Leave, Give up.

Able, *Adj. con.* Shares meaning of Capable, Good, Strong.

Abortion, *N. gr.* Links Death, Murder with Birth, Baby.

About, *Str. gr.* Around.

Above, *Adj. con., adv. con., str. gr.* Opp. Below.

Absence, *N. gr.* Partly derived from adj. con., Absent-Present. Also Loneliness, Sickness, Lateness.

Academician, *N. gr.* Scholar, Professor, Teacher.

Accident, *N. gr.* Links Car, etc., with Death, Injury, Speed.

Accordion, *N. gr. C.i.* Instrument, closest to Piano.

Acknowledge, *V. gr.* Know, Tell, Reply, Permit.

Action, *N. gr.* Motion, Running, Fight, Game, Excitement. Also a strong tendency to con. Reaction.

Active, *Adj. con.* Opp. Passive.

Actor, *N. gr.* Actress, Play. Not strongly linked with Movies, Star, etc.

Actual, *Adj. con.* Opp. False, weaker than True (via Real).

Acute, *Adj. con.* Slightly stronger than Sharp and Small. Tendency to occur in env. Pain.

Add, *V. gr.* Subtract, Multiply.

Administrative, *Adj.* Meaning given by Administration. Env. Office, Position, Job, etc.

Admiration, *N.* Strongly determined by v. Admire. Love, Like. Loyalty seems specific to Admiration, not part of Admire.

Admire, *V. gr.* Love, Like.

Adopt, *V. gr.* Take. Env. Children.

Adversary, *N. gr.* Opponent, Law (Lawyer).

Advice, *N. gr.* Help, Opinion. Linked with Mother and other people. Env. Consent.

Affection, *N. gr.* Love.

Affirm, *V. con., gr.* Opp. Deny. Confirm, Reassure, State.

Affluence, *?* Distribution shows no well-structured meaning. Confused with Influence. For those for whom it has structural meaning, gr. Wealth.

Afford, *V. gr.* Links Buy, Pay, and Spend.

Afraid, *Adj. con.?* Weak opp. Unafraid. Determined by n. gr. including Fear, Anger, Anxiety.

Age, *N.* Defined by adj. con. Young-Old, Old-New. Weakly structured with Beauty, Death, Youth.

Aggravation, *N. gr.* Annoyance.

Agreement, *N. gr.* Contract, Harmony, Pact.

Agriculture, *N.* Strongly determined by Farm.

Aid, *N. or v. gr.* Help. Env. First.

Air, *N. gr.* Earth, Water Linked with Breathe. Env. Plane.

Airplane, *N.* Defined by v. gr. Fly, Ride, Crash. Not linked with gr. Vehicles.

Ale, *N. gr.* Beer.

Alibi, *N. gr.* Excuse, Story, Lie, Crime.

Alive, *Adj. con.* Opp. Dead.

All, *Adj. con.* Stronger than Many, weaker than Entire, Total, Every.

Allege, *V. gr.* Accuse, Assert, Suppose.

Alley, *N. gr.* Links Street, Back Yard, Trash.

Alone, *Adj. con.* Opp. Together.

Alphabet, *N. gr.* Letters.

Also, *Str. gr.* Too, And, Plus, Besides.

Alter, *V. gr., n. gr.* V. Change, Fix. N. Church, God, Sacrifice (*sic*).

Altitude, *N gr.* Links Height (High) with Airplane, Mountain.

Amass, *V. gr.* Gather, Group, Accumulate.

Amazing, *Adj. con.* Stronger than Strange, Unusual, Good, and True respectively.

Ambition, *N. gr.* Work, Success, Achievement.

America, *N. gr.* Links Country, Government, Home, and Freedom. Gr. Russia, Europe.

American, *Adj.* Determined by America. Env. Flag, Citizen. Weakly opp. Russian and weakly gr. Russian, German, Indian.

Amongst, *Str. gr.* Between, Among, Within, In.

An, *Str. gr.* A, The.

Anarchy, *N. gr.* Links Government, Revolution.

Ancient, *Adj. con.* Stronger than Old. Weakly opp. Modern.

And, *Str. gr.* But, Or, So.

Angry, *Adj.* Stronger than Mad. No opp. Derived from n. gr. Anger, Fear, Anxiety, etc.

Angular, *Adj.* No str. meaning. Env. Velocity, Momentum.

Animal, *N. gr.* Man. Concept name for Dog, Cat, etc. Concept coextensive with formal definition Mammal.

Ankle, *N. gr.* Foot, Leg.

Announcer, *N. gr.* Links Program, Talk, News. Env. Radio.

Ant, *N. gr.* C.i. Insect or Bug.

Antelope, *N. gr.* C.i. Animal Close to Deer.

Anxiety, *N. gr.* Fear, Anger. C.I. Emotion.

Anyway, *Str. gr.* So, Well, Yes, Anyhow.

Anywhere, *Str. gr.* Here, There, Somewhere, Now.

Apparition, *N. gr.* Ghost, Dream.

Apple, *N. gr.* C.i. Fruit. Env., C.i. Pie, Tree.

Apply, *V. gr.* Use, Do. Env. Job.

Appreciate, *V. gr.* Like, Enjoy.

Apprentice, *N. gr.* Links Helper, Trade, and Shop. Env. Sorcerer's.

Appropriate, *Adj. con.* Weaker than Right, Good.

Are, *Str. gr.* Am, Aren't, Is, Were.

Argon, *N. gr.* Krypton. C.i. Gas.

Argue, *V. gr.* Fight, Debate, Agree.

Arise, *V.* Only in env. Bed, Morning.

Arithmetic, *N. gr.* Math, Numbers.

Arm, *N. gr.* Leg, Head.

Army, *N. gr.* Navy, Soldier.

Arrive, *V. gr.* Come, Leave.

Arrow, *N.* Env. Bow, Indian.

Art, *N. gr.* Links Music, Painting, Beauty, Picture.

Ascend, *V. gr.* Descend, Climb. Env. Stairs.

Ascribe, *V. gr.* Attribute, Write, Give.

Asparagus, *N. gr.* C.i. Food, Vegetable. No close examples. Unpleasant.

Astern, *Adj. con.?* Back. Env. Ship.

At, *Str. gr.* In, On, To.

Atlantic, *N. gr.* C.i. Ocean. Pacific.

Atom, *N. gr.* Env. Bomb. Molecule, Physics, Nucleus.

Attention, *?* Env. Pay.

Attract, *V. gr.* Pull, Detract, Repel.

Attractive, *Adj. con.* Env. Girl (male sample). Weaker than Beautiful. Stronger than Pretty.

Attorney, *N. gr.* Law, Lawyer, Trial.

Auditorium, *N. gr.* Gymnasium, Hall.

Australia, *N. gr.* C.i. Country, c.i. Continent.

Automobile, *N. gr.* Car. Env. Accident. Accident is strongly grouped with Car, Automobile, and Speed.

Average, *Adj. con.* Stronger than Poor, Bad. Not, however, neutral, but slightly negative on Poor-Weak and Good-Bad con.

Await, *V. gr.* Wait, Stop.

Awake, *Adj.* Opp. (?) Asleep.

Away, *Str. gr.* Far, Near, From.

B

Baby, *N. gr.* Child, Mother.

Back, *Adj. con., adv. con.* Opp. Front.

Background, *N. con.* Opp. Foreground.

Backward, *Adj. con., adv. con.* Opp. Forward.

Bad, *Adj. con.* Opp. Good. Not so strong as Evil.

Badge, *N. gr.* Links Police, Cap, and Authority.

Badger, *N. gr.* C.i. Animal. Close to Beaver. Env. Wisconsin (Conn. sample).

Bag, *N. gr.* Sack, Box.

Baghdad, *N. gr.* C.i. (weak) City. Also, strongly env. India (*sic*).

Bake, *V. gr.* Cook. Env. Cake.

Balance, *N. gr., v. gr.* Weight, Scales. Also, Carry. Env. Books.

Ball, *N. gr.* Bat, Game, Baseball.

Ballet, *N. gr.* Dance, Music, Opera.

Balloon, *N. gr.* Very weak tendency gr. Circus, Dirigible.

Banana, *N. gr.* C.i. Fruit. Close to Apple.

Band, *N. gr.* Music, Noise, Drums.

Bang, *?, V. gr.* Gr. Boom. Also v. gr. (to have) Sex, Intercourse (male sample).

Bank, *N. gr.* Money.

Bare, *Adj. con.* Weaker than Naked. Stronger than Empty. Weak opp. Covered.

Bark, *N. gr., v. gr.* Dog, Tree, Bite.

Barley, *N. gr.* C.i. Grain. Oats, Wheat, Rye.

Barn, *N. gr.* Links Farm, Animal, Cow, Chicken.

Barrel, *N. gr.* Box, Rifle, Muzzle (probably two otherwise distinct gr.). Env. Beer.

Base, *N. gr., n. con.* Ball, Game. Also Bottom, Top. Also con. Acid (college sample).

Baseball, *N. gr.* C.i. Game. Close to Football.

Basilica, *N. gr.* Church, Catholic Church.

Basket, *N. gr.* Box, Container. Env. Weaving.

Basketball, *N. gr.* C.i. Game. Closest to Baseball.

Bath, *N. gr.* Links Water, Soap, Shower.

Be, *Str. gr.* Am, Is, Was.

Bear, *N. gr.* C.i. Animal. Close to Muskrat, Lion.

Beard, *N. gr.* Whiskers. Also related Shave, Tough, Old.

Beast, *N. gr.* Animal, Man.

Beat, *V. gr.* Hit.

Beautiful, *Adj. con.* Stronger than Pretty. Env. Girl (male sample).

Beauty, *N. gr.* Love, Nature.

Beaver, *N. gr.* C.i. Animal. Closest to Bear.

Because, *Str. gr.* If, Since, So.

Become, *Str. gr.* Be, Happen.

Bed, *N. gr.* Sleep belongs in one fairly distinct group, Chair in another.

Bedtime, *N. gr.* Sleep, Pillow, Sheet, Night. Env. Story.

Beef, *N. gr.* Meat, Cattle.

Been, *St. gr.* Was, Be, Has.

Beer, *N. gr.* Ale, Whiskey.

Bees, *N. gr.* Birds, Flowers. In singular, c.i. Insect.

Before, *Str. gr.* After, Then, Now.

Beggar, *N. gr.* Thief, Bum.

Behind, *Adv., adj., str. gr., n. gr.* Front, Back, Under, Ahead, Bottom.

Beleaguer, *?* Confused with League. Siege.

Belgium, *N. gr.* C.i. Country. Germany, France. Env. Congo.

Belly, *N. gr.* Stomach, Fat.

Below, *Adv. con., adj. con.* Opp. Above.

Bend, *V. gr.* Break, Twist. Env. Over.

Bent, *Adj. con.* Opp. Straight, Crooked.

Berry, *N. gr.* C.i. Fruit. Strawberry, Cherry.

Best, *Adj. con.* Stronger than Better. Opp. Worst.

Better, *Adj. con.* Stronger than Good. Opp. Worse.

Bible, *N. gr.* Church, Religion.

Big, *Adj. con.* Opp. Little. Slightly stronger than Large.

Bill, *N. gr.* Cash, Money. Also, evidence of influence of proper name.

Billiards, *N. gr.* Pool, Game.

Bird, *N. gr.* Concept of which best example is Robin. Structured with Cat and with Insect, though the latter case is probably the result of the homonyms of Fly.

Bitter, *Adj. con.* Opp. Sweet.

Bituminous, *Adj.* No clear structural meaning. Env. Coal.

Black, *Adj. con., adj. gr.* Opp. White. Gr. with Blue, Red, Purple.

Blessing, *N. gr.* God, Priest, Church, Grace.

Blind, *Adj. gr.* Deaf, Crippled.

Blink, *V. gr.* Wink, Flash. Env. Eyes.

Blissful, *Adj. con.* Stronger than Happy, Quiet.

Block, *N. gr., v. gr.* Toy, Tackle. An unusual number of associates to this word are descriptors.

Blood, *N. gr.* Plasma, Corpuscle. Also Accident. Env. Red.

Blotch, *N. gr.* Spot, Mess, Smear.

Blotter, *N. gr.* Links Desk with Pen.

Blow, *N. gr., v. gr.* Hit, Suck.

Blue, *Adj. gr.* C.i. Color. Yellow, Green, and Red. Str. of Color is fundamentally primaries vs. non-primaries. Env. Sky.

Boat, *N. gr.* Ship, Sail, Trip.

Body, *N. gr.* Mind, Person, Soul, Man.

Bolivia, *N. gr.* C.i. Country, South American Country.

Bolt, *N. gr., v. gr.* Nut. Fasten. Env. Lightning.

Bone, *N. gr.* Marrow, Flesh, Skeleton, Skin.

Book, *N. gr.* Links Story, Novel, and School.

Bore, *V. gr.* Links Drill and Tire (v.).

Boring, *Adj. con.* Stronger than Dull, Tired.

Born, *V. gr.* Die, Live.

Both, *Str. gr., adj. gr.* Two, One, None, Neither. Env. Together.

Bottom, *Adj. con., n. gr.* Opp. Top. Side, Top, Edge.

Boulder, *N. gr.* Rock, Stone, Mountain.

Bounce, *V. gr.* Jump. Env. Ball.

Bow, *N.* Env. (?) Arrow.

Box, *N. gr.* Bag, Carton.

Boy, *N. gr.* Girl, Man, Woman.

Brat, *N. gr.* Kid, Child, Brother, Sister.

Brave, *Adj.?* Not clearly con. Possibly located on Strong-Weak con. Str. with Courageous, Heroic.

Bread, *N. gr.* C.i. Food. Close to Butter, Wine, Milk.

Break, *V. gr.* Shatter, Smash, Destroy.

Breast, *N. gr.* Links Woman, Skin, and Sex (male sample). Also, Chest. Env. Chicken.

Breeze, *N. gr.* Wind, Air.

Bridge, *N. gr.* Road, Game, Cards.

Brief, *Adj. con.* Stronger than Short.

Bright, *Adj. con.* Stronger than Light. Opp. Dull, stronger than Smart.

Broad, *N. gr.* Girl (male sample). Possibly, more generally opp. Narrow.

Broken, *Adj.* No apparent con. Env. Leg, Bone, Promise.

Bronze, *N. gr.* C.i. Metal. Gold, Copper.

Brook, *N. gr.* Stream, Water. Env. Trout.

Brother, *N. gr.* Sister, Father, Mother.

Brotherhood, *N. gr.* Fraternity (male college sample). Also env. Man (with possible str.).

Brown, *Adj. gr.* C.i. Color. Closest to Yellow, Red, Gray.

Buddhism, *N. gr.* C.i. Religion.

Buffalo, *N. gr.* C.i. Animal. Env. Indian, (the) West.

Bug, *N. gr.* Insect. Examples are Fly, Ant, Spider.

Building, *N. gr.* House, Office, School.

Built, *Adj. con.* Equivalent to Stacked. Stronger than Pretty (male sample).

Bull, *N. gr.* C.i. Animal. Cow. Env. Moose, Fight.

Bullet, *N. gr.* Gun, Pistol.

Bumpy, *Adj. con.* Not so extreme as Rough.

Bungalow, *N. gr.* House, Cottage.

Buoy, *N. gr.* Marker, Dock, Lighthouse.

Burgess, *N. gr.* Middle Class, Bourgeois. Env. House.

Burn, *V. gr.* Destroy, Hurt. Env. Fire.

Busy, *Adj. con.* Stronger than Active.

But, *Str. gr.* And, If, Or, Because.

Butter, *N. gr.* Bread, Milk, Cheese. C.i. Food.

Buttercup, *N. gr.* C.i. Flower. Strongly determined by descriptor Yellow.

Button, *N. gr.* Coat, Hook, Thread.

Buy, *V. con.* Sell.

By, *Str. gr.* For, At, Beside, From, Near.

C

Cabbage, *N. gr.* C.i. Vegetable. Lettuce. Env. Head.

Cabinet, *N. gr.* President, Government. Also, Drawer, Desk. Env. Maker.

Cake, *N. gr.* C.i. Food. Candy, Ice Cream.

Call, *N. or v. gr.* Yell, Talk. Env. Telephone (?).

Calm, *Adj. con.* Quiet, Smooth.

Came, *V. gr.* Went, Gone, Come.

Camp, *N. gr.* Links Summer, Scouts, and Tent. Env. Out.

Campus, *N. gr.* College, University.

Can, *Str. gr., n. gr.* Do, May, Will. Also, Bottle, Container, Box.

Canada, *N. gr.* C.i. Country. Env. North.

Canary, *N. gr.* C.i. Bird. Env. Yellow.

Candy, *N. gr.* C.i. Food. Cake, Ice Cream. Strong env. Sweet; suggests that all attributes but Sweet ignored.

Cap, *N. gr.* Hat, Head.

Capitalist, *N. gr., n.; or adj. con.* Str. gr. American, Money, Wall Street, Banking. Con. Communist.

Capsule, *N. gr.* Pill, Vitamin. Env. Space.

Car, *N. gr.* Auto, Automobile, Speed. Links these with Accident.

Care, *N. or v. gr.* Help, Aid. Env. Package.

Careful, *Adj. con.* Opp. Careless.

Careless, *Adj. con.* Opp. Careful.

Caress, *N. or v. gr.* Love, Kiss.

Carnage, *N. gr.* Meat, Body, Flesh. Only infrequently Pillage (which is confused with Pillow), or Battle, etc.

Carrot, *N. gr.* C.i. Vegetable, Food. Peas, Beets. Env. Rabbit.

Case, *N. gr.* Bag, Box. Also, Law, Court, etc.

Cast, *N. gr.* Play, Actor.

Cat, *N. gr.* C.i. Animal. Dog, Mouse.

Caterpillar, *N. gr.* C.i. Insect. Worm. Env. Tractor.

Caught, *V. gr.* Catch, Trap(ped).

Cause, *N. con.* Opp. (?) Effect.

Caution, *N. gr.* Stop, Sign, Care, Detour.

Cave, *N. gr.* Links Hole, Closet. Env. Dark, Man.

Cent, *N. gr.* Penny, Dollar.

Certain, *Adj. gr.?* Same, Particular, Sure. Neither Sure nor Certain seems to have associative con.,

though Same does. Str. not determined clearly by extant data.

Certainty, *?.* Derived from Certain, Sure, etc.

Chair, *N. gr.* Table, Desk, Couch, Bed.

Chain, *N. gr.* Link(s), Anchor.

Champion, *N. gr.* Winner, Fighter, Champ.

Change, *N. gr.* Money, Coin. As v. not clearly determined.

Chapel, *N. gr.* Church.

Character, *N. gr.* Play, Actor.

Chargeable, *?* Apparently from Charge (v.).

Charitable, *Adj.* Env. only, Organization. Perhaps str. weakly, Kind.

Charlatan, *N. gr.* Crook, Bum.

Charm, *N. gr.* Beauty, Poise. Env. Bracelet.

Chase, *V. gr.* Run, Follow, Catch.

Cheap, *Adj. con.* Opp. Expensive.

Check, *N. gr.* Money, Bill.

Cherry, *N. gr.* C.i. Fruit. C.i. Tree. Env. Red.

Chief, *N. gr.* Head, Tribe, Leader. Env. Indian.

Child, *N. gr.* Man, Body, Kid, Mother, Parents.

Chill, *Adj. con.* Probably from Chilly. More extreme than Cold.

Chip, *N. gr.?* Block, Wood. Env. Shoulder, Potatoes.

Choice, *N. gr.* Decision, Selection.

Chops, *N. gr.* C.i. Food. Meat, Steak. Env. Lamb.

Chosen, *Adj.* Env. One, Few.

Chow, *N. gr.* Food, Chinese Food. Env. Mein.

Christmas, *N. gr.* C.i. Holiday. Easter. Env. Tree, Carol.

Church, *N. gr.* Religion, God, Bible.

Cigarette, *N. gr.* Tobacco, Cigar, Pipe. Concept name for particular brands. Also, links these with Cancer. Env. Smoke.

Circle, *N. gr.* Square, Triangle. Env. Round.

Circumstance, *N. gr.* Situation, Condition.

City, *N. gr.* Town.

Claim, *V. gr., n. gr.* Take, Say, etc. Also, Mine, Gold. V. gr. linked to Money.

Clang, *?* Bang. Env. Bells. Possible str. Noise, Sound.

Class, *N. gr.* School, Hour, Group, Students (college sample). Env. Room.

Classical, *Adj.* Env. Music. Weakly determined by Old.

Clean, *Adj. con.* Opp. Dirty.

Clear, *Adj. con.* Opp. Hazy, Unclear. Also, determined by Clean.

Clemency, *N. gr.* Pardon, Mercy, Leniency.

Climb, *V. gr.?* Fall, Walk. Env. Mountain, Hill, Ladder.

Climbing, *V. gr.* Derived from Climb.

Clock, *N. gr.* Links Time, Wall, Hands.

Close, *Adj. con., v. con.* Approximately Near. Opp. Open.

Closet, *N. gr.* Links Room, Cupboard, Drawer, Clothes. Env. Door. Also, see Cave.

Cloth, *N. gr.* Dress, Clothes, Silk, Clothing, Material, Coat, etc.

Clothes, *N. gr.* See Cloth. Also, concept name for Coat, Skirt, etc.

Cloud, *N. gr.* Sky, Rain, Sun.

Club, *N. gr.* Fraternity. Also, Bat. (College sample.)

Coal, *N.?* Env. Black. Strongly determined by single adj. attribute.

Coarse, *Adj. con.* Determined by Rough, also Hard.

Coat, *N. gr.* Hat, Tie, Jacket (male sample).

Cocoa, *N. gr.* Chocolate.

Cocoon, *N. gr.* Moth, Butterfly, Bug.

Coexistence, *N. gr.* Peace, War.

Coin, *N. gr.* Money, Bill. Concept name for Nickel, Dime.

Cold, *Adj. con.* Opp. Hot.

Collar, *N. gr.* Links Shirt, Neck, etc. Env. Dog.

Collection, *N. gr.* Group, Things, Assortment. Env. Stamps.

Color, *N. gr.* Concept name for Red, etc.

Colorful, *Adj. con.* Stronger than Happy, Pretty, Bright.

Colossal, *Adj. con.* More extreme than Huge.

Come, *V. gr.* Go, Went.

Comfort, *N. gr.* Ease, Rest.

Comfortable, *Adj. con.* Easy, Soft, Good. Also, Uncomfortable.

Commingle, *V.* Weakly str. gr., Mix, Mingle. Probably determined by Mingle.

Common, *Adj. con.* Usual, Ordinary.

Communist, *N. gr.* Red (n.), Russia, Socialist. Con. Capitalist.

Compact, *N. gr.* Car, Automobile (male sample). Also, Powder, Mirror.

Companion, *N. gr.* Friend, Pal.

Company, *N. gr.* Business, Group, Corporation.

Complete, *Adj. con.* Opp. Incomplete.

Composure, *N.?* Confused with Posture. Weak str. seems to derive from Composed as adj.

Compound, *N.* Chemistry, Element (college sample). Env. Fracture.

Concord, *?* Env. Grape.

Confetti, *N. gr.?* Links Parade, Party, Paper.

Connoisseur, *N. gr.* Wine, Gourmet.

Consequence, *N. gr.* Result, Trouble.

Consider, *V. gr.* Ponder, Contemplate, Think.

Considerable, *Adj. con.* More than Many, less than All.

Consist, *V. gr.* Make, Compose, Contain.

Constant, *Adj. con.* Same.

Contented, *Adj. con.* Less extreme than Happy. Satisfied.

Contentedly, *Adv. con.* Weaker than Happily.

Continually, *Adv. con.* Determined by Always (adv.).

Controversy, *N. gr.* Argument, Fight.

Cook, *V. gr.* Bake, Eat. Env. Food.

Cool, *Adj. con.* Less extreme than cold. Colloquial usage as in "cool clothes." is Env. too scattered to determine str.

Cop, *N. gr.* Police, Law, Badge.

Copper, *N. gr.* C.i. Metal. Iron, Gold.

Cordial, *N. gr.* Liquor, Cocktail. C.i. Drink. Adj. use not obvious.

Cork, *N. gr.* Links Bottle, Stopper, Champagne.

Cormorant, *N. gr.* C.i. Bird. Surprisingly well str.

Corporation, *N. gr.* Business, Company.

Correct, *Adj. con.* Approximately same as Right.

Cost, *N. gr.* Price, Money, Expense. Only weakly str. in v. gr. Pay, etc.

Cotton, *N. gr.* C.i. Cloth. Wool.

Couch, *N. gr.* Sofa, Bed, Chair. All these linked with Sleep.

Could, *Str. gr.* Would, Should.

Couldn't, *Str. gr.* Wouldn't.

Counterpoint, *P* Env. Point. Practically no str. with Music, or musical terms generally (male sample).

Country, *N. gr.* City, Nation, Farm. Also, concept name, Canada, etc.

Courage, *N. gr.* Strength, Fear.

Course, *N. gr.* Subject, Studies, Class (college sample).

Court, *N. gr.* Trial, Law.

Courtesy, *N. gr.* Kindness, Politeness, Respect.

Cow, *N. gr.* C.i. Animal. Env. Milk.

Coward, *P* Env. Afraid, Scared.

Cowardly, *Adj.P* The potential con. Brave-Cowardly does not seem to exist strongly in association. Largely determined by n. gr., Fear, etc.

Coyote, *N. gr.* C.i. Animal. Wolf, Dog.

Cozy, *Adj. con.* Occurs on Warm, Soft, and Good con.

Cradle, *N. gr.* Bed, Carriage. Env. Baby.

Crawl, *N. gr.* Walk, Creep, Swim.

Cream, *N. gr.* Milk, Coffee, Sugar. Env. Ice.

Creation, *N. gr.* God, World, Man. Only weakly Invention, etc. (College sample.)

Creek, *N. gr.* River, Stream, Water.

Crest, *N. gr.* Top, Hill, Peak, Mountain. Less with Seal, Emblem.

Crew, *N. gr.* Links Men with Ship, Boat.

Criminal, *N. gr.* Links Law, Prison, Police. Also, Crook, Gangster.

Cringe, *P* Str. with n. gr. Fear, Pain.

Crook, *N. gr.* Bum, Gangster.

Crooked, *Adj. con.* Opp. Straight.

Cruel, *Adj. con.* Potential con. Kind-Cruel not evident. Cruel determined by Bad, Hard, Wrong, etc.

Cruise, *N. gr.* Links Trip with Ship, Boat.

Crumb, *P* Env. Cake, Bread. Possibly weak n. gr. with Bum, etc.

Crush, *V. gr.* Smash, Break, Hurt.

Cud, *?* Env. Cow, Chew.

Cull, *?* Clang (?) association with Gull. Hence, str. with Bird, Chicken, Bill, etc., which occur in response distribution.

Curious, *Adj. con.* More extreme than Different. No evidence of str. with Inquiring, etc.

Currant, *N. gr.* Berry, Grape, Fruit, Raisin. Env. Jelly. Perhaps C.i. Jelly.

Current, *Adj. con.* More extreme than New. No evidence of n.

Curtain, *N. gr.* Window, Drapes, Shade.

Cushion, *N. gr.* Chair, Pillow, Couch. Env. Soft.

Cut, *V. gr.* Slice, Hurt, Knife. These all linked with Blood.

Cute, *Adj. con.* Approximately Pretty, Little. Env. Girl.

D

Dad, *N. gr.* Mom, Mother, Father.

Dainty, *Adj. con.* Env. Girl (male sample). Shares meaning of Small, Pretty.

Daisy, *N. gr.* C.i. Flower. Pansy.

Dame, *N. gr.* Girl, Woman.

Damper, *N. gr.* Fireplace, Chimney.

Dancing, *N. gr.* Gerundive form dominates associations. Str. Music, Records, Singing.

Danker, *N. gr.* Fear, Accident. Meaning not well determined with existing data.

Dare, *V. gr.* Challenge, Try, Do.

Dark, *Adj. con.* Opp. Light.

Dart, *N. gr.* Arrow, Blowgun. No evidence of v.

Date, *N. gr.* Girl, Chick, Dance (male sample).

Day, *N. gr.* Day, Night, Morning, Evening, Afternoon.

Dead, *Adj. con.* Opp. Alive.

Deal, *V. gr.* Buy, Bet, Give. Env. Cards.

Dear, *?* Env. Wife, John, Abbey, etc.

Death, *N. gr.* Life, Destruction, Sorrow, Disease.

Debris, *N. gr.* Rubbish, Garbage, Trash.

Decorum, *V., sic.* Confused with Decorate.

Deep, *Adj. con.* Opp. Shallow.

Deer, *N. gr.* C.i. Animal. Antelope.

Defeat, *N. gr.* War, Victory.

Deformed, *V. or adj. gr.* Crippled.

Delicacy, *N. gr.* Concept name for Caviar, *Pâté,* etc.

Delicate, *Adj. con.* Shares meaning of Soft, Small.

Delicious, *Adj. con.* Stronger than Good. Env. Food.

Delightful, *Adj. con.* Stronger than Happy.

Demagogue, *?* No apparent str., save possibly with Tyrant. Env. God, suggests weakly str. meaning.

Dependent, *Adj. con.* Opp. Independent.

Depressed, *Adj. con.* More extreme than Sad.

Depression, *N. gr.* Recession, Money. Only slight evidence of str. with Emotion gr.

Depth. *N. gr.* Height, Width. Env. Deep.

Describe, *V. gr.* Show, Tell, Explain.

Desert, *N. gr.* Sand, Cactus, Oasis.

Desirable, *Adj. con.* Stronger than Nice, Good.

Desire, *V. gr.* Wish, Want, Need.

Desk, *N. gr.* Table, Chair, Lamp.

Desperately, *Adj.?* Env. Needed, Lonely.

Despoil, *V. gr.* Determined by Spoil, Ruin.

Destination, *N. gr.* Journey, Trip.

Determine, *V. gr.* Insist, Do.

Develop, *V.?* Env. Picture, Film.

Deviation, *N. gr.* Change, Perversion.

Devil, *N. gr.* Evil, Sin, Death, Satan, Hell, God. Env. Red, Bad.

Devotion, *N. gr.* Prayer, Religion. Env. Love.

Diadem, *N. gr.* Jewel, Crown, Necklace.

Did, *V. gr.* Do, Done, Will.

Differ, *?* Env. From.

Different, *Adj. con.* Opp. Same. This con. yields Similar, Dissimilar, Strange, Familiar, etc.

Difficult, *Adj. con.* Stronger than Hard.

Difficulty, *N. gr.* Hardship, Sorrow, Hardness.

Dignity, *N. gr.* Honor, Respect.

Dim, *Adj. con.* Not so extreme as Dark.

Dimension, *?* Env. Three, Third.

Dinner, *N. gr.* Supper, Lunch, Food. Env. Eat.

Direct, *Adj. con.* Determined by Straight. Weak con. Indirect.

Dirt, *N. gr.* Mud, Ground, Filth.

Dirty, *Adj. con.* Opp. Clean.

Discipline, *N. gr.* Punishment, School. Little evidence of v. gr. Env. Strict.

Disease, *N. gr.* Death, Illness.

Dish, *N. gr.* Plate, Food, Pan, Spoon.

Disorganized, *V. gr.* Organized, Confused, Disrupted. Strong evidence that v. gr. determined by underlying v. and not adj. in nature.

Dispense, *?* Env. With.

Dispose, *V. gr.* Throw, Rid, Kill.

Disseminate, *?* Primary is Apart.

Dissimilar, *Adj. con.* Determined by Different.

Distant, *Adj. con.* More extreme than Far.

Dizzy, *Adj.?* Sick, Giddy.

Do, *V. gr., str. gr.* Don't, Make, Can, Will. Env. Not.

Dock, *N. gr.* Boat, Wharf, Pier.

Doctor, *N. gr.* Sickness, Medicine, Nurse, Lawyer.

Does, *V. gr., str. gr.* Do, Did, Doesn't.

Dog. *N. gr.* Cat.

Doggedly, *?* Distribution too scattered to determine str. Form class not consistent.

Dome, *N. gr.* Steeple, Roof.

Done, *V. gr., str. gr., adj?* Do, Did. Shares meaning of Complete.

Donkey, *N. gr.* Ass, Mule, Horse. Only weakly c.i. Animal.

Dollar, *N. gr.* Money, Cents, Bill.

Doodle, *V. gr.* Scribble, Write.

Door, *N. gr.* Window, Knob, Room.

Doorpost, *N. gr.* Doorway, Window, Sill.

Dot, *N. gr.* Point, Dash, Spot.

Dough, *N. gr.* Bread, Cake, Pie. Also, Money, etc.

Doughnut, *N. gr.* C.i. Food. Coffee. Env. Hole.

Down, *Adv. con., str. gr.* Opp. Up. Adv. con. dominates; only very weakly str. with prepositions.

Drag, *N. gr., v. gr.* Girl, Stag (college male sample). Also, Pull. Env. Race.

Draw, *V. gr.* Paint, Write. Env. Picture.

Dream, *V. gr. or n. gr.* Sleep, Fantasy.

Dress, *N. gr.* Clothes, Clothing, Girl, Woman.

Drill, *V. gr.* March. Also, Hammer.

Drink, *V. gr., n. gr.* Sleep, Eat. Also, Coke, Liquor.

Drive, *V. gr.* Go, Walk, Ride. Env. Car.

Drop, *V. gr.* Fall, Break.

Drum, *N. gr.* Band, Noise, Instrument. Env. Beat.

Dry, *Adj. con.* Opp. Wet.

Dug, *V.?* Env. Hole.

Dull, *Adj. con.* Shares meaning of Dim. Also, weak con. Sharp.

Dullness, *N. gr.* Boredom, Sharpness.

Dumb, *Adj. con.* Weak opp. Smart. Similar to Stupid.

Dungeon, *N. gr.* Cell, Prisoner, Jail, Castle.

Duty, *N. gr.* Honor, Work, Obligation.

Dyer, *?* Responses too scattered to determine str.

E

Each, *Adj. con.* Less extreme than All, more than Many.

Ear, *N. gr.* Eye, Nose.

Early, *Adj. con.* Opp. Late.

Earth, *N. gr.* C.i. Planet. Also, Ground, Dirt.

East, *Adj. con.* Opp. West. East-West nearly orthogonal to North-South. There is a slight tendency for East to relate to North and West to South.

Easy, *Adj. con.* Opp. Hard.

Eat, *V. gr.* Drink, Sleep. Env. Food.

Economy, *N. gr.* Budget, Money.

Edge, *?* Env. Cliff.

Edinburgh, *N.?* Env. Scotland.

Edit, *V.?* Env. Papers. Possibly str. Censor, Write.

Egyptian, *N. gr.* Egypt, Pyramid, Pharaoh, Nasser.

Eight, *N. gr.* C.i. Number.

Either, *Str. gr.* Or, Neither.

Ellipse, *N. gr.* Circle.

Elm, *N. gr.* C.i. Tree.

Elopement, *N. gr.* Marriage, Engagement.

Else, *Str. gr.* Or, Where, Other, But.

Elsie, *?* Env. Cow.

Empty, *Adj. con.* Opp. Full.

Encourage, *V. gr.* Help, Aid. Only weakly related to Discourage.

Enemy, *N. gr.* Friend, Foe.

Enfeeble, *?* The primary is Weak.

Engine, *N. gr.* Car, Motor, Machine.

Engineering, *N. gr.* Science, Math, probably env. Student.

Enjoyment, *N. gr.* Entertainment, Pleasure, Fun.

Entire, *Adj. con.* More extreme than All or Total.

Envious, *Adj.?* Jealous. No clear str. other than relation to Jealous. Through Jealous, related to Emotion gr.

Equal, *Adj. con.?* Weakly related to Same (Identical, etc.). Env. Opportunity.

Equivocal, *?* Weak primary of Equal. Responses otherwise scattered.

Erupt, *V. gr.* Explode. Env. Volcano.

Especially, *Adv. str.* Particularly, Mostly. Env. Nice, If.

Essence, *?* Scattered responses. Weak primary, Being.

Europe, *N. gr.* C.i. Continent. America.

Eve, *?* Env. Adam, Christmas.

Even, *Adj. con.* Similar to Smooth. Not a clear con. Odd.

Evening, *N. gr.* Morning, Night.

Ever, *Adj. con.* Similar to Always.

Everybody, *?* con. Str. close to Every. Env. not evident in association.

Evil, *Adj. con.* More extreme than Bad.

Evoke, *V. gr.* Elicit, Cause, Emit (college sample, currently enrolled in psychology).

Exactly, *Adv. gr.* Precisely, Accurately. This gr. probably basically a con. derived from adj. con. Right-Wrong.

Examine, *V. gr.* Heal.

Exceptionally, *Adv.* Env. Good, Well, Brilliant. Only very infrequently env. Bad.

Exciting, *Adj. con.* Shares meaning of Happy, Good.

Exhaust, *N. gr.* Fumes, Intake.

Exhibit, *V. gr., n. gr.* Display, Show. Also, Paintings, etc.

Exist, *V. gr.* Be, Live, Survive.

Exile, *N. gr.* Prisoner, Napoleon.

Exorbitant, *Adj. con.* More extreme than Expensive.

Expense, *N. gr.* Cost, Money.

Explosion, *N. gr.* Fire, Dynamite, Fireworks.

Expose, *V. gr.* Uncover, Bare, Show.

Extraordinary, *Adj. con.* Shares meaning of Different. Not a clear con. Ordinary.

Extravagant, *Adj. con.* Shares meaning of Rich, Expensive.

Eye, *N. gr.* Ear, Nose, Mouth.

F

Face, *N. gr.* Nose, Head.

Fact, *N. gr.* Knowledge, Truth, Fiction.

Fail, *V. gr.* Pass, Flunk, Try.

Faint, *?* Response scattered. Most frequent, Smell, Dizzy.

Fair, *Adj. con.?* Responses scattered. Seems to share meaning of Good, Pretty, and Right.

Fairy, *N. gr.* Queer, Homosexual. Also, env. Tale.

Faith, *N. gr.* Religion, Hope, Love.

Faithfulness, *N. gr.* Loyalty, Truth.

Fall, *N. gr., v. gr.* Autumn, Spring, Winter. Env. Down.

Fallen, *V., adj.* Str. Drop, Hurt. Also, env. Down, Angel, Idol.

False, *Adj. con.* Opp. True.

Fame, *N. gr.* Fortune, Honor.

Familiar, *Adj. con.* Shares meaning of Same. Env. Face.

Family, *N. gr.* Friends, Home, Love.

Famous, *Adj. con.* Shares meaning of Good and Rich.

Fan, *N. gr.* Air, Air Conditioning, Heater.

Fancy, *Adj. con.* Opp. Plain.

Fantastical, *Adj. con.* Shares meaning of Different, Strange.

Far, *Adj., adv. con.* Opp. Near.

Farm, *N. gr.,* Animal, Barn, Country.

Farther, *Adj. con.* More extreme than Far.

Fast, *Adj. con.* Opp. Slow.

Fat, *Adj. con.* Thick. Opp. Thin. Also shares meaning of Ugly.

Fatal, *Adj. Env.* Death, Accident.

Fateful, *Adj. Env.* Day. Perhaps str. Bad.

Father, *N. gr.* Mother, Dad, Son, Daughter.

Fathom, *N. gr.* Depth, Ocean.

Fatigue, *N. gr. Env.* Tired.

Fault, *N. gr.* Mistake, Error.

Favorite, *Adj. con.* More extreme than Good. Nearly equal Best.

Fear, *N. gr.* Anger, Anxiety, Worry, Hatred.

Feather, *N.?* Env. Light, Soft.

Feel, *N. gr.* Touch, Smell, Sense.

Feeling, *N. gr.* Emotion, Sensation.

Fellow, *N. gr.* Friend, Chum, Boy.

Female, *N. gr.* Male, Woman, Girl.

Ferocious, *Adj.?* Str. Wild. Env. Lion.

Fertile, *Adj.?* Env. Soil.

Fete, *N. gr.* Feast, Festival, Holiday.

Fever, *N. gr.* Temperature, Heat.

Few, *Adj. con.* Opp. Many.

Fight, *N. gr., v. gr.* Battle, Hit, Punch, Fist.

Figure, *N. gr.* Shape, Build. Env. Girl.

Fill, *V. con.?* Some evidence str. opp. Empty.

Filth, *N. gr.* Dirt, Garbage.

Finance, *N. gr.* Money, Bank, Loan.

Find, *V. gr.* Lose, Search.

Fine, *Adj. con.* More extreme than Good. Less than Best.

Finger, *N. gr.* Hand, Toe, Thumb.

Fire, *N. gr.* Flame, Water, Heat.

Fireworks, *N. gr.* Explosion, Fire.

Firm, *N. gr., adj. con.* Company, Business, etc. Also, not so extreme as Hard.

First, *Adj. con.* Opp. Last.

Fish, *N. gr.* Concept name, Trout. Sea, Ocean, Water.

Fist, *N. gr.* Hand, Knuckle, Fight.

Fit, *?* Env. Tight.

Five, *N. gr.* C.i. Number.

Fixed, *V. gr.* Repaired, Fired (?).

Fixture, *N. gr.* Lamp, Ceiling. Env. Light.

Flag, *?* Env. Pole, American.

Flare, *N. gr.* Light, Fire.

Flat, *Adj. con.* Similar to Smooth.

Flax, *N. gr.* Wheat, Straw, Wool.

Flea, *N. gr.* C.i. Bug (also, Insect). Fly. Env. Dog.

Flock, *?* Env. Sheep, Geese, Birds.

Flood, *N. gr.* Water, Storm, River.

Floor, *N. gr.* Ceiling, Wall, Rug.

Floral, *?* Str. Flowers, Garden, Florist. Str. as n.

Flow, *N. gr., v. gr.* Water, Stream, Move.

Flower, *N. gr.* Concept name, Rose, etc.

Fluffy, *Adj. con.* More extreme than Soft. Also, White.

Flutter, *V. gr., n. gr.?* Fly, Flap. Also, str. Bird, Butterfly, Wing, etc.

Fly, *N. gr., v. gr.?* C.i. Bug, Insect. Also, Bird, Airplane.

Flying, *N. gr.* Str. Bird, Airplane.

Food, *N. gr.* Drink, Dinner. Env. Eat.

Fool, *N. gr.* Clown, Jester. See Deceive.

Foolish, *Adj. con.* Shares meaning of Stupid, Careless.

Foot, *N. gr.* Shoe, Toe.

Football, *N. gr.* C.i. Game. Baseball, Stadium.

For, *Str. gr.* Against, With, To, By.

Force, *N. gr.* Strength, Power.

Foreign, *Adj. con.* More extreme than Different. Env. Country.

Forester, *N. gr.* Woodsman, Tree, Ranger.

Forget, *V. gr.* Learn, Remember.

Forgiveness, *N. gr.* Sin, Mercy.

Form, *N. gr.?* Shape, Body, Build.

Former, *Adj. con.* Opp. Latter.

Forty-six, *N. gr.* C.i. Number.

Forward, *Adv. con.* Opp. Backward.

Four, *N. gr.* C.i. Number.

Fox, *N. gr.* C.i. Animal Wolf, Dog.

Fragile, *Adj.?* Soft. Env. Break.

Frame, *?* Env. Picture, Window, House.

Fraud, *N. gr.* Cheat, Swindle, Fake.

Freckle, *N. gr.* Pimple, Skin.

Free, *?* Primary is Easy.

Freedom, *N. gr.* Liberty, Slavery, Security.

Freely, *Adv.?* Easily, Loosely.

Freeze, *?* More extreme than Cold. Thaw, Melt, Chill.

Fresh, *Adj. con.* More extreme than New.

Friendly, *Adj. con.* Nice, Good. Env. Person.

Friendship, *N. gr.* Love, Loyalty.

Frieze, *?* Env. Cold (*sic*).

Frigid, *Adj. con.* More extreme than Cold.

Fright, *N. gr.* Fear, Scare.

From, *Str. gr.* To, Here, There, Away, By, On, etc.

Front, *Adj. con.* Opp. Back.

Frown, *N. gr.* Smile, Worry, Wrinkle.

Fruit, *N. gr.* Concept name, Orange, Apple. Str. Vegetable.

Full, *Adj. con.* Opp. Empty.

Fun, *N. gr.* Enjoyment, Joy, Play.

Funny, *Adj.?* Shares meaning of Happy. Env. Joke. Also, probably str. Crazy, etc.

Fur, *N. gr.* Animal, Coat, Hair. Env. Soft.

Furnace, *N. gr.* Heat, Fire.

Further, *Adj., adv. con.* Farther.

Futurity, *N.?* Weakly str. Race, Horse. Env. Future.

G

Gable, *N. gr.* Roof, House. Env. Clark.

Gain, *V. gr.* Lose, Achieve, Win.

Gallon, *N. gr.* Pint, Quart.

Game, *N. gr.* Concept name, Chess, Football, Ball. Env. Play.

Garage, *N. gr.* Links Car, Auto, and Mechanic.

Garden, *N. gr.* Flower, Plant, Summer.

Garment, *N. gr.* Clothes, Coat, Dress.

Gate, *N. gr.* Fence, Door.

Gay, *Adj. con.* More extreme than Happy.

General, *N. gr.* Army, Officer, Soldier. Little evidence of adj.

Generally, *Adv.?* Usually, Mostly. Possible Seldom-Often con.

Gentility, *N. gr.* Gentleness, Softness, Gentleman.

Gentle, *Adj. con.* Good, Soft, Warm, Kind.

Gentleman, *N. gr.* Lady, Women, Man.

Germ, *N. gr.* Disease, Bacteria, Bug.

Get, *V. gr.* Take, Receive.

Gift, *N. gr.* Present, Box.

Girl, *N. gr.* Boy, Woman.

Give, *V. gr.* Take, Receive, Obtain.

Glad, *Adj. con.* Happy.

Glamour, *N. gr.* Beauty, Actress.

Glass, *?* Env. Drink, Water, Clear.

Glitter, *V. gr.* Sparkle, Shine.

Globe, *N. gr.* Earth, World. Env. Round.

Glory, *N. gr.* Fame, Honor.

Glove, *N. gr.* Hand, Mitten.

Glow, *V. gr.* Shine, Light.

Glower, *V. gr.* (*sic*). Light, Shine. (Compare Bloomfield's remarks on *gl* words.)

Glue, *N.?* Env. Stick.

Glut, *?* Eat, Fat.

Gnat, *N. gr.* C.i. Bug, Insect. Fly.

Go, *V. gr.* Stop, Walk, Travel. Env. Around, To, On.

Goal, *N. gr.* Ambition, Aim, Achievement.

Goat, *N. gr.* C.i. Animal. Sheep.

God, *N. gr.* Heaven, Church, Man.

Gold, *N. gr.* Silver, Money, C.i. Metal.

Golden, *Adj.?* Yellow, Bright.

Golf, *N. gr.* C.i. Sport, Game. Env. Ball, Club.

Gone, *V. gr.* Left, Went, Go.

Good, *Adj. con.* Opp. Bad.

Gorilla, *N. gr.* Ape, Monkey. C.i. Animal.

Government, *N. gr.* Democracy. United States, Politics.

Grace, *N. gr.* Prayer, God. Env. Meal.

Grammar, *N. gr.* School, English, Book.

Grand, *Adj. con.* More extreme than Big or Good.

Grape, *N. gr.* Fruit, Wine. C.i. Fruit (?).

Grapefruit, *N. gr.* C.i. Fruit. Env. Sour, Breakfast.

Grass, *N. gr.* Lawn, Tree. Env. Green.

Grasshopper, *N. gr.* C.i. Insect, Bug. Ant.

Gray, *Adj. gr.* C.i. Color. White, Black, Brown, Blue.

Great, *Adj. con.* More extreme than Big or Good.

Greatly, *Adv.* Largely.

Greedily, *Adv.* Hungrily.

Green, *Adj. gr.* C.i. Color. Orange, Red, Yellow, Blue.

Grief, *N. gr.* Sorrow, Sadness, Death.

Grisly, *?* Env. Bear (*sic*). Also, confused with Greasy.

Ground, *N. gr.* Earth, Dirt. Also, evidently str. with Potential, Electricity (college male, heavily engineering sample).

Grow, *V.?* Env. Up, Tall.

Guide, *N. gr.* Leader, Chief, Indian.

Gun, *N. gr.* Bullet, Pistol.

Gunpowder, *N. gr.* Explosion, Fireworks, Fire. Only weakly str. with Gun, etc.

H

Hair, *N. gr.* Head, Skin.

Half, *Adj. ? con.* Opp. Whole.

Hall, *N. gr.* Corridor, House, Closet.

Halt, *V. gr.* Stop, Go.

Hammer, *N. gr.* Nail, Sickle. C.i. Tool.

Hamster, *N. gr.* C.i. Animal. Mouse.

Hand, *N. gr.* Foot, Arm, Finger.

Handful, *?* Response distrbution includes Money, Few. No evidence of str.

Handle, *N. gr.* Hold, Touch. Env. Ax, Door.

Hang, *V. gr.* Die, Kill. Env. Rope.

Happily, *Adv.* Env. Married.

Happy, *Adj. con.* Opp. Sad.

Hard, *Adj. con.* Opp. Soft, Easy.

Hardhearted, *Adj.?* Cruel.

Hardware, *?* Env. Store.

Harsh, *Adj. con.* Loud, Hard, Bad.

Harvest, *N. gr.* Crops, Food. Env. Moon.

Has, *V. str. gr.* Had, Have, Been.

Hat, *N. gr.* Head, Coat.

Hate, *V. gr.* Love, Fear, Like.

Hatred, *N. gr.* Love, Anger, Fear. C.i. Emotion.

Have, *V. gr.* Hold, Get.

Haystack, *?* Env. Needle.

Hazy, *Adj.?* Gray. Possible opp. Clear.

He, *Str. gr.* She, Her, Him.

Head, *N. gr.* Body, Shoulders, Neck.

Headache, *N. gr.* Pain, Sickness, Env. Hurt.

Health, *N. gr.* Happiness, Life. Env. Good.

Health, *Adj. con.?* Possible opp. Sick, or possible str. with Well in Well-Sick con.

Hear, *V. gr.* See, Listen, Sound.

Heartiness, *?* Response distribution includes Healthy, Laughter.

Heat, *N. gr.* Cold, Fire.

Heaven, *N. gr.* God, Earth, Sky.

Heavy, *Adj. con.* Opp. Light.

Helmet, *N. gr.* Links Hat, Head, and Soldier.

Help, *V. gr.* Aid, Call.

Her, *Str. gr.* Him, His.

Here, *Adv. con.* Opp. There.

Heretofore, *?* Before. Possible preposition or adv. str. gr.

Hesitate, *V. gr.* Wait, Stop, Delay.

Hide, *V. gr.* Seek, Find.

Hie, *?* Env. Hello, Greetings (*sic*).

High, *Adj. con.* Opp. Low.

Hiking, *V. gr.* Walking, Camping. Evidence suggests verb rather than gerund.

Hill, *N. gr.* Mountain, Valley.

Him, *Str. gr.* Her.

Hip, *N. gr.* Leg, Body.

His, *Str. gr.* Her, Hers, Him.

Hit, *V. gr., n. gr.* Run, Hurt, Strike, Ball.

Hockey, *N. gr. C.i.* Game. Skating.

Hog, *N. gr.* C.i. Animal. Pig.

Hold, *V. gr.* Take, Keep, Grip.

Hole, *N. gr.* Ground, Dirt. Env. Deep.

Hollow, *Adj. con.* Equivalent to Empty. Env. Tree.

Holy, *?* Str. with Church, God.

Home, *N. gr.* Primary link for House, Family.

Homely, *Adj. con.* Ugly. Env. Girl.

Hook, *N. gr.* Links Line, Fish, and Nail.

Hope, *V. gr., n. gr.* Want, Desire. Faith, Prayer.

Horn, *?* Env. Blow.

Horrible, *Adj.?* Terrible.

Horse, *N. gr.* Donkey. C.i. Animal.

Hospitable, *Adj.?* Friendly, Good.

Hospital, *N. gr.* Doctor, Nurse, Illness. Env. Sick.

Hot, *Adj. con.* Opp. Cold.

Hour, *N. gr.* Time, Minute.

House, *N. gr.* Home, Room.

Huge, *Adj. con.* More extreme than Big.

Huguenot, *?* Env. French.

Human, *Adj.?* Env. Being.

Humble, *Adj. con.* Poor.

Hungry, *Adj. gr.* Thirsty, Tired.

Hurt, *V. gr.* Injure, Wound. Env. Pain.

Hybrid, *?* Env. Plant, Mix.

I

I, *Str. gr.* Me, You.

Ice, *N. gr.* Water, Snow. Env. Cold, Cream.

Idle, *Adj.?* Lazy.

If, *Str. gr.* But, Or, And.

Igloo, *?* Env. Eskimo. Possible str. Eskimo.

Ignorance, *N. gr.* Stupidity, Knowledge.

Ill, *Adj. con.?* Opp. Sick in Healthy, Well, Ill arrangement. It is not clear that there is a fundamental con. here.

Immediate, *Adj. con.* More extreme than Fast.

Immediately, *Adv.* Now.

Immoral, *Adj. con.* More extreme than Evil.

Immunity, *N. gr.* Disease, Vaccine.

Impatient, *Adj. gr.* Anxious, Patient, Restless, Angry.

Importance, *N. gr.* Prestige, Status.

Important, *Adj. con.* Responses diffuse. Str. on Good, Big, Strong.

Improve, *V. gr.* Help, Work.

In, *Str. gr.* Out, On, Into. Str. with Out important enough to resemble con.

Inborn, *?* Env. Motor (*sic*).

Inch, *N. gr.* Foot, Mile, Yard.

Income, *N. gr.* Money, Salary. Taxes probably str. and env.

Incomplete, *Adj. con.* Opp. Complete.

Independent, *Adj.?* Similar to Free. Cannot str. Free from available data.

Indication, *N. gr.* Sign.

Induce, *V. gr.* Seduce, Persuade, Make.

Indulge, *V. gr.* Links Drink, Eat, and Sin.

Indulgent, *Adj.?* Env. Drinker.

Inherit, *V. gr.* Gain, Insure.

Ink, *N. gr.* Pen, Pencil. Env. Black.

Insect, *N. gr.* Concept name for Fly, Ant.

Inside, *Adj. con., adv. con.* Opp. Outside.

Insinuate, *V. gr.* Accuse, Tell.

Instantaneous, *Adj. con.* More extreme than Fast.

Instrument, *N. gr.* Concept name, Piano, Trumpet.

Insulation, *N. gr.* Wire, Electricity.

Insurance, *N. gr.* Money, Security.

Interesting, *Adj.?* Env. Book, etc.

Interstate, *Adj.?* Env. Commerce.

Ire, *N. gr.* Anger, Fear, Wrath.

Irish, *Adj. gr. or n. gr.* English, Spanish.

Iron, *N. gr.* C.i. Metal. Steel.

Irritate, *N. gr.* Anger, Annoy.

Is, *V. str. gr.* Are, Was, Be.

Isis, *?* Env. Goddess.

Islet, *N. gr.* Island, Sea.

It, *Str. gr.* They, Them, That, She.

J

Jail, *N. gr.* Prison, Crime, Criminal.

Jazz, *N. gr.* Music, Concert. Also, Concert possible env.

Jealousy, *N. gr.* Belongs to Emotion gr. Hatred, Anger.

Jelly, *N. gr.* Jam, Bread.

Jet, *?* Env. Plane.

Join, *V. gr.* Group (possible env.), Tie.

Joint, *N. gr.* Elbow, Hip.

Joy, *N. gr.* Happiness, Pleasure, Sorrow, Merriment.

Judgment, *N. gr.* Str. weakly with Law, Trial.

Juice, *?* Env. Orange, Tomato.

Jump, *V. gr.* Leap, Run.

June, *N. gr.* C.i. Month. July, Summer.

Just, *Adj. con.* Right.

Justice, *N. gr.* Law, Mercy, Truth. Env. Peace.

Justification, *N. gr.* Rationalization, Law.

K

Keep, *V. gr.* Hold, Have, Find.

Key, *N. gr.* Lock, Door.

Keyboard, *N. gr.* Piano, Typewriter.

Kill, *V. gr.* Murder, Die.

Kind, *Adj. con.* Some meaning determined by Good, some by Soft.

Kindly, *?* Almost the same response distribution as Kind.

King, *N. gr.* Queen, Crown.

Kingdom, *?* Env. Come.

Kiss, *N. gr., v. gr.* Love, Hug, Env. Girl.

Kitchen, *N. gr.* Stove, Sink.

Knee, *N. gr.* Leg, Elbow, Foot.

Knife, *N. gr.* Fork, Spoon. Env. Cut.

Know, *V. gr.* Learn, Understand.

Knowledge, *N. gr.* Intelligence, Books, School.

Knuckle, *N. gr.* Wrist, Hand, Fist.

L

Lad, *N. gr.* Boy, Lass, Child.

Lady, *N. gr.* Man, Gentleman, Woman.

Lake, *N. gr.* River, Water.

Lamb, *N. gr.* Sheep, Wool. No evidence of c.i. Animal.

Lamp, *N.?* Env. Light(?).

Lance, *N. gr.* Spear, Dart, Sword.

Land, *N. gr.* Sea, Water, Earth.

Lapse, *?* Env. Time.

Larceny, *N. gr.* Crime, Theft, Thief.

Large, *Adj. con.* Opp. Small.

Lass, *N. gr.* Girl, Boy, Lad.

Last, *Adj. con.* Opp. First.

Lave, *V. gr., n. gr.* Wash, Bathe. Also, Lava, Volcano (*sic*).

Lean, *Adj. con.* Thin.

Learn, *V. gr.* Study, Know.

Leather, *N.?* Shoe, Belt.

Left, *Adj. con.* Opp. Right.

Leg, *N. gr.* Arm, Foot.

Legendary, *Adj. con.* Old. Env. Story, Myth.

Leisure, *N. gr.* Pleasure. Env. Time.

Lemon, *N. gr.* C.i. Fruit. Orange. Env. Sour.

Lend, *V. gr.* Borrow, Give.

Leper, *?* Primary is Sickness.

Lessen, *V. gr.* Decrease, Reduce.

Lesson, *?* Env. Learn, Music.

Lettuce, *N. gr.* C.i. Vegetable. Tomato, Cabbage.

Level, *Adj. con.* Smooth.

Liberty, *N. gr.* Freedom, Peace.

Lice, *N. gr.* C.i. Bug(s). Also, Rats, Mice.

Lie, *V.?* Env. Down.

Life, *N. gr.* Death. Possible n. con. with Death.

Like, *V. gr.* Love, Hate.

Light, *Adj. con.* Opp. Dark.

Lily, *N. gr.* C.i. Flower.

Limit, *V. gr., n. gr.* Stop, End.

Lion, *N. gr.* C.i. Animal. Tiger.

Lipstick, *?* Env. Red.

Liquor, *N. gr.* Beer, Drink (also, possible env.).

Little, *Adj. con.* Opp. Big.

Lively, *Adj. con.* Alive.

Living, *Adj. con.* Alive.

Lizard, *N. gr.* Snake, Reptile. Reptile possible concept name.

Lock, *N. gr., v. gr.* Key, Door. Also, Close.

Log, *N. gr.* Wood, Tree, Lumber.

London, *N. gr.* C.i. City. Paris. Env. England.

Long, *Adj. con.* Opp. Short.

Look, *V. gr.* See, Listen.

Loose, *Adj. con.* Opp. Tight.

Lost, *Adj. con.* Opp. Found.

Loud, *Adj. con.* Opp. Soft. Env. Noise.

Low, *Adj. con.* Opp. High.

Lower, *Adj. con., v. gr.* Opp. Higher. Also, Reduce, Carry.

Luggage, *N. gr.* Baggage, Travel, Trip.

M

Mad, *Adj. gr.?* Angry, Afraid, Crazy. Also, env. Magazine.

Made, *V. gr.* Did, Make, Build.

Magically, *?* Distribution scattered. Possibly str. Magic, Magician.

Maid, *N. gr.* C.i. Servant. Butler.

Mail, *N. gr.* Stamp, Letters (possible env.).

Mainly, *Adv. str. gr.* Usually, Chiefly. Env. Because.

Major, *N. gr., adj. con.* Army, Colonel, General. Also, opp. Minor.

Make, *V. gr.* Build.

Male, *Adj. con.* Opp. Female.

Mallet, *N. gr.* Croquet, Hammer. No evidence of c.i. Tool.

Man, *N. gr.* Woman, Boy, Girl.

Manage, *V. gr.* Handle, Control.

Manner, *?* Env. Way.

Mantel, *N. gr.* Fireplace.

Many, *Adj. con.* Opp. Few. Scale displaced so that Many close to Few.

Maple, *N. gr.* C.i. Tree.

Marble, *N. gr.* Stone.

Mark, *V. gr.* Grade, Write. Possibly n. gr. also.

Married, *Adj. con.* Opp. Single.

Marry, *V. gr.* Love, Divorce.

Martyr, *?* Primary is Saint.

Masonic, *Adj.?* Env. Temple, Lodge.

Mass, *N. gr.* Church, Service, Sermon. Also, Weight, Gravity.

Match, *N. gr.* Cigarette. Little evidence of v.

Mate, *N. gr., v. gr.* Wife, Girl. Also, Marry, Love.

Matter, *N. gr.* Mind, Energy.

Maturity, *N. gr.* Age, Father.

May, *V. str. gr., n. gr.* Can, be, etc. Also, June, April.

Maybe, *Adv. str. gr.* Perhaps, Possibly, Probably. Env. Not. These words are probably undimensionally scaled.

Mean, *Adj.* More extreme than Bad. Also, Average. Also, Angry, Mad.

Meanwhile, *Str. gr.* Now, While.

Measles, *N. gr.* Mumps, Disease. (Disease possible concept name.)

Meat, *N. gr.* Food, Steak.

Meet, *V.?* Env. People.

Melancholy, *Adj. con.* Sad.

Melodrama, *N. gr.* Drama, Play, Opera.

Melody, *N. gr.* Song, Music.

Men, *N. gr.* Women, Ladies, Boys.

Merriment, *N. gr.* Joy, Fun, Happiness, Contentment.

Merry, *Adj. con.* Happy.

Messy, *Adj. con.* More extreme than Dirty.

Middle, *?* Perhaps str. with Center, Top, End, Side.

Might, *V. str. gr.* Could, Can, May.

Mighty, *Adj.?* May be str. with Strong, or possible env. Strong.

Mil, *?* Env. Million, Millimeter, etc.

Mile, *N. gr.* Foot, Inch.

Militia, *N. gr.* Army, Minutemen (?).

Milk, *N. gr.* Links Cow with Food. Env. Drink.

Mind, *N. gr.* Body, Matter.

Miner, *N.?* Env. Coal.

Mineral, *N. gr.* Metal, Rock, Oil.

Minister, *N. gr.* Church, Priest.

Minnesota, *N. gr.* C.i. State.

Minor, *N. gr., adj. con.* Child, Adult. Also, opp. Major.

Mirror, *N. gr.* Links Image with Wall.

Miss, *V. str.?* Hit. Also, Girl.

Mississippi, *N. gr.* C.i. River. Missouri. (Data obtained before civil-rights disputes.)

Misuse, *?* Distribution includes Wrong, Words.

Moan, *V. gr.* Groan, Cry.

Mob, *N. gr.* Gang, Crowd.

Moderation, *?* Responses scattered. Primary, Little.

Modern, *Adj. con.* Stronger than New.

Moist, *Adj. con.* Wet.

Momentum, *N. gr.* Force, Energy, Speed.

Money, *N. gr.* Dollar, Bank, Bills.

Mongrel, *N. gr.* Dog, probably Puppy.

Monk, *N. gr.* Monastery, Priest.

Monsoon, *N. gr.* Storm, Wind, Rain.

Monument, *?* Env. George Washington.

Mood, *N.?* Env. Bad.

Moon, *N. gr.* Sun, Stars.

Moose, *N. gr.* C.i. Animal. Deer.

Moral, *Adj. con.* Good. No clear evidence of con. with Immoral.

Morning, *N. gr.* Night, Evening, Afternoon.

Mosquito, *N. gr.* C.i. Bug. Fly. Env. Bite.

Moth, *N. gr.* C.i. Bug. Butterfly.

Mother, *N. gr.* Father, Dad, Child, Daughter.

Motion, *N. gr.* Movement, Speed.

Mountain, *N. gr.* Hill, Valley.

Mouse, *N. gr.* C.i. Animal. Cat, Rat.

Mouth, *N. gr.* Nose, Teeth.

Move, *V. gr.* Stop, Go, Stay.

Movement, *N. gr.* Motion, Activity.

Much, *Adj. con.* More extreme than Many.

Mud, *N. gr.* Dirt.

Mug, *N.?* Env. Beer.

Museum, *N. gr.* Art, Auditorium, Painting.

Music, *N. gr.* Song, Sound, etc.

Muskrat, *N. gr.* C.i. Animal. Rat.

Must, *V. str. gr.* Will, Have, Do.

Mystery, *N. gr.* Novel, Story, Plot.

N

Nail, *N. gr.* or *v. gr.* Hammer, Pin.

Name, *N. gr.* Person, Friend.

Narrative, *N. gr.* Story, Book.

Narrow, *Adj. con.* Opp. Wide.

Nation, *N. gr.* Country. Concept name, United States.

Nationalist, *Adj.?* Env. China.

Native, *Adj. con., n. gr.* Opp. Foreign. Str. Indians, Foreigner, Alien.

Natural, *Adj.?* Distribution scattered and env. Primary, Science.

Nature, *N. gr.* God, Trees.

Navy, *N. gr.* Army, Air Force.

Near, *Adj. con.* Opp. Far.

Neck, *V. gr., n. gr.* Kiss, Hug. Also, Head.

Negro, *Adj. con.* Black. Very little evidence of Negro as n. (Caucasian sample).

Nest, *N. gr.* Bird, Tree.

Net, *?* Env. Fish, Hair, Tennis.

Neurosis, *N. gr.* Psychosis, Disease.

News, *N. gr.* Television, Paper. Also, probably env. Paper.

Next, *Adj.?* Env. Time.

Niagara, *?* Env. Falls.

Nice, *Adj. con.* Good. Also, Pretty.

Nicely, *Adv.* Determined by Good.

Night, *N. gr.* Day, Noon.

Nine, *N. gr.* C.i. Number. Ten.

Noble, *Adj.* More extreme than Good.

Noise, *N. gr.* Sound, Music. Env. Loud.

Noisy, *Adj. con.* Loud.

None, *Adj. con.* More extreme than Few.

Noon, *N. gr.* Lunch, Hour, Day.

North, *N. gr.* South, East, West.

Nose, *N. gr.* Face, Nostril.

Nostril, *N. gr.* Nose.

Note, *N. gr.* Music. Also, Letter, Paper.

Nude, *Adj.?.* Env. Woman.

Numerous, *Adj. con.* More extreme than Many.

Nurse, *N. gr.* Hospital, Doctor, Patient.

O

Oat, *N. gr.* C.i. Cereal. Wheat. Env. Horse.

Obey, *V. gr.* Listen, Command.

Oblique, *Adj.?* Env. Angle.

Obscurity, *?* Unknown, Darkness as responses.

Obtain, *V. gr.* Get, Receive.

Ocean, *N. gr.* Sea, Water. Concept name, Atlantic (east-coast sample).

October, *N. gr.* C.i. Month. November.

Of, *Str. gr.* From, By, For, About.

Officer, *N. gr.* Police, Cop, Law. Weak evidence for str. Army, etc.

Oil, *N. gr.* Gas, Grease, Petroleum.

Old, *Adj. con.* Opp. New, Young.

Olive, *N. gr.* C.i. Food. Martini. Env. Green (possible str. color adj.).

On, *Str. gr.* Off, In, Under, Upon.

Once, *?* Primary, Twice.

One, *N. gr.* C.i. Number. Two.

Only, *?* Env. One.

Open, *Adj. con.* Opp. Closed. No clear evidence of str. as v.

Openly, *Adv.* Meaning derived from Open.

Opera, *N. gr.* Music, Ballet, Song.

Opposite, *Adj. con.* Different.

Optimistic, *Adj. con.?* Probably opp. Pessimistic.

Or, *Str. gr.* And, Nor, Either, But.

Oracle, *?* Responses include Speech, Delphi.

Orange, *N. gr., adj. gr.* C.i. Fruit. Apple, Green, Red, Yellow.

Order, *V. gr.* Obey, Command.

Ordinary, *Adj. con.* Same.

Organ, *N. gr.* Music, Piano. Also, Stomach.

Organize, *V. gr.* Lead, Arrange.

Orifice, *N. gr.* Opening, Mouth.

Original, *Adj. con.* First.

Othello, *?* Responses include Shakespeare, Greek (?).

Other, *Adj. con.* Different.

Ourself, *Str. gr.* Us, We, Yourself.

Out, *Str. gr.* In, Of.

Outside, *Adj. con.* Opp. Inside.

Oven, *N. gr.* Stove, Heat.

Over, *Adv. con., adj. con., str. gr.* Opp. Under. Also, Above, Here, There.

Overlap, *V. gr.* Cover, Hide.

Oxford, *N. gr.* Cambridge. Env. England, University.

Oxidation, *N. gr.* Links Chemistry and Fire.

P

Pace, *V. gr.* Walk, Run.

Page, *N. gr.* Book, Paper.

Pain, *N. gr.* Fear, Anxiety, Misery.

Paint, *V.?* Env. Red, House.

Painting, *N. gr.* Art, Picture.

Pair, *?* Str. Two. Env. Shoes.

Pant, *V. gr.* Breathe, Puff.

Panther, *N. gr.* C.i. Animal. Cat.

Pants, *N. gr.* Trousers, Clothing (possible concept name).

Paper, *N. gr.* Books, Pencil.

Parent, *N. gr.* Child, Mother, Uncle.

Parsimony, *?* Responses include Peace, Matrimony. Also, Stingy.

Part, *Adj.?* Whole, Piece, All. Evidence not clear. May be from Piece, Part, Half, Whole, to All. No study of possible relation to Many-Few scale.

Particular, *Adj.?* Special, Certain. No clear opp.

Passive, *Adj. con.* Opp. Active.

Past, *N. gr.* Present, Future, Time.

Pat, *?* Primary Girl.

Pathological, *Adj.?* Env. Science.

Patient, *N. gr.* Doctor, Nurse, Hospital. Little evidence of adj.

Patriot, *N. gr.* Loyalty, Traitor, Country, Spy.

Payroll, *N. gr.* Money, Bank.

Peace, *N. gr. or con.?* War.

Peak, *N. gr.* Mountain, Valley.

Peal, *V.?* Env. Bells, Orange.

Pear, *N. gr.* C.i. Fruit, Tree.

Pearl, *N. gr.* C.i. (?) Jewel. Diamond, Oyster.

Peek, *V. gr.* Look, See.

Peerless, *Adj.?* Str. Brave.

Pen, *N. gr.* Pencil, Ink, Paper. Env. Write.

Pencil, *N. gr.* Pen, Paper, Ink, Env. Write.

People, *N. gr.* Person(s), Crowd, Society.

Perch, *N. gr.?.* C.i. Fish. Env.(?) Bird.

Perfect, *Adj. con.* More extreme than Good.

Performance, *N. gr.* Act, Play.

Perfume, *N. gr.?* Env. Smell. Links Flower, Odor.

Perhaps, *Adv. str.* Possibly, Probably. Scaling data shows undimensional scale.

Period, *N. gr.* Time, Hour. Also, Comma, Sentence.

Persimmon, *N. gr.* C.i. Fruit. Env. Sour.

Person, *N. gr.* People, Man, Human (evidence shows Human as n.).

Personal, *Adj.?* Evidence suggests str. with Private.

Personally, *?* Str. Me, I, Mine.

Petal, *N. gr.* Leaf, Flower.

Petroleum, *N. gr.* Gas, Oil, Grease.

Philip, *?* Env. Morris.

Philosopher, *N. gr.* Thinker, Academician, Professor.

Phosphoric, *Adj.?* Env. Acid.

Piano, *N. gr.* Music, Concert. C.i. Instrument.

Pick, *V. gr.* Find, Choose.

Pickle, *N.?* Env. Sour.

Picture, *N. gr.* Links Art to Window, Wall.

Piece, *N. gr.* Part, Portion (see Part). Env. Cake, Pie.

Piecemeal, *?* Responses include Pie, Part.

Pierce, *V. gr.* Penetrate, Puncture.

Pig, *N. gr.* C.i. Animal. Hog.

Pillow, *N. gr.* Bed, Sleep.

Pin, *N. gr.* Needle, Nail, Point.

Pine, *N. gr.* C.i. Tree. Oak.

Pineapple, *N. gr.* C.i. Fruit. Grapefruit.

Pink, *Adj. gr.* Red, Blue.

Pious, *Adj.* Good (also str. with Religious, Religion, etc.).

Pistol, *N. gr.* Gun, Rifle, Bullet.

Pity, *N. gr.* Sympathy, Sorrow, Shame.

Plain, *Adj. con.* Opp. Fancy.

Plan, *V. gr.* Think, Do, Prepare.

Plane, *N. gr.* Airplane, Jet, Air. Env. Fly.

Plant, *N. gr.* Animal, Tree. Env. Green. Except for possible env. Tree, little evidence of v.

Play, *V. gr., n. gr.* Run, Walk. Env. Game. Also, Actor.

Player, *N. gr.* Game, Baseball (possible env.).

Plead, *V. gr.* Beg, Ask.

Pleasant, *Adj. con.* Good.

Pleasure, *N. gr.* Fun, Joy.

Pleiades, *?* Greek is primary, Latin in distribution. By virtue of these, str. with Greek and Latin.

Plenty, *?* Basic meaning seems to derive from Many.

Pliers, *N. gr.* Nail, Hammer. C.i. Tool.

Poetry, *N. gr.* Poet, Prose, Writer.

Point, *N. gr.* Pin, Needle. Env. Sharp. Little evidence of v.

Poke, *N. gr.* Hit, Stab.

Pony, *N. gr.* C.i. Animal. Horse.

Pool, *N. gr.* Water, Swimming (possible env.).

Poor, *Adj. con.* Opp. Rich.

Popular, *Adj.?* Env. Music.

Portion, *N. gr.* Part, Piece, Food. (See Part.)

Position, *N. gr.* Job.

Post, *?* Env. Office.

Pot, *N. gr.* Kettle, Pan, Stove.

Powder, *N. gr.?* Env. Gun, Face. Str. Explosion, Fire.

Powerful, *Adj. con.* Strong.

Practical, *Adj.?* Env. Application.

Praetor, *?* Roman is primary.

Prayer, *N. gr.* God, Church, Religion.

Precious, *Adj.?* Env. Stone, Jewel.

Preference, *N. gr.* Choice, Desire.

Pressure, *N. gr.* Force, Volume.

Prestige, *N. gr.* Status.

Pretty, *Adj. con.* Opp. Ugly.

Prick, *V. gr.* Puncture, Stick.

Priest, *N. gr.* Church, Minister, Religion.

Primer, *N. gr.* Reader, Book, School.

Prince, *N. gr.* King, Queen, Princess.

Prison, *N. gr.* Jail, Prisoner, Crime.

Prisoner, *N. gr.* Jail, Crime, Prison.

Probably, *Adv.* Scaling data suggest undimensional scale with Maybe, Possibly, Surely.

Production, *N. gr.* Play, Movie. Also, Factory.

Profession, *N. gr.* Doctor, Lawyer.

Professional, *Adj.?* Env. Doctor.

Proscription, *N. gr.* Medicine, Drug (*sic*).

Prose, *N. gr.* Poetry, Writer.

Prosper, *?* Str. with Rich, Wealth.

Proud, *Adj.?* Env. Father. Little evidence of str. Humble occurs in response distribution infrequently.

Puddle, *N. gr.* Mud, Rain, Dirt.

Punch, *V. gr.* Hit, Fight.

Puncture, *V. gr.* Pierce, Penetrate, Prick.

Puny, *Adj. con.* More extreme than Little.

Purchase, *V. gr.* Buy, Sell.

Pure, *Adj. con.* Clean.

Purple, *Adj. gr.* Blue, Green, Red.

Purpose, *N. gr.* Goal, Motive.

Push, *V. gr.* Pull, Shove.

Python, *N. gr.* C.i. Snake. Rattlesnake.

Q

Quaint, *Adj. con.* Old. Also, Different.

Quibble, *V. gr.* Argue, Fight, Hit.

Quick, *Adj. con.* More extreme than Fast.

Quiet, *Adj. con.* Basic con. may be Quiet-Noisy or Soft-Loud.

Quota, *N. gr.?* Weakly str. with Limit.

R

Rabbit, *N. gr.* C.i. Animal. Dog.

Race, *V. gr.* Run, Walk. Few responses in distribution such as White, Negro, etc.

Radiator, *N. gr.* Heat.

Rage, *N. gr. or V. gr.* Anger, Hatred, Hate.

Railway, *N. gr.* Railroad, Train (possible env.).

Rain, *N. gr.* Water, Snow, Storm, Sunshine.

Raise, *V. gr.* Lift, Climb.

Ram, *N. gr.* C.i. Animal. Sheep. Response distribution also includes Football, Hit, etc.

Ram, *N. gr.* Cat, Mouse. C.i. Animal.

Rattle, *V. gr.* Shake. Also, Baby (env. or str.?).

Rayon, *N. gr.* Silk, Nylon.

Reach, *V.?* Responses scattered. Env. For. Possible str. Grab.

Read, *V.?* Env. Books. Possible str. Write, etc.

Ready, *?* Env. Go.

Real, *Adj.* con. True. Use as adv. intensifier (Very) does not show up in associative distribution (male college sample).

Really, *Adv.* True. Str. Truly, Actually, etc. Env. Not.

Recent, *Adj.* con. New.

Reception, *N. gr.* Party.

Rector, *N. gr.* Church, Minister. Also, wide scattering of responses.

Red, *Adj. gr.* Green, Blue, Black, Pink, Orange.

Reel, *?* Fish, Rod in response distribution.

Referee, *N. gr.* Game, Umpire.

Refresh, *V. gr.* Str. Water, Drink.

Refuel, *V.?* Env. Plane, Tank.

Regarding, *?* Responses include Looking, Pertaining. May str. Look, See, etc.

Regiment, *N. gr.* Soldier, Troops.

Regular, *Adj.?* Responses scattered env.

Relax, *V. gr.* Sit, Sleep, Rest. Env. Easy.

Relaxed, *Adj.?* Responses scattered, may str. Anxious, Angry, etc. Possible con. Tense not clearly evident.

Religion, *N. gr.* Church, God.

Remember, *V. gr.* Forget, Think.

Repay, *V. gr.* Pay, Borrow.

Repeat, *?* Env. Again.

Repentance, *N. gr.* Sin, Sinner, Church.

Replant, *?* Responses include Grow, Trees, Flowers.

Report, *?* Env. Card.

Rescue, *N. gr.* Save, Help, Aid.

Resent, *V. gr.* Like, Hate.

Respectable, *Adj.?* Env. Person, Gentleman.

Rest, *V. gr.* Sleep, Sit, Relax.

Result, *N. gr. or v. gr.* End, Cause.

Retard, *V. gr.* Weakly str. Stop, Go. Also probably weakly str. Mind, Child.

Reveal, *V. gr.* Show, Tell.

Revenge, *N. gr.* Hatred, Fight.

Reverberate, *?* Responses scattered. Include Resound, Sound, Echo.

Rhyme, *N. gr.* Poem, etc.

Ribald, *?* Primary is Classic (env.?). Responses include Funny, Bold.

Rich, *Adj.* con. Opp. Poor.

Ride, *V. gr.* Walk, Travel. Env. Horse. See Rider.

Rider, *N.?* Str. with Ride, via Horse and Car.

Right, *Adj.* con. Opp. Wrong, left.

Ring, *V., n.?* Env. Bell. Str. weakly with Marriage, Wedding.

Rinse, *V. gr.* Wash, Clean.

Rise, *V. gr. or n. gr.* Fall, Stand.

River, *N. gr.* Water, Lake, Stream.

Road, *N. gr.* Car, Highway, Street.

Rob, *V. gr.* Steal.

Robbery, *N. gr.* Thief, Theft, Crime.

Rock, *N. gr.* Stone, Earth.

Rocker, *?* Primary Chair. Possibly str. Chair, Sofa, etc.

Rocky, *?* Env. Mountains.

Role, *N. gr.* Play, Actor.

Roll, *?* Env. Call.

Roof, *N. gr.* Top (also env.), House.

Room, *N. gr.* Home, House.

Rooster, *N. gr.* Hen, Chicken.

Rose, *N. gr.* C.i. Flower. No evidence of v.

Rot, *N. gr. or v. gr.* Decay.

Rough, *Adj. con.* Opp. Smooth.

Round, *Adj. con.* Opp. Square.

Rubble, *N. gr.* Trash, Dirt.

Rug, *N. gr.* Floor, Carpet.

Rugged, *Adj. con.* Rough.

Rule, *N. gr.* Law.

Run, *V. gr.* Walk, Race, Walk. Env. Away.

Rung, *N.?* Primary Ladder, possibly str.

Runner, *N.?* Env. Track, Fast.

Russian, *N. gr. or adj. gr.* Links Communist, Red, American.

Rustic, *Adj. con.* Weakly str. Old. Env. Country.

S

Sad, *Adj. con.* Opp. Happy.

Safe, *Adj. gr.?* Str. Secure.

Said, *V. gr.* Told, Say, Tell.

Sailing, *N. gr.* Boat, Water.

Salary, *N. gr.* Wage, Money, Pay.

Salt, *N. gr.* Pepper. C.i. Food. Env. Water.

Salute, *?* Primary is Flag.

Same, *Adj. con.* Opp. Different.

Sand, *N. gr.* Beach, Sea.

Sandpaper, *N.?* Env. Rough.

Satirical, *Adj.?* Str. Funny, Fun, Joy, possibly Happy-Sad.

Saucer, *N. gr.* Cup, Dish.

Save, *V. gr.* Help. Also, probably Lose.

Say, *V. gr.* Tell, Talk.

Scale, *N. gr.* Balance, Weight.

Scene, *N. gr.* Play, Spectacle.

School, *N. gr.* Teacher, Book. Env. Work.

Schoolroom, *N. gr.* Teacher, School.

Scientist, *N. gr.?* Responses scattered. Str. Professor, Doctor.

Scimitar, *N. gr.* Sword, Knife.

Scout, *?* Env. Boy.

Scow, *N. gr.?* Weakly str. Boat, Ship.

Scream, *V. gr.* Yell, Cry, Shout.

Sea, *N. gr.* Water, Ocean.

Seat, *N. gr.* Chair. Env. Car.

Secondary, *Adj.?* Env. School.

Secret, *?* Responses include Love, Mystery. No str. evident.

Secure, *Adj. gr.?* Str. Safe. No evidence of con.

Seduce, *V.?* Env. Women (male sample).

See, *V. gr.* Look, Hear, Listen.

Seek, *V. gr.* Find, Look.

Seem, *V. str. gr.* Appear, Be.

Seldom, *Adv.* Scaled with Never, Often.

Self, *?* Str. Me, My.

Sell, *V. gr.* Buy, Pay.

Sentence, *N. gr.* Word, Period.

Sepal, *P* Primary is Flower.

Series, *N.P* Env. World.

Serious, *Adj. con.* Str. Old, Sad.

Several, *Adj. con.* Between Many and Few.

Sew, *V.P* Str. Needle, Thread. Also links these with Knit.

Sex, *N. gr. or v. gr.* Love. Env. Female, Male.

Shade, *N. gr.* Lamp, Light. Also, Trees, Sun, Sunshine.

Shady, *Adj.P* Env. Trees.

Shall, *V. str. gr.* Will, Do.

Shallow, *Adj. con.* Opp. Deep.

Shark, *N. gr.* C.i. Fish. Also weakly str. Tiger, Teeth.

Sharp, *Adj. con.* Possibly opp. Dull. Con. not clear, however.

Shave, *V.P* Env. Beard. Also possibly str. Beard, Whiskers.

She, *Str. gr.* He, Her, Him, It.

Sheep, *N. gr.* C.i. Animal. Dog, Goat.

Shell, *N. gr.* Egg. Also, Clam, Oyster.

Shine, *V.P* Env. Sun, Shoes. Weakly str. Sun, Sunshine.

Ship, *N. gr.* Boat, Sea, Water.

Shoe, *N. gr.* Foot, Socks.

Shooting, *N. gr.* Gun, Rifle, Hunting.

Shop, *V. gr., n. gr.* Buy, Sell. Also, Store.

Short, *Adj. con.* Opp. Long, Tall.

Shortsighted, *Adj.P* Weakly str. Blind, Nearsighted.

Should, *V. str. gr.* Would, Ought. Env. Not.

Shout, *V. gr.* Yell, Scream.

Shove, *N. gr.* Push, Pull.

Show, *N. gr.* Movie, Picture. Only weakly v.

Shower, *N. gr.* Bath, Water.

Shrill, *Adj. con.* Loud.

Shut, *V. gr.* Close, Open, Slam.

Shyly, *Adv.* Probably based on adj. str. Shy, Timid, Bold.

Sick, *Adj. con.P* Possible con. Healthy, though not strongly so.

Sickness, *N. gr.* Health, Death.

Sign, *N. gr.* Env. Stop. Str. Signal, Light.

Signal, *N. gr.* Sign, Light.

Signify, *V.P* Env. Meaning.

Silence, *N. gr.* Quiet, Noise.

Silent, *Adj.* More extreme than Soft or Quiet.

Silk, *N. gr.* Env. Smooth. Cloth, Dress.

Similar, *Adj. con.* Close to Same.

Simple, *Adj. con.* Easy.

Sinecure, *N. gr.P* Weakly str. Job.

Sing, *V.P* Env. Song. Str. Music, Song, etc. Also weakly str. Talk.

Single, *Adj. con.* Opp. Married.

Sister, *N. gr.* Brother, Mother.

Sit, *V. gr.* Stand, Walk, Step.

Size, *P* Str. with Big, Large, Small, etc. Possibly concept name for Big-Little con. Response dist. suggests more Big than Small.

Skid, *V. gr.* Slide, Stop.

Skiing, *N. gr.* Sport, Snow, Sledding.

Skirt, *N. gr.* Dress, Clothing (C.i.).

Sky, *N. gr.* Env. Blue. Heavens, Star, Moon, Sun.

Slash, *V. gr.* Cut, Slice.

Sledding, *N. gr.* Skiing, Snow.

Slight, *Adj. con.* Smaller than Little, bigger than Tiny.

Slime, *N. gr.* Dirt, Mud. Env. Slippery.

Slip, *V. gr.* Slide, Fall (male sample).

Sloppy, *Adj. con.* Dirty.

Sloth, *N. gr.* C.i. Animal. Pig.

Slow, *Adj. con.* Opp. Fast.

Slumber, *N. gr.* Sleep, Bed.

Small, *Adj. con.* Opp. Big.

Smart, *Adj. con.* Weak opp. Dumb. Intelligent.

Smear, *V. gr.* Mess, Spread.

Smoke, *V.?* Env. Cigarettes. Also, str. with Cigarettes, Cigars, etc.

Smooth, *Adj. con.* Opp. Rough.

Snail, *N.?* Env. Slow. Weakly str. Bug, Insect, Worm.

Sneer, *V. gr. or n. gr.* Laugh, Snicker.

Snow, *N. gr. or v. gr.* Rain, Ice. Env. White.

So, *Str. gr.* If, Therefore, And. Env. What.

Sober, *Adj. con.* Opp. Drunk.

Soccer, *N. gr.* C.i. Game. Football.

Social, *Adj.?* Responses scattered. Env. Security.

Socialism, *N. gr.* Communism.

Sofa, *N. gr.* Chair, Bed, Couch.

Soft, *Adj. con.* Opp. Hard. Also, in Quiet-Noisy, Loud-Soft con.

Soil, *N. gr.* Dirt.

Sold, *V. gr.* Bought, Sell, Buy.

Some, *Adj. con.* Between Considerable and Many on Many-Few con.

Somebody, *Str. gr.* Anyone, Someone, Anybody.

Sometimes, *Adv. str. gr.* Scaled with no strong con. with Never, Always, etc.

Song, *N. gr.* Music, Dance, Sing, Singing.

Soon, *Adv.* Str. by Fast-Slow. Also, forms adv. str. gr. (Immediately, etc.) scaled but without con. on Fast.

Sore, *Adj.?* Env. Throat, Hurts.

Sorrow, *N. gr.* Grief, Sadness, Death.

Soul, *N. gr.* Body, Mind.

Sound, *N. gr.* Noise, Music.

Sour, *Adj. con.* Opp. Sweet.

Souse, *N. gr.?* Apparently str. Drunk, Spouse, Wife (?).

South, *N. gr.* North, West, East.

Speak, *V. gr.* Talk, Listen.

Spear, *N. gr.* Sword, Dart, Knife.

Special, *Adj. con.?* Weakly str. Different.

Spectacle, *N. gr.* Scene, Sight, Glasses.

Speech, *N. gr.* Talk, Words.

Speed, *?* Str. with Fast, also with Motion. Clearly not a name for Fast-Slow con. All str. relations with Fast, Speedy, etc., not with Slow, Stop, etc.

Speedy, *Adj. con.* Fast.

Spent, *V. gr.* Paid, Spend.

Spider, *N. gr.* C.i. Bug, Insect. Env. Web.

Spit, *?* Primary is Saliva.

Splendid, *Adj. con.* Very good.

Spoken, *V. gr.* Speak, Written.

Spool, *N. gr.* Thread.

Sports, *N. gr.* Games. Concept name, Football, Basketball.

Spread, *N. gr. or v. gr.* Str. Butter, Jelly.

Spring, *N. gr.* Summer, Fall, Winter.

Square, *Adj. con.* Opp. Round.

Staccato, *N. gr.?* Str. Music, Piano.

Stagecoach, *?* Env. Western.

Stalk, *? also v. gr.* Env. Corn. Also, Hunt, Animal.

Stand, *V. gr.* Sit, Step.

Stars, *N. gr.* Night, Moon, Heaven.

Startle, *V. gr.* Surprise, Jump, Scare.

Starved, *Adj. gr.?* Str. Hungry. Also str. Food, Eat.

Statement, *N. gr.* Links Sentence and Fact.

Stay, *V. gr.* Leave, Go, Remain.

Steal, *V. gr.* Rob, Take.

Steel, *N. gr.* C.i. Metal. Iron. Env. Hard.

Stem, *N. gr.* Plant, Leaf, Flower (also probably env.).

Step, *V. gr.* Env. Up, Down. Stand, Sit.

Stevedore, *?* Primary is Ship.

Sticky, *Adj.?* Env. Glue.

Stocky, *Adj. con.* Fat, Short, and Strong.

Stomach, *N. gr.* Food, Eat. Also, Liver, etc. Env. Ache.

Stop, *V.?* Go. Env. Sign.

Story, *N. gr.* Book (also probably env.).

Stout, *Adj. con.* Fat.

Stove, *N. gr.* Heat, Oven. Env. Hot.

Straight, *Adj. con.?* Env. Forward, Line. Also, opp. Crooked.

Strange, *Adj. con.* Different.

Stratagem, *N. gr.* Plan, Strategy.

Stream, *N. gr.* River, Water.

Street, *N. gr.* Road, Car.

Strengthen, *V. gr.* Weaken, Help.

Strife, *N. gr.* Fight, War.

String, *N. gr., v. gr.* Rope. Also, Hang.

Stroke, *?* Env. Swim, Heart. Possible str. Pet.

Strong, *Adj. con.* Weak.

Struck, *V. gr.* Strike, Hit.

Strung, *V. gr.* Hung, String.

Study, *V. gr.* Learn, Work.

Stupid, *Adj. con.* Dumb.

Subtract, *V. gr.* Add, Divide. Env. Numbers.

Suburb, *N. gr.* City, Town.

Success, *N. gr.* Failure, Happiness, Wealth.

Such, *Str. gr.* That, This. Env. As.

Sudden, *Adj. con.* Very Fast.

Sugar, *N. gr.* Coffee, Salt. Env. Sweet.

Summer, *N. gr.* Winter, Spring, Env. Hot.

Summon, *N. gr.* (*sic*). Judge, Law, Jury.

Sun, *N. gr.* Moon, Sky, Sunshine, Light.

Sunshine, *N. gr.* Links Light, Rain, Heat, Summer, etc.

Supplementary, *Adj. gr.* Complementary, Extra, Added, Additional. All these may have as str. basis, More-Less.

Support, *V. gr.* Hold, Help, Lift.

Sure, *Adj.?* Str. Certain. Perhaps related to Same-Different con.

Surface, *N. gr.?* Top. Env. Smooth, Hard.

Suspend, *V. gr.* Hang, String.

Sweep, *V. gr.?* Perhaps str. with Clean, but Clean distribution shows little evidence of v.

Sweet, *Adj. con.* Opp. Sour.

Sweetly, *Adv.?* Str. Good, also Sweet.

Swim, *V. gr.* Sink, Swim, Float. Env. Water.

Sword, *N. gr.* Dart, Knife, Spear.

Swung, *V. gr.* Swing, Hit.

Symphony, *N. gr.* Music, Sound. Env. Orchestra.

T

Table, *N. gr.* Chair, Desk.

Tack, *N. gr.* Nail, Pin, Hammer (little suggestion of v.).

Take, *V. gr.* Steal, Give, Receive, Took.

Talk, *V. gr.* Speak, Listen.

Tall, *Adj. con.* Opp. Short.

Tang, *?* Primary is Orange (brand name?).

Tangible, *Adj. con.* Shares meaning of Real, Hard.

Tango, *N. gr. or v. gr.* C.i. Dance (?). Waltz.

Taste, *V. gr.* Smell, Feel, Touch. Little evidence of n. gr.

Tea, *N. gr.* Coffee. C.i. Drink (?).

Teaspoonful, *?* Env. Sugar.

Teeth, *N. gr.* Mouth, Gums, Tongue. Also, env. White.

Tell, *V. gr.* Say, Talk.

Temper, *N. gr.* Anger, Rage.

Tempo, *?* Primary is Music.

Tend, *V.?* Env. Toward.

Tenderness, *N. gr.* Love.

Tennis, *?* Env. Ball, Racket.

Tense, *Adj. gr.?* Anxious, Scared, Frightened. Emotion gr.

Tenure, *?* Env. Office.

Terrier, *N. gr.* C.i. Dog. Boxer.

Test, *N. gr.* Exam. Env. Hard.

Testimony, *N. gr.* Trial, Court.

Tetanus, *? N. gr.?* Env. Shot. Possible str. Disease, Infection.

Texture, *?* Str. with adj., Rough, Soft, Coarse. Perhaps concept name for Rough-Smooth con.

That, *Str. gr.* This, Them.

The, *Str. gr.* A, An, That.

Theory, *N. gr.* Idea, Science.

There, *Adv. con., str. gr.* Possible opp. Here. Also, That, This.

They, *Str. gr.* Them, We, Us.

Thick, *Adj. con.* Opp. Thin.

Thief, *N. gr.* Robber, Crime.

Thin, *Adj. con.* Opp. Thick.

Thing, *N. gr.* Object, Something.

Think, *V. gr.* Study, Learn.

This, *Str. gr.* That, There, Those.

Thitherward, *Adv.?* Primary is Towards.

Thorough, *Adj. con.* Complete.

Thought, *N. gr.* Idea, Mind. Linked with v. gr., Think, Learn.

Thread, *N. gr., v. gr.* Needle, String, Sew.

Throw, *V.?* Env. Away, Ball.

Tie, *V., n. gr.* Env. Knot. Also, str. Shirt, Coat.

Tiger, *N. gr.* C.i. Animal. Lion.

Time, *N. gr.* Clock, Hour, Day. Also, env. Magazine.

Tint, *N. gr. or v. gr.* Color, Dye.

Tiny, *Adj. con.* More extreme than Little.

Tire, *N. gr.* Car, Tube. Little evidence of v.

Tired, *Adj.?* Str. Relaxed. Apparently part of Emotion gr. Also, linked with Sleep, Rest.

Tissue, *?* Env. Paper.

Title, *N. gr.* Links Book, Name.

To, *Str. gr.* From, At, For.

Toe, *N. gr.* Foot, Heel, Shoe.

Together, *Adj. con.* Opp. Alone.

Toil, *N. gr., v. gr.* Work, Labor.

Tolerant, *Adj. con.* Easy, Good.

Tone, *N. gr.* Music, Sound, Noise.

Tonight, *N. or adv. gr.* Tomorrow, Today, Yesterday.

Took, *V. gr.* Take, Steal (Stolen).

Tooth, *N. gr.* Mouth, Tongue. Less env. to White than Teeth. Env. Ache.

Top, *Str. as con.* Opp. Bottom.

Torso, *N. gr.* Body, Breast.

Torture, *V. gr., n. gr.* Hurt, Kill. Also, Pain, Punishment.

Touch, *V. gr.* Feel, Smell.

Tough, *Adj. con.* More extreme than Rough, Hard.

Tower, *N.?* Env. High.

Town, *N. gr.* City, Village.

Track, *N. gr.* Team (possible env.), Race (college sample).

Traffic, *?* Env. Light.

Train, *N. gr.* Car, Trip, Railroad.

Transformation, *N. gr.* Str. with Transform, Change.

Trap, *V. gr.* Catch, Kill.

Travel, *N. gr., v. gr.* Go, Car, Trip, Plane, etc.

Treasure, *P* Env. Chest.

Treat, *P* Trick is primary.

Tree, *N. gr.* Grass, Bush, Plant.

Tremendous, *Adj. con.* Bigger than Huge.

Trick, *N. gr., v. gr.* Magic, Game, Fool.

Trip, *N. gr.* Travel, Vacation.

Trough, *P* Env. Water.

Trout, *N. gr.* C.i. Fish. Bass.

Truce, *N. gr.* War, Peace.

Truck, *N. gr.* Car, Bus.

True, *Adj. con.* Opp. False.

Trunk, *P* Env. Elephant, Tree.

Truth, *N. gr.* Lies, Honesty, Beauty.

Try, *V. gr.* Fail, Win.

Tune, *N. gr.* Song, Music.

Tunnel, *N.P* Env. Dark.

Turn, *V. gr.P* Env. Around. Twist, Bend.

Tutor, *N. gr., v. gr.* Teach, Teacher, Study.

Twelve, *N. gr.* C.i. Number. Thirteen.

Twist, *V. gr.* Turn, Bend (data obtained prior to 1960).

Typhoid, *N. gr.* Disease, Germ.

Typical, *Adj. con.* Same.

Tyrannical, *Adj.P* Env. King.

U

Ugly, *Adj. con.* Opp. Pretty.

Unconsciously, *Adv. con.P* Opp.(P) Consciously.

Underwent, *V.P* Env. Surgery.

Uniform, *N. gr.* Army, Soldier.

Union, *N. gr.* Links Labor, Matrimony.

Unite, *V. gr.* Join, Combine.

Unjust, *Adj. con.* Wrong. Also, Bad.

Unprofitable, *Adj.P* Env. Business.

Unstable, *Adj.P* Env. Compound.

Up, *Adv., adj. con.* Opp. Down.

Upholstery, *N. gr.* Furniture, Chair.

Upon, *Str. gr.* On, In, Into.

Upper, *Adj. con.* Opp. Lower.

Upwards, *Adv. con.* Opp. Downwards.

Use, *P* Responses scattered. Seems to be mainly v. with possible str. with Make, Do.

Usher, *N. gr.* Movie.

Usual, *Adj. con.* Same.

V

Vacate, *V. gr.* Leave, Empty.

Valley, *N. gr.* Hill, Mountain.

Valuable, *Adj.P* Str. with Expensive, Money.

Various, *Adj. con.* Numerous. Also, Different.

Vast, *Adj. con.* Bigger than Large. Also, Wide.

Veal, *N. gr.* Env. Cutlet. Str. Meat, Chops. Possible c.i. Food.

Vegetable, *N. gr.* Fruit. Also, concept name for Carrot, etc. C.i. Food.

Velocity, *N. gr.* Speed, Motion. More related to Fast than Slow.

Velvet, *N. gr.P* Env. Soft, Smooth. Str. Cloth, Silk.

Venice, *N. gr.* Rome, Italy. C.i. City.

Very, *Adv.* Env. Much. On an adv. intensifier scale. Less than Extremely.

Vessel, *N. gr.* Ship, Boat.

Victim, *N. gr.* Murder, Accident.

View, *N. gr.* Scene, Picture.

Village, *N. gr.* Town, City.

Vinegar, *N.?* Env. Sour.

Violence, *N. gr.* War, Destruction.

Violin, *N. gr.* C.i. Instrument. Music, Viola.

Virginal, *Adj.?* Env. Girl. Little evidence of Instrument.

Voice, *N. gr., v. gr.?* Str. Sound, Music, Tone. Also, Sing, Hear, etc.

Vulture, *N. gr.* C.i. Bird. Buzzard.

W

Wagon, *?* Env. Wheels, Train.

Wait, *V. gr.* Go, Stay.

Wake, *?* Env. Up.

Walk, *V. gr.* Run.

Wall, *N. gr.* Room, Picture, Window.

Walnut, *N. gr.* C.i. Tree. Nut, Peanut.

Waltz, *N. gr. or v. gr.* C.i. Dance. Music, Tango.

Want, *V. gr.* Wish, Need, Desire.

War, *N. gr.* Peace, Death, Fight.

Warehouse, *N. gr.* Building, House, Storage.

Warm, *Adj. con.* Less extreme than Hot.

Warmth, *N. gr.* Heat, Love.

Warrior, *N. gr.* Indian, Soldier, War.

Was, *V. str. gr.* Is, Has, Been.

Wash, *?* Env. Clean.

Wasp, *N. gr.* Bee, Fly. C.i. Bug.

Watch, *N. gr., v. gr.* Time, Clock. Weaker str. with Look, Listen.

Water, *N. gr.* Env. Cool, Wet, Glass. Also, str. with Ocean, River, Air.

Wave, *N. gr., v.?* Ocean, Water. Env. Hand.

Wayfarer, *N. gr.* Traveler, Wanderer.

We, *Str. gr.* They, Us, You.

Weak, *Adj. con.* Opp. Strong.

Weal, *?* Primary is Wheel.

Weapon, *N. gr.* Links Gun, Knife, and Fight.

Wear, *V.?* Env. Clothes.

Weather, *N. gr.* Storm, Climate. Env. Bad, Cold.

Web, *?* Env. Spider.

Wedding, *N. gr.* Marriage, Ring.

Week, *N. gr.* Day, Month, Year.

Week end, *?* Env. Fun.

Weigh, *?* Str. with Scales, Pounds, and Weight.

Weird, *Adj. con.?* Str. on Same-Different con. Probably on other con. as well.

Well, *N.?* Env. Water, Deep. Only weakly Good.

Went, *V. gr.* Gone, Left.

Were, *V. str. gr.* Was, Did, Have.

West, *N. gr.* East, North, South.

Wet, *Adj. con.* Opp. Dry.

What, *Str. gr.* Which, Who, Why, Where.

When, *Str. gr.* Now, Where, Then.

Whether, *Str. gr.* Or, If, Because. Linked through these to And, But, etc.

Whetstone, *?* Primary is Knife.

White, *Adj. con.* Opp. Black. Also, str. with Yellow, Red, etc.

Who, *Str. gr.* When, What, Why.

Whole, *Adj. con.* Opp. Part.

Whom, *Str. gr.* Who.

Why, *Str. gr.?* Primary is Because. Also, env. Not. Str. weakly with When, How.

Wide, *Adj. con.* Opp. Narrow.

Width, *N. gr.* Length, Breadth, Depth, Height.

Wife, *N. gr.* Husband, Mother, Girl.

Wig, *N. gr.* Toupee, Hat, Head.

Wild, *Adj.?* Env. Horse, Animal. Very little evidence of possible con. with Tame. Str. with Ferocious. Possibly an Emotion gr. word.

Wile, *?* Primary is Away (*sic*).

Will, *V. str. gr. n.* Shall, Do. Also, evidence in distribution for n.

Wind, *N. gr.* Rain, Storm.

Window, *N. gr.* Env. Pane. Door, Room.

Wine, *?* Env.(*?*) Drink. Or possibly c.i. Drink.

Wing, *N. gr.* Bird, Airplane, Fly.

Winnow, *?* Primary is Minnow. Also, Fish, Window occur in distribution. No evidence of dictionary meaning.

Winter, *N. gr.* Summer, Fall, Spring. Env. Cold.

Wise, *Adj. con.* Smart. Also, Old.

Wish, *V. gr.* Want, Desire, Hope.

With, *?* Env. Out, Her, etc. Unlike most str. words, elicits mostly env. associates.

Wolf, *N. gr.* C.i. Animal. Dog, Fox.

Woman, *N. gr.* Man, Girl.

Won, *V. gr.* Win, Lose, Lost, Beat.

Wonderful, *Adj. con.* More extreme than Good.

Wood, *N. gr.* Tree, Forest, Oak.

Word, *N. gr.* Dictionary, Sentence.

Work, *V. gr.* Env. Hard. Play, Study. Little evidence of n.

Worker, *N. gr.* Labor, Man.

Worn, *?* Env. Out.

Worship, *N. gr.* Env. God. Also, str. God, Church, Prayer.

Worst, *Adj. con.* Extreme for Bad.

Worth, *Adj. con.* Good.

Would, *V. str. gr.* Should, Could.

Wrath, *N. gr.* Anger, Rage, Fear.

Wreck, *?* Env. Ship.

Wrong, *Adj. con.* Opp. Right.

Wrote, *V. gr.* Write. Also, str. with Story, Letter, Book.

Wrought, *?* Env. Iron.

Wyoming, *N. gr.* C.i. State. Colorado.

Y

Yard, *?* Env. Stick.

Yell, *V. gr. or n. gr.* Scream, Shout.

Yellow, *Adj. gr.* Red, Green, Blue.

Yield, *V. gr.* Give, Make.

Yolk, *?* Env. Egg.

Yonder, *?* Primary is There.

You, *Str. gr.* Me, Your, I, He.

Young, *Adj. con.* Opp. Old.

Your, *Str. gr.* My, Mine.

Yourself, *Str. gr.* Myself, You, Me.

Z

Zebra, *N. gr.* Env. Striped. C.i. Animal, Horse.

Zulu, *?* Primary is Native.

❧ *Index*

The Structure of Associations in Language and Thought
by James Deese

designer : Cecilie Smith
typesetter : Monotype Composition Co.
typefaces : Caledonia (text), Bodoni Bold (display)
printer : John D. Lucas Printing Company
paper : Perkins and Squier GM
binder : Moore & Co., Inc.
cover material : Columbia Riverside Linen